P9-BZV-022

# GREAT CANADIAN SPEECHES

## WORDS THAT SHAPED A NATION

EDITED BY
BRIAN BUSBY

Capella

# CONTENTS



---


This edition published in 2008 by
Arcturus Publishing Limited
26/27 Bickels Yard, 151–153 Bermondsey Street
London SE1 3HA





ISBN: 978-1-84193-957-5

Printed in China

ive by careful

# Introduction

On 16 March 1886, the Member of Parliament for Quebec East rose in the House of Commons and began a speech which would earn him the epithet 'Silver-Tongued Laurier' in the country's English-language press. Wilfrid Laurier's subject was the execution of Louis Riel. It was, he argued, a wrongful penalty; one carried forward without cause or forethought by a government which should rightly hold the blame for the dual tragedies of the Red River and North-West Rebellions. In presenting his argument, the future Prime Minister drew on history, precedent, procedure, Parliament and the law. It was several hours before he would yield the floor. Following the speech, Edward Blake, the leader of the Liberal Party, told the House that Laurier had delivered a speech which in his humble opinion 'was the finest parliamentary speech ever pronounced in the Parliament of Canada since Confederation'.

Blake made his claim when Confederation was in its ninth year; thirteen decades later, his words hold true.

Laurier lived at a time in which both sides of the House featured Members possessing great eloquence and oratorical skill. Across the aisle, Sir John A. Macdonald, displayed a different yet equally effective style, incorporating humour and a good measure of verbal jousting. These two men were typical orators of their age in that they were thoroughgoing. In his informal and spontaneous speech in the Halifax Hotel, made with enthusiasm in response to a toast to 'Colonial Union', Macdonald sets forth ideas, arguments and ideals which would in part contribute to the existence and substance of the British North America Act. Though it would not have been considered a lengthy speech in its day, Macdonald's words number more than three times those delivered by Brian Mulroney in his first report on the Meech Lake Accord 123 years later.

It is not possible to consider the speeches printed on these pages without recognizing a patent decline. Where once was expressiveness and ardour and reflection, we today so often encounter mere reportage and tired, clichéd expressions of partisanship and patriotism. Though skill and substance may be lacking in certain selections, each endures as a record of an important and often pivotal event in Canada's story. The victory speech delivered by Kim Campbell at the 1993 Progressive Conservative convention could hardly be held up as an example of great oratory; nevertheless it is significant as one delivered by a politician who had moments earlier been chosen to be the country's first woman Prime Minister.

Campbell's speech is one of over a dozen included here which were delivered either in whole or in part in French. Fluency in both official languages has come to be expected of political leaders at the federal level, though this was not always the norm. Prime Minister William Lyon Mackenzie King delivered his 1942 radio address on the conscription plebiscite in English, leaving a member of his staff to present the French-language translation of his speech.

Radio and television broadcasts excepted, a speech is not made in a vacuum; there is an immediate response. The audience may disrupt, it may contribute; even silence has an effect. In speaking the orator receives a reaction, yet this often rests unrecorded due to the limitations of the printed word. Barring disruption, as in the case of Lester Pearson's 1964 address to the Royal Canadian Legion, rarely is there a written record of the subject's interaction with his audience. Written transcription does not record René Lévesque's attempts to speak over the chants of *'Le Québec aux Québécois!'* that accompanied the Parti Québécois victory in the 1976 provincial election, or the fact that Jacques Parizeau joined in on the very same mantra, incorporating it into his concession speech on the evening of the second Quebec referendum.

Rambling and unfocused, Parizeau's address is best remembered for his comments concerning *'l'argent puis des votes ethniques'*, words that have become part of the national consciousness, and yet a complete transcript of his speech was never provided by the press. Today's newspapers ape the broadcasters, focusing on the print equivalent of the sound bite. Indeed, the last of these speeches to have been printed in its entirety by a newspaper was Pierre Elliott Trudeau's House of Commons address on the abolition of capital punishment, published in the 16 June 1976 edition of *The Globe and Mail*.

In his *Against the Current: Selected Writings, 1939–1996*, Trudeau includes just ten sentences from his historic speech. All ninety-nine sentences are included here. With three exceptions – Laurier on the Riel execution, Macdonald on the Pacific Scandal and Lucien Bouchard on the Bloc Québécois as the Official Opposition – the speeches in this volume are presented in their entirety. Thus, we have Charles de Gaulle's infamous 1967 speech from the balcony of Montreal City Hall ending not with *'Vive le Québec libre!'*, as is so often presented, but with the pronouncements that followed: *'Vive le Canada français! Et vive la France!'*

The words spoken by General de Gaulle on that hot July evening were wholly his own. The same can be said with equal certainty for those spoken by Louis Riel at his trial, and the speeches delivered at the Paul Sauvé Arena by Trudeau and René Lévesque. The remarks made by Macdonald and Laurier included in these pages were not penned by others. Of other leaders we cannot be so definite; it is one talent of the speechwriter that he remains unnoticed. It needs be pointed out, however, that many of the figures included here achieved their position due in part to their skill at composition and delivery. A member of the St. Mary's Collegiate Institute Debating Society, Arthur Meighen's first electoral victory was to the position of Secretary in the school's Literary Society. Sixteen years later, his rhetorical skills were credited with a surprise win in his 1908 election to the House of Commons. Once in Ottawa, he drew the attention of Laurier, who remarked 'Borden has found a man at last'.

Laurier understood the power of the spoken word, and wielded it with a skill unmatched by any other.

Brian Busby
Vancouver, November 2007

# CONFEDERATION

"The question of 'Colonial Union' is one of such magnitude that it dwarfs every other question on this portion of the continent. It absorbs every idea as far as I am concerned. For twenty long years I have been dragging myself through the dreary waste of colonial politics. I thought there was no end, nothing worthy of ambition; but now I see something which is well worthy of all I have suffered in the cause of my little country."

*- Sir John A. Macdonald, 1864*

## Sir John A. Macdonald

A Reply to the Toast 'Colonial Union'

*The Halifax Hotel, Halifax, 12 September 1864*

**'Everything, gentlemen, is to be gained by union, and everything to be lost by disunion.'**

**With the prominence given the Charlottetown Conference in Canadian history, it is often forgotten that meetings followed immediately in Halifax, Saint John and Fredericton. On the second evening following the adjournment in Charlottetown a banquet was hosted by the Nova Scotia government in the dining hall of the Halifax Hotel. There glasses were raised in a toast to 'Colonial Union'.**

**The reply presented here reflects the passion and reason which energized the future Prime Minister in his pursuit of Confederation. Macdonald addresses the need for a strong central government, an 'intercolonial railway', and the benefits of union in dealing with the might of the United States, then at war with what he terms the 'Southern Republic', the Confederate States of America.**

**Macdonald begins his speech with a reference to his colleagues from the Canadas, George-Étienne Cartier and George Brown, with whom he had formed the Grand Alliance. The 'gallant admiral' is Sir James Hope, Vice-Admiral of the North American Station in Halifax.**

My friends and colleagues, Messrs Cartier and Brown, have returned their thanks on behalf of the Canadians for the kindness bestowed upon us, and I shall therefore not say one word on that subject, but shall approach the question more immediately before us. I must confess to you, sir, and to you, gentlemen, that I approach it with the deepest emotion.

The question of 'Colonial Union' is one of such magnitude that it dwarfs every other question on this portion of the continent. It absorbs every idea as far as I am concerned. For twenty long years I have been dragging myself through the dreary waste of colonial politics. I thought there was no end, nothing worthy of ambition; but now I see something which is well worthy of all I have suffered in the cause of my little country. This question has now assumed a position that demands and commands the attention of all the colonies of British America. There may be obstructions, local difficulties may arise, disputes may occur, local jealousies may intervene, but it matters not – the wheel is now revolving, and we are only the fly on the wheel, we cannot delay it – the union of the colonies of British America, under one sovereign, is a fixed fact.

Sir, this meeting in Halifax will be ever remembered in the history of British America, for here the delegates from the several provinces had the first opportunity of expressing their sentiments. We have been unable to announce them before; but now let me say that we have arrived unanimously at the opinion that the union of the provinces is for the advantage of all, and that the only question that remains to be settled is, whether that union can be arranged with a due regard to sectional and local interests. I have no doubt that such an arrangement can be effected, that every difficulty will be found susceptible of solution, and that the great project will be successfully and happily realized.

What were we before this question was brought before the public mind? Here we were in the neighbourhood of a large nation – of one that has developed its military power in a most marvellous degree – connected by one tie only, that of common allegiance.

True it was we were states of one sovereign, we all paid allegiance to the great central authority; but as far as ourselves were concerned there was no political connection, and we were as wide apart as British America is from Australia. We had only the mere sentiment of a common allegiance, and we were liable, in case England and the United States were pleased to differ, to be cut off, one by one, not having any common means of defence.

I believe we shall have at length an organization that will enable us to be a nation and protect ourselves as we should. Look at the gallant defence that is being made by the Southern Republic – at this moment they have not much more than four millions of men – not much exceeding our own numbers – yet what a brave fight they have made, notwithstanding the stern bravery of the New Englander, or the fierce elan of the Irishman.

We are now, I say, nearly four millions of inhabitants, and in the next decennial period of taking the census, perhaps we shall have eight millions of people, able to defend their country against all comers. But we must have one common organization – one political government.

It has been said that the United States government is a failure. I don't go so far. On the

*Sir John A. Macdonald, the first Prime Minister of Canada*

contrary, I consider it a marvellous exhibition of human wisdom. It was as perfect as human wisdom could make it, and under it the American States greatly prospered until very recently; but being the work of men it had its defects, and it is for us to take advantage by experience, and endeavour to see if we cannot arrive by careful study at such a plan as will avoid the mistakes of our neighbours.

In the first place, we know that every individual state was an individual sovereignty – that each had its own army and navy and political organization – and when they formed themselves into a confederation they only gave the central authority certain specific powers, reserving to the individual states all the other rights appertaining to sovereign powers. The dangers that have arisen from this system we will avoid if we can agree upon forming a strong central government – a great central legislature – a constitution for a union which will have all the rights of sovereignty except those that are given to the local governments. Then we shall have taken a great step in advance of the American republic. If we can only attain that object – a vigorous general government – we shall not be New Brunswickers, nor Nova Scotians, nor Canadians, but British Americans, under the sway of the British sovereign.

In discussing the question of colonial union, we must consider what is desirable and practicable; we must consult local prejudices and aspirations. It is our desire to do so. I hope that we will be enabled to work out a constitution that will have a strong central government, able to offer a powerful resistance to any foe whatever, and at the same time will preserve for each province its own identity – and will protect every local ambition; and if we cannot do this, we shall not be able to carry out the object we have now in view.

In the conference we have had, we have been united as one man – there was no difference of feeling – no sectional prejudices or selfishness exhibited by any one; – we all approached the subject feeling its importance – feeling that in our hands were the destinies of a nation; and that great would be our sin and shame if any different motives had intervened to prevent us carrying out the noble object of founding a great British monarchy, in connection with the British Empire, and under the British Queen.

That there are difficulties in the way would be folly for me to deny; that there are important questions to be settled before the project can be consummated is obvious; but what great subject that has ever attracted the attention of mankind has not been fraught with difficulties? We would not be worthy of the position in which we have been placed by the people, if we did not meet and overcome these obstacles.

I will not continue to detain you at this late period of the evening, but will merely say that we are desirous of a union with the Maritime provinces on a fair and equitable basis: that we desire no advantage of any kind, that we believe the object in view will be as much in favour as against these Maritime colonies. We are ready to come at once into the most intimate connection with you. This cannot be fully procured, I admit, by political union simply. I don't hesitate to say that with respect to the intercolonial railway, it is understood by the people of Canada that it can only be built as a means of political union for the colonies. It cannot be denied that the railway, as a commercial enterprise, would be of comparatively little commercial advantage to the people of Canada. Whilst we have the Saint Lawrence in summer, and the American ports in time of peace, we have all that is requisite for our purposes.

We recognise, however, the fact that peace may not always exist, and that we must have some other means of outlet if we do not wish to be cut off from the ocean for some months in the year. We wish to feel greater security – to know that we can have assistance readily in the hour of danger. In the case of a union, this railway must be a national work, and Canada will cheerfully contribute to the utmost extent in order to make that important link without which no political connection can be complete.

What will be the consequence to this city, prosperous as it is, from that communication? Montreal is at this moment competing with New York for the trade of the great West. Build the road and Halifax will soon become one of the great emporiums of the world. All the great resources of the West will come over the immense railways of Canada to the bosom of your harbour. But there are even greater advantages for us all in view. We will become a great nation, and God forbid that it should be one separate from the United Kingdom of Great Britain and Ireland.

There has been a feeling that because the old colonies were lost by the misrule of the British government, every colony must be lost when it assumes the reins of self-government. I believe, however, as stated by the gallant admiral, that England will hold her position in every colony – she will not enforce an unwilling obedience by her arms; but as long as British Americans shall retain that same allegiance which they feel now, England will spend her last shilling, and spill her best blood like wine in their defence.

In 1812 there was an American war because England impressed American seamen. Canadians had nothing to do with the cause of the quarrel, yet their militia came out bravely and did all they could for the cause of England. Again, we have had the Oregon question, the Trent difficulty – question after question in which the colonies had no interest – yet we were ready to shoulder the musket and fight for the honour of the mother country.

It has been said that England wishes to throw us off. There may be a few doctrinaires who argue for it, but it is not the feeling of the people of England. Their feeling is this – that we have not been true to ourselves, that we have not put ourselves in an attitude of defence, that we have not done in Canada as the English have done at home. It is a mistake: Canada is ready to do her part. She is organizing a militia; she is expending an enormous amount of money for the purpose of doing her best for self-protection.

I am happy to know that the militia of Nova Scotia occupies a front rank; I understand by a judicious administration you have formed here a large and efficient volunteer and militia organization. We are following your example and are forming an effective body of militia, so that we shall be able to say to England, that if she should send her arms to our rescue at a time of peril, she would be assisted by a well disciplined body of men.

Everything, gentlemen, is to be gained by union, and everything to be lost by disunion. Everybody admits that union must take place some time. I say now is the time. Here we are now, in a state of peace and prosperity – now we can sit down without any danger threatening us, and consider and frame a scheme advantageous to each of these colonies. If we allow so favourable an opportunity to pass, it may never come again; but I believe we have arrived at such a conclusion in our deliberations that I may state without any breach of confidence – that we all unitedly agree that such a measure is a matter of the first necessity, and that only a few (imaginary, I believe) obstacles stand in the way of its consummation.

I will feel that I shall not have served in public life without a reward, if before I enter into private life, I am a subject of a great British American nation, under the government of her majesty, and in connection with the empire of Great Britain and Ireland.

## Joey Smallwood

On Newfoundland and Confederation

*The Colonial Building, Saint John's, 28 October 1946*

***'Confederation I will support if it means a lower cost of living for our people. Confederation I will support if it means a higher standard of living for our people. Confederation I will support if it means strength, stability and security for Newfoundland.'***

**A failed candidate in the 1932 Newfoundland general election, the Newfoundland National Convention provided Smallwood with a second chance at entry into a life in politics. Here Smallwood presents what is foremost an economic argument for Newfoundland's entry into Confederation – considered and rejected some eight decades previously.**

**In the speech, he makes mention of three nineteenth-century Newfoundland politicians: Prime Ministers Patrick Morris and John Kent; and Sir William Carson, 'The Great Reformer', who in the early part of the century had fought for representative government. Confronted with the realities of the mid-twentieth century, Smallwood claims, these men would have desired the linking of Newfoundland with 'the democratic, developing mainland of the New World'.**

Our people's struggle to live commenced on the day they first landed here, four centuries and more ago, and has continued to this day. The struggle is more uneven now than it was then, and the people view the future now with more dread than they felt a century ago. The newer conceptions of what life can be, of what life should be, have widened our horizons and deepened our knowledge of the great gulf which separates what we have and are from what we feel we should have and be. We have been taught by newspapers, motion pictures, radios and visitors something of the higher standards of well-being of the mainland of North America; we have become uncomfortably aware of the low standards of our country, and we are driven irresistibly to wonder whether our attempt to persist in isolation is the root cause of our condition.

We have often felt in the past, when we learned something of the higher standards of the mainland, that such things belonged to another world, that they were not for us. But today we are not so sure that two yardsticks were designed by the Almighty to measure the standards of well-being: one yardstick for the mainland of the continent; another for this island which lies beside it. Today we are not so sure, not so ready to take it for granted, that we Newfoundlanders are destined to accept much lower standards of life than our neighbours of Canada and the United States. Today we are more disposed to feel that our manhood, our very creation by God, entitles us to standards of life no lower than those of our brothers on the mainland.

Our Newfoundland is known to possess wealth of considerable value and variety. Without at all exaggerating their extent, we know that our fisheries are in the front rank of the world's marine wealth. We have considerable forest, water power and mineral resources. Our Newfoundland people are industrious, hard-working, frugal, ingenious and sober. The combination of such natural resources and such people should spell a prosperous country enjoying high standards of living. This combination should spell fine, modern, well-equipped homes; lots of health-giving food; ample clothing; the amenities of modern New World civilization; good roads, good schools, good hospitals, high levels of public health and private health; it should spell a vital, prosperous, progressive country.

It has not spelt any such things. Compared with the mainland of North America, we are fifty years, in some things one hundred years, behind the times. We live more poorly, more shabbily, more meanly. Our life is more a struggle. Our struggle is tougher, more naked, more hopeless. In the North American family, Newfoundland bears the reputation of having the lowest standards of life, of being the least progressive and advanced, of the whole family.

We all love this land. It has charm that warms our hearts, go where we will; a charm, a magic, a mystical tug on our emotion that never dies. With all her faults, we love her. But a metamorphosis steals over us the moment we cross the border that separates us from other lands.

As we leave Newfoundland, our minds undergo a transformation: we expect, and we take for granted, a higher, more modern way of life such as would have seemed ridiculous or even avaricious to expect at home. And as we return to Newfoundland, we leave that higher standard behind, and our minds undergo a reverse transformation. We have grown so accustomed to our own lower standards and more antiquated methods and old-fashioned conveniences that we readjust ourselves unconsciously to the meaner standards under which we grew up. We are so used to our railway and our coastal boats that we scarcely see them; so used to our settlements and roads and homes and schools and hospitals and hotels and everything else that we do not even see their inadequacy, their backwardness, their seaminess.

We have grown up in such an atmosphere of struggle, of adversity, of mean times, that we are never surprised, never shocked, when we learn that we have one of the highest rates of tuberculosis in the world; one of the highest infant mortality rates in the world; one of the highest rates of beriberi and rickets in the world.

We take these shocking facts for granted. We take for granted our lower standards, our poverty. We are not indignant about them. We save our indignation for those who publish such facts. For with all our complacency, with all our readiness to receive, to take for granted and even to justify these things amongst ourselves, we are, strange to say, angry and hurt when these shocking facts become known to the outside world.

We are very proud of our Newfoundland people. We all admire their strength, their skill, their adaptability, their resourcefulness, their industry, their frugality, their sobriety and their warm-hearted, simple generosity.

We are proud of them, but are we indignant? Does our blood boil when we see the lack of common justice with which they are treated? When we witness the long, grinding struggle they have? When we see the standards of their life? Have we compassion in our hearts for them? Or are we so engrossed, so absorbed, in our own struggle to live in this country that our social conscience has become toughened, even case-hardened? Has our own hard struggle to realize a modest competence so blinded us that we have little or no tenderness of conscience left to spare for the fate of the tens of thousands of our brothers so very much worse off than ourselves?

In the present and prospective world chaos, with all its terrible variety of uncertainty, it would be cruel and futile, now that the choice is ours, to influence the handful of people who inhabit this small island to attempt independent national existence.

The earnings of our 65,000 families may be enough, in the years ahead, to support them half-decently and at the same time support the public services of a fair-sized municipality. But will those earnings support independent national government on an expanding, or even the present, scale?

Except for a few years of this war and a few of the last, our people's earnings never supported them on a scale comparable with North American standards, and never maintained a government even on the pre-war scale of service. Our people never enjoyed a good standard of living and never were able to yield enough taxes to maintain the government. The difference was made up by borrowing or grants-in-aid.

We can indeed reduce our people's standard of living: we can force them to eat and wear and use and have much less than they have; and we can deliberately lower the level of governmental services. Thus, we might manage precariously to maintain independent national status. We can resolutely decide to be poor but proud. But if such a decision is made, it must be made by the 60,000 families who would have to do the sacrificing, not the 5,000 families who are confident of getting along pretty well in any case.

We have, I say, a perfect right to decide that we will turn away from North American standards of public services and condemn ourselves as a people and government deliberately to long years of struggle to maintain even the little that we have. We may, if we wish, turn our backs upon the North American continent, beside which God placed us, and resign ourselves to the meaner outlook and shabbier standards of Europe, 2,000 miles across the ocean. We can do this, or we can face the

*Joey Smallwood signing the 11 December 1948 agreement admitting Newfoundland into Confederation. Sir Albert Walsh, future Lieutenant-Governor is seated at Smallwood's left*

fact that the very logic of our situation on the surface of the globe impels us to draw close to the progressive outlook and dynamic living standards of this continent.

Our danger, so it seems to me, is that of nursing delusions of grandeur. We remember the stories of small states that valiantly preserved their national independence and developed their own proud cultures, but we tend to overlook the fact that comparison of Newfoundland with them is ludicrous.

We are not a nation. We are merely a medium-size municipality, a mere miniature borough of a large city. Doctor William Carson, Patrick Morris and John Kent were sound in the first decades of the nineteenth-century when they advocated cutting the apron strings that bound us to the government of the United Kingdom. But the same love of Newfoundland, the same Newfoundland patriotism, that inspired their agitation then would now, if they lived, drive them to carry the agitation to its logical conclusion of taking the next step of linking Newfoundland closely to the democratic, developing mainland of the New World.

There was indeed a time when tiny states lived gloriously. That time is now ancient European history. We are trying to live in the mid-twentieth century, post-Hitler New World. We are living in a world in which small countries have less chance than ever before of surviving.

We can, of course, persist in isolation, a dot in the shore of North America, the funks of the North American continent, struggling vainly to support ourselves and our greatly expanded public services. Reminded continually by radio, movie and visitor of greatly higher standards of living across the gulf we can shrug incredulously or dope ourselves into the hopeless belief that such things are not for us.

By our isolation from the throbbing vitality and expansion of the continent, we have been left far behind in the march of time, the 'sport of historic misfortune', the 'Cinderella of the Empire'. Our choice now is to continue in blighting isolation or seize the opportunity that may beckon us to the wider horizons and higher standards of unity with the progressive mainland of America.

I am not one of those, if any such there be, who would welcome federal union with Canada at any price. There are prices which I, a Newfoundlander whose ancestry in this country reaches back for nearly two centuries, am not willing that Newfoundland should pay. I am agreeable to the idea that our country should link itself federally with that great British nation, but I am not agreeable that we should ever be expected to forget that we are Newfoundlanders with a great history and a great tradition of our own.

I agree that there may be much to gain from linking our fortunes with that great nation, but I insist that as a self-governing province of the Dominion, we should continue to enjoy the right to our own distinctive culture. I do not deny that once we affiliated with the Canadian federal union, we should in all fairness be expected to extend the scope of our loyalty to embrace the federation as a whole. I do not deny this claim at all, but I insist that as a constituent part of the federation, we should continue to be quite free to hold to our love of our own dear land.

Nor am I one of those, if there be any such, who would welcome union with Canada without regard for the price that the Dominion might be prepared to pay.

I pledge myself to this House and to this country that I will base my ultimate stand in this whole question of Confederation upon the nature of the terms that are laid before the convention and the country. If the terms are such as clearly to suggest a better Newfoundland for our people, I shall support and maintain them. If they are not of such a nature, I shall oppose them with all the means I can command.

In the price we pay and the price we exact, my only standard of measurement is the welfare of the people. This is my approach to the whole question of federal union with Canada. It is in this spirit that I move this resolution today.

Confederation I will support if it means a lower cost of living for our people.

Confederation I will support if it means a higher standard of living for our people.

Confederation I will support if it means strength, stability and security for Newfoundland.

I will support Confederation if it gives us democratic government. I will support Confederation if it rids us of commission government. I will support Confederation if it gives us responsible government under conditions that will give responsible government a real chance to succeed. Confederation I will support if it makes us a province enjoying privileges and rights no lower than any other province.

These, then, are the conditions of my support of Confederation: that it must raise our people's standard of living, that it must give Newfoundlanders a better life, that it must give our country stability and security and that it must give us full, democratic responsible government under circumstances that will ensure its success.

I believe that this move will lead to a brighter and happier life for our Newfoundland people. If you adopt this resolution, and Canada offers us generous terms, as I believe she will, and Newfoundland decides to shake off her ancient isolation, I believe with all my heart and mind that the people will bless the day this resolution was moved.

With God's grace, let us move forward for a brighter and happier Newfoundland.

## Louis Saint-Laurent

Address on the Entry of Newfoundland into Confederation

*Parliament Hill, Ottawa, 1 April 1949*

**'In greeting you as fellow citizens we do not feel that you in Newfoundland have ever been strangers.'**

**Negotiations for union of Newfoundland with Canada, begun under Mackenzie King, concluded during the first months of Saint-Laurent's term in office. The Prime Minister made a speech below the Peace Tower after listening to a public radio broadcast of Sir Albert Walsh being sworn into office as Lieutenant-Governor of the new province.**

**In Saint-Laurent's address he welcomes Gordon Bradley, the first Newfoundlander to sit in Cabinet. Bradley had been a delegate to the National Convention and had served as its Chairman.**

**The E.J. Pratt poem from which the Prime Minister quotes is 'Newfoundland Seamen', written two months earlier in honour of the former colony's entry into Confederation.**

**After completing his remarks, Saint-Laurent was given a stonemason's mallet and chisel with which he cut the first line of Newfoundland's coat of arms into an arch beneath the tower.**

I should like to direct my first words today to the people of the new Canadian province of Newfoundland. I know I am speaking for the people of the other nine provinces when I say that we welcome you warmly as fellow Canadians.

In greeting you as fellow citizens we do not feel that you in Newfoundland have ever been strangers. In peace we have been happy to live and work beside you. In two wars we have been glad you were in our company and we in yours. We have the same traditions and the same way of life. We are both proud of our association in the British Commonwealth of Nations. We have shared – and continue to share – a common loyalty to His Majesty the King.

At this time, when we are taking a major step in the life of Newfoundland and of all Canada, the people of the nine older provinces and those of Newfoundland are equally aware that one circumstance that has contributed to union is our common loyalty to His Majesty the King. That common loyalty will continue to be one of the most important forces in the life of our united nation. With those thoughts in mind, I asked His Excellency the Governor General to convey a message this morning – the first full day of the new union – to His Majesty, King George VI. The message reads as follows:

> On the occasion of the entry of Newfoundland into Confederation as a province of Canada I send to your Majesty, on behalf of the Government and people of Canada, the expression of our devoted loyalty together with our sincere good wishes to you and to Her Majesty the Queen. The people of Canada, those of Newfoundland and those of the other provinces of Canada, now one nation under the Crown, are happy to learn of Your Majesty's improvement in health, and join in wishing you a speedy recovery.

The union we celebrate today was not concluded without the most careful consideration by representatives of both Canada and Newfoundland.

In 1947, when the delegation from your National Convention came to Ottawa to see if a satisfactory basis could be found for the political union, we were pleased. We had no hesitation in making it clear that we would welcome union. But we recognized the decision was one for you to make yourselves. We were happy when you, the people of Newfoundland, decided by a free vote that you favoured union. And we are happy today to have the union completed.

In welcoming you as partners in the Canadian Nation, we, of the rest of Canada, feel you are joining a good country – a country of which you will come to be as proud as we are. Canada is a country with a distinctive character and distinctive qualities.

Our nation in its origin is a union of two great races that have joined their talents without merging their identities. The union includes peoples of many other national origins. Our country covers a vast area between two oceans, with great differences of soil and climate and industry. But from end to end of Canada there is an ever deepening sense of community of interest and of purpose. We have a common pride in being Canadians. We are proud of Canada's past and of the record of our men and women in peace and in war. We are confident of our country's future. We feel that our nation can hold its head high among the nations of the world.

With the pleasure we have in welcoming you of Newfoundland as Canadians today, there is mingled a feeling that you could have joined no better nation. The formal union is completed today. But the real union – the union of hearts and minds – took place in the recent terrible war, in which Canadians and Newfoundlanders were so closely joined.

It is not only in war that we have come to know and appreciate the qualities of the people of Newfoundland. During the centuries since the original settlement of Newfoundland, the people of your island have met the forces of nature, on sea and on land. In adversity and in prosperity they have developed qualities of heart and spirit for which they are renowned.

Some of those qualities are referred to by your native son E. J. Pratt who has written:

*Prime Minister Louis Saint-Laurent and Newfoundland National Council Chairman Sir Albert Walsh shake hands following the signing of the agreement admitting Newfoundland to Confederation*

> This is their culture, this – their master passion
> Of giving shelter and of sharing bread,
> Of answering rocket signals in the fashion
> Of losing life to save it. In the spread
> Of time – the Gilbert-Grenfell-Bartlett span –
> The headlines cannot dim their daily story,
> Nor calls like London! Gander! Teheran!
> Outplay the drama of the sled and dory.

In becoming a province of Canada, you in Newfoundland will not lose your own identity, of which you are all so justly proud.

A Canadian province is not a mere administrative unit of the central government. Each of our provinces has its won distinctive political existence and political traditions. Within its field of jurisdiction, the provincial legislature is as sovereign as the Parliament of Canada is within its field. The provincial legislature has jurisdiction over education; property and civil rights; charitable, local and municipal institutions. To the province, also, falls the primary responsibility for public health and social welfare.

In entrusting such jurisdiction to the province, the Fathers, in their wisdom, left to the province the primary responsibility for the protection of the family, the school, the church, the very foundations of our society.

Our constitution thus assures to each province that it may preserve its ancient traditions, its own culture and all those distinctive characteristics which add variety and colour to our national life.

Newfoundland today enters Confederation as a full and equal partner with the older provinces. It is my hope and belief that in the future the advantages of the union will be increasingly recognized by the great majority of the people of Newfoundland and of all Canada.

We are completing our union at a troubled time for all people who believe in freedom and democracy and who hope for peace. The free and peace-loving countries of the North Atlantic Community are at the present moment taking steps, within the Charter of the United Nations, to band themselves together for greater security against any would-be aggressor.

Newfoundland is in the very centre of the North Atlantic Community. Canada as a whole occupies a large part of the North Atlantic area. The nations of that whole area will be more secure in the new North Atlantic association. In the same way, Canada and Newfoundland will have greater security in being bound together in federal union. From today all Canadians, old and new, will work as one to preserve peace and to win security. And in a world where free people can work in security and peace, the opportunities for the enlarged Canada, with its ten provinces, are immense.

Among our people there are some who still do not have that standard of life we think all Canadians should have. There are some who still do not enjoy an adequate degree of social security. We shall not cease to work for a larger measure of prosperity and security for all our people in all parts of Canada.

But while there is yet room for improvement, there is no country in the world where that improvement is more possible, or indeed, more certain. The wealth of Canada is the wealth of half a continent. The talents and the energies of our people are those of free men who work together for the benefit of all. Our wealth, our talents, our energy, and our co-operation constitute the promise of our country.

The people of Newfoundland, who have today become citizens of Canada, will share with the people of the rest of Canada in the work and in the wealth of our nation. Together, we shall strive, under God's guidance, and with confidence in our future, to build a greater and a better land.

In conclusion, I welcome as a colleague in the Government of Canada, the Honourable Gordon Bradley of Newfoundland who this morning was sworn to the Privy Council and becomes Secretary of State of Canada.

I should like to give to the Newfoundlanders of yesterday, who are Canadians today, the assurance that, in addressing to them these words of welcome in English, I do so quite as much in the name of their new compatriots whose mother tongue is French, as in the name of those whose language is English.

They belong now to a nation whose two principal races have both retained their attachment to the traditions, to the culture, and to the language of their ancestors. That is the best guarantee to our new fellow-citizens that their entry into this new nation will not lose for them their own ancestral patrimony, but that, on the contrary, it will make its contribution with ours to the common good of all Canadian citizens.

## Pierre Elliott Trudeau

Remarks at the Proclamation Ceremony

*Parliament Hill, Ottawa, 17 April 1982*

**'...what we are celebrating today is not so much the completion of our task, but the renewal of our hope – not so much an ending, but a fresh beginning.'**

The Constitution Act, 1982, was the fulfilment of a long sought goal of Trudeau's to 'retrieve what is properly ours'. His first attempt, the 1971 Victoria Charter, had failed after Quebec Premier Robert Bourassa withdrew his support and presented an alternate proposal. Trudeau later blamed the about-face for the rise of the Parti Québécois and the Meech Lake Accord. Another decade passed before the next attempt at patriation.

The signing of the act took place on a cold, rainy Saturday, before a crowd of over thirty thousand. Rain began to fall as Trudeau began his speech and it wasn't long before the rumbling of thunder could be heard. While some commentators wrote that the thunder added force to Trudeau's words, others considered the inclement weather as an omen.

Your Majesty, Your Royal Highness, Excellencies, fellow Canadians, *mes chères compatriots*, today, at long last, Canada is acquiring full and complete national sovereignty. The Constitution of Canada has finally come home. The most fundamental law of the land will now be capable of being amended in Canada, without any further recourse to the Parliament of the United Kingdom.

In the name of all Canadians, may I say how pleased and honoured we are that Your Majesty and Your Royal Highness have journeyed to Canada to share with us this day of historic achievement.

For more than half a century, Canadians have resembled young adults who leave home to build a life of their own, but are not quite confident enough to take along all their belongings. We became an independent country for all practical purposes in 1931, with the passage of the Statute of Westminster. But by our own choice, because of our inability to agree upon an amending formula at that time, we told the British Parliament that we were not ready to break this last colonial link.

After fifty years of discussion we have finally decided to retrieve what is properly ours. It is with happy hearts, and with gratitude for the patience displayed by Great Britain, that we are preparing to acquire today our complete national sovereignty. It is my deepest hope that Canada will match its new legal maturity with that degree of political maturity which will allow us all to make a total commitment to the Canadian ideal.

I speak of a Canada where men and women of aboriginal ancestry, of French and British heritage, of the diverse cultures of the world, demonstrate the will to share this land in peace, in justice, and with mutual respect. I speak of a Canada which is proud of, and strengthened by its essential bilingual destiny, a Canada whose people believe in sharing and in mutual support, and not in building regional barriers.

I speak of a country where every person is free to fulfill himself or herself to the utmost, unhindered by the arbitrary actions of governments.

The Canadian ideal which we have tried to live, with varying degrees of success and failure for a hundred years, is really an act of defiance against the history of mankind. Had this country been founded upon a less noble vision, or had our forefathers surrendered to the difficulties of building this nation, Canada would have been torn apart long ago. It should not surprise us, therefore, that even now we sometimes feel the pull of those old reflexes of mutual fear and distrust.

Fear of becoming vulnerable by opening one's arms to other Canadians who speak a different language or live in a different culture.

Fear of becoming poorer by agreeing to share one's resources and wealth with fellow citizens living in regions less favoured by nature.

The Canada we are building lies beyond the horizon of such fears. Yet it is not, for all that, an unreal country, forgetful of the hearts of men and women. We know that justice and generosity can flourish only in an atmosphere of trust.

For if individuals and minorities do not feel protected against the possibility of the tyranny of the majority, if French-speaking Canadians or native peoples or new Canadians do not feel they will be treated with justice, it is useless to ask them to open their hearts and minds to their fellow Canadians.

Similarly, if provinces feel that their sovereign rights are not secure in those fields in which they have full constitutional jurisdiction, it is useless to preach to them about co-operation and sharing.

The constitution which is being proclaimed today goes a long way toward removing the reasons for the fears of which I have spoken.

We now have a charter which defines the kind of country in which we wish to live, and guarantees the basic rights and freedoms which each of us shall enjoy as a citizen of Canada.

It reinforces the protection offered to French-speaking Canadians outside Quebec, and to English-speaking Canadians in Quebec. It recognizes our multicultural character. It upholds the equality of women and the rights of disabled persons.

The constitution confirms the longstanding division of powers among governments in Canada, and even strengthens provincial jurisdiction over natural resources and property rights. It entrenches the principle of equalization, thus helping less wealthy provinces to discharge their obligations without excessive taxation. It offers a way to meet the legitimate demands of our

*Prime Minister Pierre Elliott Trudeau and Queen Elizabeth II signing the Constitution Act, 1982*

native peoples. And, of course, by its amending formula, it now permits us to complete the task of constitutional renewal in Canada.

The Government of Quebec decided that it wasn't enough. It decided not to participate in this ceremony, celebrating Canada's full independence. I know that many Quebecers feel themselves pulled in two directions by that decision. But one need look only at the results of the referendum in May, 1980, to realize how very strong is the attachment to Canada among the people of Quebec. By definition, the silent majority does not make a lot of noise; it is content to make history.

History will show, however, that in the guarantees written into the Charter of Rights and Freedoms, and in the amending formula – which allows Quebec to opt out of any constitutional arrangement which touches upon language and culture, with full financial compensation – nothing essential to the originality of Quebec has been sacrificed.

Moreover, the process of constitutional reform has not come to an end. The two orders of government have made a formal pledge to define more precisely the rights of native peoples. At the same time, they must work together to strengthen the Charter of Rights, including language rights in the various provinces. Finally, they must try to work out a better division of powers among governments.

It must, however, be recognized that no constitution, no Charter of Rights and Freedoms, no sharing of powers can be a substitute for the willingness to share the risks and grandeur of the Canadian adventure. Without that collective act of the will, our constitution would be a dead letter, and our country would wither away.

It is true that our will to live together has sometimes appeared to be in deep hibernation; but it is there nevertheless, alive and tenacious, in the hearts of Canadians of every province and territory. I wish simply that the bringing home of our Constitution marks the end of a long winter, the breaking up of the ice-jams and the beginning of a new spring. For what we are celebrating today is not so much the completion of our task, but the renewal of our hope – not so much an ending, but a fresh beginning.

Let us celebrate the renewal and patriation of our Constitution; but let us put our faith, first and foremost, in the people of Canada who will breathe life into it.

It's in that spirit of faith, and of confidence, that I join with Canadians everywhere in sharing this day of national achievement. It is in their name, Your Majesty, that I now invite you, the Queen of Canada, to give solemn proclamation to our new Constitution.

# REBELLION AND RESISTANCE

> **Blood! Blood! Blood! Prisons, scaffolds, widows, orphans, destitution, ruin; these are what fill the blank in the administration of this Government of the affairs of the North-West.**
>
> *- Sir Wilfrid Laurier, 1886*

## Louis Riel

His Final Statement, The *Queen versus Louis Riel*

*Court Room, Regina, 31 July 1885*

### 'I hope with the help of God I will maintain calmness and decorum as suits this honourable court...'

**Coming a mere eighteen years after Confederation, the *Queen versus Louis Riel* ranks amongst the most significant court cases in Canadian history. Its impact continues to echo in relations between francophone, anglophone and Métis Canadians.**

**The leader of the failed North-West Rebellion, in July 1885 Riel was indicted with six counts of treason. During the subsequent trial, against the wishes of their client, his attorneys focused increasingly on an insanity defence.**

**Riel was limited to two lengthy speeches in which he defended his actions and affirmed the rights of the Métis, referred to here as 'half-breeds'. Among those the resistance leader mentions are priests and doctors, all of whom presented evidence to indicate that Riel was insane. Charles Nolin, also mentioned, was a cousin and former confidant. A witness for the prosecution, Nolin testified that Riel's goal was to divide Canada into separate countries. 'Exovedate', included in the statement, was a neologism created by Riel and used to describe his council in the resistance.**

**This final speech was delivered at the conclusion of the five-day trial. Hours later, the jury found the defendant guilty. Though mercy was recommended, Hugh Richardson, magistrate for the District of Saskatchewan in the North-West Territories, sentenced Riel to death. He was hanged on 16 November 1885 in Regina.**

Your Honours, gentlemen of the jury: It would be easy for me today to play insanity, because the circumstances are such as to excite any man, and under the natural excitement of what is taking place to-day (I cannot speak English very well, but am trying to do so, because most of those here speak English), under the excitement which my trial causes me would justify me not to appear as usual, but with my mind out of its ordinary condition. I hope with the help of God I will maintain calmness and decorum as suits this honourable court, this honourable jury.

You have seen by the papers in the hands of the Crown that I am naturally inclined to think of God at the beginning of my actions. I wish if you – I – do it you won't take it as a mark of insanity, that you won't take it as part of a play of insanity. Oh, my God, help me through Thy grace and the divine influence of Jesus Christ. Oh, my God, bless me, bless this honourable court, bless this honourable jury, bless my good lawyers who have come seven hundred leagues to try to save my life, bless also the lawyers for the Crown, because they have done, I am sure, what they thought their duty. They have shown me fairness which at first I did not expect from them. Oh, my God, bless all those who are around me through the grace and influence of Jesus Christ our Saviour, change the curiosity of those who are paying attention to me, change that curiosity into sympathy with me. The day of my birth I was helpless and my mother took care of me although she was not able to do it alone, there was someone to help her to take care of me and I lived. Today, although a man, I am as helpless before this court, in the Dominion of Canada and in this world, as I was helpless on the knees of my mother the day of my birth.

The North-West is also my mother, it is my mother country and although my mother country is sick and confined in a certain way, there are some from Lower Canada who came to help her to take care of me during her sickness and I am sure that my mother country will not kill me more than my mother did forty years ago when I came into the world, because a mother is always a mother, and even if I have my faults if she can see I am true she will be full of love for me.

When I came into the North-West in July, the first of July 1884, I found the Indians suffering. I found the half-breeds eating the rotten pork of the Hudson Bay Company and getting sick and weak every day. Although a half-breed, and having no pretension to help the whites, I also paid attention to them. I saw they were deprived of responsible government, I saw that they were deprived of their public liberties. I remembered that half-breed meant white and Indian, and while I paid attention to the suffering Indians and the half-breeds I remembered that the greatest part of my heart and blood was white and I have directed my attention to help the Indians, to help the half-breeds and to help the whites to the best of my ability. We have made petitions, I have made petitions with others to the Canadian Government asking to relieve the condition of this country. We have taken time; we have tried to unite all classes, even, if I may speak, all parties. Those who have been in close communication with me know I have suffered, that I have waited for months to bring some of the people of the Saskatchewan to an understanding of certain important points in our petition to the Canadian Government and I have done my duty. I believe I have done my duty. It has been said in this box that I have been egotistic. Perhaps I am egotistic. A man cannot be individuality without paying attention to himself. He cannot generalize himself, though he may be general. I have done all I could to make good petitions with others, and we have sent them to the Canadian Government, and when the Canadian Government did answer, through the Under Secretary of State, to the Secretary of the Joint Committee of the Saskatchewan, then I began to speak of myself, not before; so my particular interests passed after the public interests. A good deal has been said about the settlement and division of lands a good deal has been said about that. I do not think my dignity today here would allow me to mention the foreign policy, but if I was to explain to you or if I had been allowed to make the questions to witnesses, those questions would have appeared in an altogether different light before the court and jury. I do not say that my lawyers did not put the right questions. The observations I had the honour to make to the court the day before yesterday were good, they were absent of the situation, they did not know all the small circumstances as I did. I could mention a point, but that point was leading to so many that I could not have been all the time suggesting. By it I don't wish it understood that I do not appreciate the good works of my lawyers, but if I were to go into all the details of what has taken place, I think I could safely show you that what Captain Young said that I am aiming all the time at practical results was true, and I could have proved it. During my life I have aimed at practical results. I have writings, and after my death I hope that my spirit will bring practical results.

The learned lawyers for the Crown have produced all the papers and scribbling that was under their hands. I thank them for not having brought out those papers which are so particular to myself, though as soon as they saw what they were they should not have looked at them. I have written not books, but many things. All my papers were taken. I destined the papers to be published, if they were worth publishing, after my death. I told Parenteau, one of the prisoners, to put all my books underground. He did not do it. At that time they acknowledged my orders, that is why I say so. He did not put my books away in time and I am not sorry. I say, I thank the learned lawyers for the Crown for having reserved so many things; and if, by the almighty power of God, I go free from this trial, I have such confidence in British fairness that all my papers will be returned me, at least the originals – and if copies are wanted I will be willing to give them.

No one can say that the North-West was not suffering last year, particularly the Saskatchewan, for the other parts of the North-West I cannot say so much. But what I have done, and risked, and to which I have exposed myself, rested certainly on the conviction, I had to do, was called upon to do something for my country.

It is true, gentlemen, I believed for years I had a mission, and when I speak of a mission you will understand me not as trying to play the roll of insane before the grand jury so as to have a verdict of acquittal upon that ground. I believe that I have a mission, I believe I had a mission at this very time. What encourages me to speak to you with more confidence in all the imperfections of my English way of speaking, it is that I have yet and still that mission, and with the help of God, who is in this box with me. And He is on the side of my lawyers, even with the honourable court, the Crown and the jury, to help me, and to prove by the extraordinary help that there is a Providence today in my trial, as there was a Providence in the battles of the Saskatchewan.

I have not assumed to myself that I had a mission. I was working in Manitoba first, and I did all I could to get free institutions for Manitoba. They have those institutions today in Manitoba, and they try to improve them, while myself, who obtained them, I am forgotten as if I was dead. But after I had obtained, with the help of others, a constitution for Manitoba, when the Government at Ottawa was not willing to inaugurate it at the proper time, I have worked till the inauguration should take place, and that is why I have been banished for five years. I had to rest five years, I was willing to do it. I protested, I said: 'Oh, my God, I offer You all my existence for that cause, and please to make of my weakness an instrument to help men in my country.' And seeing my intentions, the late Archbishop Bourget said: 'Riel has no narrow views, he is a man to accomplish great things,' and he wrote that letter of which I hope that the Crown has at least a copy. And in another letter, when I became what doctors believed to be insane, Bishop Bourget wrote again and said: 'Be ye blessed by God and man and take patience in your evils.' Am I not taking patience? Will I be blessed by man as I have been by God?

I say that I have been blessed by God, and I hope that you will not take that as a presumptuous assertion. It has been a great success for me to come through all the dangers I have in that fifteen years. If I have not succeeded in wearing a fine coat myself I have at the same time the great consolation of seeing that God has maintained my view; that He has maintained my health sufficiently to go through the world, and that he has kept me from bullets, when bullets marked my hat. I am blessed by God. It is this trial that is going to show that I am going to be blessed by man during my existence, the benedictions are a guarantee that I was not wrong when by circumstances I was taken away from adopted land to my native land. When I see British people sitting in the court to try me, remembering that the English people are proud of that word 'fair-play', I am confident that I will be blesssed by God and by man also.

Not only Bishop Bourget spoke to me in that way, but Father Jean Baptiste Bruno, the priest of Worcester, who was my director of conscience, said to me: 'Riel, God has put an object into your hands, the cause of the triumph of religion in the world, take care, you will succeed when most believe you have lost.' I have got those words in my heart, those words of J. B. Bruno and the late Archbishop Bourget. But last year, while I was yet in Montana, and while I was passing before the Catholic church, the priest, the Reverend Father Frederick Ebeville, curate of the church of the Immaculate Conception, at Benton, said to me: 'I am glad to see you. Is your family here?' I said: 'Yes.' He said: 'Go and bring them to the altar, I want to bless you before you go away.' And with Gabriel Dumont and my family we all went on our knees at the altar. The priest put on his surplice and he took holy water and was going to bless us. I said: 'Will you allow me to pronounce a prayer while you bless me?' He said: 'Yes, I want to know what it is.' I told him the prayer. It is speaking to God: 'My Father, bless me according to the views of Thy Providence which are bountiful and without measure.' He said to me: 'You can say that prayer while I bless you.' Well, he blessed me and I pronounced that prayer for myself, for my wife, for my children, and for Gabriel Dumont.

When the glorious General Middleton fired on us during three days, and on our families, and when shells went and bullets went as thick as mosquitoes in the hot days of summer, when I saw my children, my wife, myself and Gabriel Dumont were escaping, I said that nothing but the blessing without measure of Father Frederick Ebeville could save me – and that can save me today from these charges. The benediction promised to me surrounded me all the time in the Saskatchewan, and since it seems to me that I have seen it.

Captain Deane, Corporal Prickert, and the corporal of the guard who have been appointed over me have been so gentle while the papers were raging against me shows that nothing but the benediction of God could give me the favour I have had in remaining so respected among these men. Today when I saw the glorious General Middleton bearing testimony that he thought I was not insane, and when Captain Young proved that I am not insane, I felt that God was blessing me, and blotting away from my name the blot resting upon my reputation on account of having been in the lunatic asylum of my good friend Doctor Roy.

*Louis Riel addressing the jury. The 'Court Room', so described in the charges laid against the Métis leader, was in fact a privately owned building that had been rented for the trial.*

I have been in an asylum, but I thank the lawyers for the Crown who destroyed the testimony of my good friend Doctor Roy, because I have always believed that I was put in the asylum without reason. Today my pretension is guaranteed, and that is a blessing too in that way. I have also been in the lunatic asylum at Longue Pointe, and I wonder that my friend Doctor Lachapelle, who took care of me charitably, and Doctor Howard are not here. I was there perhaps under my own name.

Even if I was going to be sentenced by you, gentlemen of the jury, I have this satisfaction if I die… that if I die I will not be reputed by all men as insane, as a lunatic. A good deal has been said by the two reverend fathers, André and Fourmand. I cannot call them my friends, but they made no false testimony. I know that a long time ago they believed me more or less insane. Father Fourmand said that I would pass from great passion to great calmness. That shows great control under contradiction, and according to my opinion and with the help of God I have that control. Mister Charles Nolin, when he went into the box, did not say that he was sworn with me in all the affairs that I did. Far from taking them as insane affairs, he was in them under the cover of an oath with four of us. He did not say that in the box. My word is perhaps not testimony, but if he was asked in the box to say if there was an oath taken he could not deny it, and he would have to name the four men, and he would have to name himself. When he speaks of resigning a contract in my favour, I did not ask it, the Government would not give it to me; besides, he was engaged in a movement against the Government, and to take a contract from the Government was certainly a weakness upon his part, and I told him not to compromise his cause, and I told him to withdraw instead of going ahead till we saw if we were going to be listened to at all. He wanted me to make a bargain and renounce my American citizenship. I told him that it was a matter of more strength that I should be an American citizen, not that I want to make any ground of it, but as it took place naturally and as the fact existed I wanted to take advantage of it as such. I told him: 'It is of advantage for you that you should have me an American citizen. I have no bargain to make with you about my American papers, no bargain on such a matter as that.' Mister Charles Nolin speaks of my ambition, and other witnesses also. There are men among the prisoners who know that last year Mister Renez and Mister Joseph Fourget came to the Saskatchewan and said that I could have a place in the council if I wanted it, and that it was a good chance for the half-breeds of the Saskatchewan. If I had been so anxious for position I would have grasped at this place, but I did not, and Mister Nolin has some knowledge of that, I speak of those things to defend my character, as it has been said that I am egotistical.

The agitation in the North-West Territories would have been constitutional, and would certainly be constitutional today if, in my opinion, we had not been attacked. Perhaps the Crown has not been able to find out the particulars, that we were attacked, but as we were on the scene it was easy to understand. When we sent petitions to the Government, they used to answer us by sending police, and when the rumours were increasing every day that Riel had been shot here or there, or that Riel was going to be shot by such and such a man, the police would not pay any attention to it. I am glad that I have mentioned the police, because of the testimony that has been given in the box during the examination of many of the witnesses. If I had been allowed to put questions to the witnesses, I would have asked them when it was I said a single word against a single policeman or a single officer. I have respected the policemen, and I do today, and I have respected the officers of the police; the paper that I sent to Major Crozier is a proof it: 'We respect you, Major.' There are papers which the Crown has in its hands, and which show that demoralization exists among the police, if you will allow me to say it in the court, as I have said it in writing.

Your Honours, gentlemen of the jury, if I was a man of today perhaps it would be presumptuous to speak in that way, but the truth is good to say, and it is said in a proper manner, and it is without any presumption, it is not because I have been libelled for fifteen years that I do not believe myself something. I know that through the grace of God I am the founder of Manitoba. I know that though I have no open road for my influence, I have big influence, concentrated as a big amount of vapour in an engine. I believe by what I suffered for fifteen years, by what I have done for Manitoba and the people of the North-West, that my words are worth something. If I give offence, I do not speak to insult. Yes, you are the pioneers of civilization, the whites are the pioneers of civilization, but they bring among the Indians demoralization. Do not be offended, ladies, do not be offended, here are the men who can cure that evil; and if at times I have been strong against my true friends and fathers, the reverend priests of the Saskatchewan, it is because my convictions are strong. There have been witnesses to show that immediately after great passion I could come back to the great respect I have for them.

One of the witnesses here, George Ness, I think, said that I spoke of Archbishop Taché, and told him that he was a thief. If I had had the opportunity I proposed I would have questioned him as to what I said, so that you would understand me. I have known Archbishop Taché as a great benefactor, I have seen him surrounded by his great property, the property of a widow, whose road was passing near. He bought the land around, and took that way to try and get her property at a cheap price. I read in the Gospel: 'Ye Pharisees with your long prayers devour the widows.' And as Archbishop Taché is my great benefactor, as he is my father, I would say because he has done me an immense deal of good, and because there was no one who had the courage to tell him, I did, because I love him, because I acknowledge all he has done for me; as to Bishop Grandin, it was on the same grounds. I have other instances of Bishop Taché, and the witness could have said that the Reverend Father Moulin: 'When you speak of such persons as Archbishop Taché, you ought to say that he made a mistake, not that he committed robbery.' I say that we have been patient a long time, and when we see that mild words only serve as covers for great ones to do wrong, it is time when we are justified in saying that robbery is robbery everywhere, and the guilty ones are bound by the force of public opinion to take notice of it. The one who has the courage to speak out in that way, instead of being an outrageous man, becomes in fact a benefactor to those men themselves, and to society.

When we got to the church of Saint Anthony on the 18th, there was a witness who said,

I think George Ness, that I said to Father Moulin, 'You are a Protestant.' According to my theory I was not going to speak in that way, but I said that we were protesting against the Canadian Government, and that he was protesting against us, and that we were two protestants in our different ways.

As to religion, what is my belief? What is my insanity about that? My insanity, your Honours, gentlemen of the jury, is that I wish to leave Rome aside, inasmuch as it is the cause of division between Catholics and Protestants. I did not wish to force my views, because in Batoche to the half-breeds that followed me I used the word, *carte blanche*. If I have any influence in the New World it is to help in that way and even if it takes two hundred years to become practical, then after my death that will bring out practical results, and then my children's children will shake hands with the Protestants of the New World in a friendly manner. I do not wish these evils which exist in Europe to be continued, as much as I can influence it, among the half-breeds. I do not wish that to be repeated in America. That work is not the work of some days or some years, it is the work of hundreds of years.

My condition is helpless, so helpless that my good lawyers – and they have done it by conviction; Mister Fitzpatrick in his beautiful speech has proved, he believed, I was insane – my condition seems to be so helpless that they have recourse to try and prove insanity to try and save me in that way. If I am insane, of course I don't know it; it is a property of insanity to be unable to know it. But what is the kind of mission that I have? Practical results. It is said that I had myself acknowledged as a prophet by the half-breeds. The half-breeds have some intelligence. Captain Young, who has been so polite and gentle during the time I was under his care, said that what was done at Batoche, from a military point of view was nice, that the line of defence was nice, that showed some intelligence.

It is not to be supposed that the half-breeds acknowledged me as a prophet if they had not seen that I could see something into the future. If I am blessed without measure I can see something into the future, we all see into the future more or less. As what kind of a prophet would I come, would it be a prophet who would all the time have a stick in his hand, and threatening – a prophet of evil? If the half-breeds had acknowledged me as a prophet, if on the other side priests come and say that I am polite, if there are general officers, good men, come into this box and prove that I am polite, prove that I am decent in my manner, in combining all together you have a decent prophet. An insane man cannot withhold his insanity. If I am insane my heart will tell what is in me.

Last night, while I was taking exercise, the spirit who guides and assists me and consoles me told me that 'tomorrow somebody will come *t'aider*', five English and one French word: '*t'aider*', that is to help you. I am consoled by that. While I was recurring to my God, to our God, I said, but woe to me if you do not help me, and these words came to me in the morning, in the morning someone will come *t'aider*, that is today. I said that to my two guards and you can go for the two guards. I told them that if the spirit that directs me is the spirit of truth it is today that I expect help. This morning the good doctor who has care of me came to me and said you will speak today before the court. I thought I would not be allowed to speak;

those words were given to me to tell me that I would have liberty to speak. There was one French word in it, it meant I believe that there was to be some French influence in it, but the most part English. It is true that my good lawyers from the Province of Quebec have given me good advice.

Mister Nolin came into the box and said that Mister Riel said that he had a noise in his bowels and that I told him that it meant something. I wish that he had said what I said, what I wrote on the paper of which he speaks, perhaps he can yet be put in the box. I said to Nolin, 'Do you hear?' Yes, I said there will be trouble in the North-West, and was it so or not? Has there been no trouble in the North-West? Besides Nolin knows that among his nationality, which is mine, he knows that the half-breeds as hunters can foretell many things, perhaps some of you have a special knowledge of it. I have seen half-breeds who say, my hand is shaking, this part of my hand is shaking you will see such a thing today, and it happens. Others will say I feel the flesh on my leg move in such a way, it is a sign of such a thing, and it happens. There are men who know that I speak right. If the witness spoke of that fact which he mentioned, to show that I was insane he did not remember that perhaps on that point he is insane himself, because the half-breed by the movement of the hand, sometimes of his shoulders, sometimes his legs, can have certain knowledge of what will happen. To bring Sir John to my feet, if it was well reported it would appear far more reasonable than it has been made to appear. Mister Blake, the leader of the opposition, is trying to bring Sir John to his feet in one way. He never had as much at stake as I had, although the Province of Ontario is great it is not as great as the North-West.

I am glad that the Crown have proved that I am the leader of the half-breeds in the North-West. I will perhaps be one day acknowledged as more than a leader of the half-breeds, and if I am I will have an opportunity of being acknowledged as a leader of good in this great country.

One of the witnesses said that I intended to give Upper Canada to the Irish. If he had no mystery he would have seen that Upper Canada could not be given to the Irish without being given to England. He rested only upon his imagination.

There is another thing about the partition of lands into sevenths. I do not know if I am prepared to speak of it here because it would become public information. There is so much at stake that if I explained that theory Canada would not very long remain in quiet.

Captain Deane has seen my papers – I have sent them somewhere but he has seen them – and after seeing them he came there and said that I was an intelligent man, and pretty shrewd. I have written these documents and they are in the hands of those whom I trust. I do not want to make them public during my trial; what I have made public during the sixty days we were in arms at Batoche.

There have been three different times when the council decided to send men to the States to notify the nationalities to come to our assistance, but these three delegations waited for my orders and have not started; why? Because I had an object.

The half-breeds also knew that I told them that they would be punished, that I did not say it of my own responsibility, but that I said it in the same way as I have told them other things. It was said to me that the nation would be punished. Why? Because she had consented to leave Rome too quick. What was the meaning of that? There was a discussion about too quick; they said that they should do it at once. Too quick does not mean too soon, if we say yes, it shows no consideration to the man. If God wants something, and if we say 'yes', that is not the way to answer him. He wants the conscience to say: 'yes, oh my God, I do Thy will'. And because the half-breeds quickly separated from Rome, in such a quick manner, it was disagreeable to God and they were punished – and I told them it would happen; fifty of those who are there can prove it. But, you will say, you did not put yourself as a prophet? The ninth-century is to be treated in certain ways, and it is probably for that reason I have found the word 'Exovedate'. I prefer to be called one of the flock. I am no more than you are, I am simply one of the flock, equal to the rest. If it is any satisfaction to the doctors to know what kind of insanity I have, if they are going to call my pretensions insanity, I say humbly, through the grace of God, I believe I am the prophet of the New World.

I wish you to believe that I am not trying to play insanity; there is in the manner, in the standing of a man, the proof that he is sincere, not playing. You will say, what have you got to say? I have to attend to practical results. Is it practical that you be acknowledged as a prophet? It is practical to say it. I think that if the half-breeds have acknowledged me, as a community, to be a prophet, I have reason to believe that it is beginning to become practical. I do not wish, for my satisfaction, the name of prophet. Generally that title is accompanied with such a burden, that if there is satisfaction for your vanity, there is a check to it. To set myself up as Pope, no, no. I said I believed that Bishop Bourget had succeeded in spirit and in truth. Why? Because while Rome did not pay attention to us, he, as a bishop, paid attention to us.

You have given me your attention, your Honours; you have given me your attention, gentlemen of the jury, and this great audience. I see that if I go any further on that point I will lose the favour you have granted me up to this time, and as I am aiming all the time at practical results, I will stop here, master of myself, through the help of God. I have only a few more words to say, your Honours. Gentlemen of the jury, my reputation, my liberty, my life, are at your discretion. So confident am I, that I have not the slightest anxiety, not even the slightest doubt, as to your verdict. The calmness of my mind concerning the favourable decision which I expect, does not come from any unjustifiable presumption upon my part. I simply trust, that through God's help, you will balance everything in a conscientious manner, and that, having heard what I had to say, that you will acquit me. I do respect you, although you are only half a jury, but your number of six does not prevent you from being just and conscientious. Your number of six does not prevent me giving you my confidence, which I would grant to another six men. Your Honour, because you appointed these men, do not believe that I disrespect you. It is not by your own choice; you were authorized by those above you, by the authorities in the North-West. You have acted according to your duty, and while it is, in our view, against the guarantees of liberty, I trust the Providence of God will bring out good of what you have done conscientiously.

Although this court has been in existence for the last fifteen years, I thought I had a right to be tried in another court. I do not disrespect this court. I do respect it, and what is called by my learned and good lawyers, the in competency of the court must not be called in disrespect, because I have all respect.

The only things I would like to call your attention to before you retire to deliberate are: first, that the House of Commons, Senate and Ministers of the Dominion, and who make laws for this land and govern it, are no representation whatever of the people of the North-West; second, that the North-West Council generated by the federal Government has the great defect of its parent; third, the number of members elected for the Council by the people make it only a sham representative legislature and no representative government at all.

British civilization which rules today the world, and the British constitution has defined such government as this is which rules the North-West Territories as irresponsible government, which plainly means that there is no responsibility. And by all the science which has been shown here yesterday you are compelled to admit if there is no responsibility, it is insane.

Good sense combined with scientific theories lead to the same conclusion. By the testimony laid before you during my trial witnesses on both sides made it certain that petition after petition had been sent to the federal Government, and so irresponsible is that government to the North-West that in the course of several years besides doing nothing to satisfy the people of this great land, it has even hardly been able to answer once or to give a single response. That fact would indicate an absolute lack of responsibility, and therefore insanity complicated with paralysis.

The Ministers of an insane and irresponsible government and its little one – the North-West Council – made up their minds to answer my petitions by surrounding me slyly and by attempting to jump upon me suddenly and upon my people in the Saskatchewan. Happily when they appeared and showed their teeth to devour, I was ready: that is what is called my crime of high treason, and to which they hold me today. Oh, my good jurors, in the name of Jesus Christ, the only one who can save and help me, they have tried to tear me to pieces.

If you take the plea of the defence that I am not responsible for my acts, acquit me completely, since I have been quarrelling with an insane and irresponsible government. If you pronounce in favour of the Crown, which contends that I am responsible, acquit me all the same. You are perfectly justified in declaring that having my reason and sound mind, I have acted reasonably and in self-defence, while the Government, my accuser, being irresponsible, and consequently insane, cannot but have acted wrong, and if high treason there is it must be on its side and not on my part.

*His Honour*: Are you done?

*Riel*: Not yet, if you have the kindness to permit me your attention for a while.

*His Honour*: Well, proceed.

*Riel*: For fifteen years I have been neglecting myself. Even one of the most hard witnesses on me said that with all my vanity, I never was particular to my clothing; yes, because I never had much to buy any clothing. The Reverend Father André has often had the kindness to feed my family with a sack of flour – and Father Fourmand. My wife and children are without means, while I am working more than any representative in the North-West. Although I am simply a guest of this country – a guest of the half-breeds of the Saskatchewan – although as a simple guest, I worked to better the condition of the people of the Saskatchewan at the risk of my life, to better the condition of the people of the Saskatchewan at the risk of my life, to better the condition of the people of the North-West, I have never had any pay. It has always been my hope to have a fair living one day. It will be for you to pronounce. If you say I was right, you can conscientiously acquit me, as I hope through the help of God you will. You will console those who have been fifteen years around me only partaking in my sufferings. What you will do in justice to me, in justice to my family, in justice to my friends, in justice to the North-West, will be rendered a hundred times to you in this world, and to use a sacred expression, life everlasting in the other.

I thank your Honour for the favour you have granted me in speaking. I thank you for the attention you have given me, gentlemen of the jury, and I thank those who have had the kindness to encourage my imperfect way of speaking the English language by your good attention. I put my speech under the protection of my God, my Saviour, He is the only one who can make it effective. It is possible it should become effective, as it is proposed to good men, to good people, and to good ladies, also.

## Sir Wilfrid Laurier

### On the Execution of Louis Riel and the North-West Rebellion

*The House Of Commons, Ottawa, 16 March 1886*

***'...the great mass of the people believed that mercy should have been extended to all the prisoners, Riel included...'***

**Sir Wilfrid Laurier spoke many times about Louis Riel both in the House of Commons and without. It was Laurier's contention, and that of the Liberal Party as a whole, that the blame for the North-West Rebellion rested not on the executed Riel, nor on the Métis settlers and those of European descent, but with the government of Sir John A. Macdonald.**

**Delivered entirely in English, this particular speech, perhaps Laurier's strongest, was key in convincing Liberal leader Edward Blake that the Member of Parliament for Quebec East should be his successor.**

**Here Laurier uses his knowledge of history to great effect, quoting Henry IV of France and comparing Riel's sentence to that handed to John Byng, the British Admiral who was executed for not having 'done his utmost' during the Seven Years' War.**

**The Parti National referred to here was a provincial party composed primarily of Quebec liberals. Its greatest success came in the wake of the Riel execution, when it attracted a number of disaffected provincial Conservatives. The Parti National formed the provincial government in 1887, but was dismissed due to scandal four years later.**

**Presented here is the first fifth of Laurier's great speech.**

Mister Speaker, since no one on the other side of the House has the courage to continue this debate, I will do so myself. The Minister of Public Works stated that the Government were ready and anxious to discuss this question, and is this an evidence of the courage they pretend to possess? Sir, in all that has been said so far, and that has fallen from the lips of honourable gentlemen opposite, there is one thing in which we can all agree, and one thing only – we can all agree in the tribute which was paid to the volunteers by the Minister of Public Works when he entered into a defence of the Government. The volunteers had a most painful duty to perform, and they performed it in a most creditable manner to themselves and the country. Under the uniform of a soldier there is generally to be found a warm and merciful heart. Moreover, our soldiers are citizens who have an interest in this country: but when they are on duty they know nothing but duty. At the same time it can fairly be presumed that when on duty the heart feels and the mind thinks; and it may be fairly presumed that those who were on duty in the North-West last spring thought and felt as a great soldier, a great king, King Henry IV of France, thought and felt when engaged in battle for many years of his life, in fighting his rebellious subjects. Whenever his sword inflicted a wound he used these words:

> The King strikes thee, God heal thee!

It may be presumed that perhaps our soldiers, when fighting the rebellion, were also animated by a similar spirit, and prayed to God that he would heal the wounds that it was their duty to inflict, and that no more blood should be shed than the blood shed by themselves. The Government, however, thought otherwise. The Government thought that the blood shed by the soldiers was not sufficient, but that another life must also be sacrificed. We heard the Minister of Public Works attempting to defend the conduct of the Government, and stating that its action in this matter was a stern necessity which duty to our Queen and duty to our country made inevitable.

Mister Speaker, I have yet to learn – and I have not learned it from anything that has fallen from the lips of gentlemen opposite – that duty to Queen and country may ever prevent the exercise of that prerogative of mercy which is the noblest prerogative of the Crown. The language of the honourable gentleman was not the first occasion when responsible or irresponsible advisers of the Crown attempted to delude the public, and perhaps themselves as well, into the belief that duty to Queen and country required blood, when mercy was a possible alternative.

When Admiral Byng was sentenced to be shot for no other crime than that of being unfortunate in battle, there were men at the time, who said to the King that the interests of the country required that the sentence should be carried out, though the court, which had convicted him, strongly recommended him to mercy. Those evil counsels prevailed, and the sentence was carried out; but the verdict of history, the verdict of posterity – posterity to which honourable gentlemen now appeal – has declared long ago that the carrying out of the sentence against Admiral Byng was a judicial murder. And I venture to predict, Mister Speaker, that the verdict of history will be the same in this instance.

In every instance in which a Government has carried out the extreme penalty of the law, when mercy was suggested instead, the verdict has been the same.

Sir, in the province to which I belong, and especially amongst the race to which I belong, the execution of Louis Riel has been universally condemned as being the sacrifice of a life, not to inexorable justice, but to bitter passion and revenge.

And now, Sir, before going any further, it is fitting that, perhaps, I should address myself at once to the state of things which has sprung up in Quebec from the universal condemnation of the Government not only by their foes, but by their friends as well.

The movement which has followed the execution of Riel has been strangely misconceived, or I should say, has been wilfully misrepresented. The Tory press of Ontario at once turned bitterly and savagely upon their French allies of twenty-five years or more. They assailed them not only in their action but in their motives. They charged them with being animated with nothing less than race prejudices ; they not only charged their former friends, but the whole French race as well, that the only motive which led them to take the course they did in the matter of Riel, was simply because Riel was of French origin. They charged against the whole race that they would step between a criminal and justice, the moment the criminal was one of their own race. They charged against the whole French race that they would prevent the execution of the law the moment the law threatened one of their own.

Mister Speaker, in this matter I am not desirous of following the example which has been set before us by honourable gentlemen opposite of citing copious newspaper extracts, although I could cite extracts of the most bitter nature that ever was penned, of *The Mail* newspaper and other Tory organs against French Canadians. I will not import into this debate any more acrimony than can be avoided, but I simply quote a single paragraph from *The Mail* and one of the most moderate which will show the general spirit of the attacks made upon us. On the 7th of December last, *The Mail* wrote as follows, speaking of the French Canadians:

> Their leaders are paying us back at the present time by asserting that they should have the right of suspending the operation of law against treason whenever they choose to demand its suspension in the interests of a traitor of French origin, even though he may have been twice guilty.

Sir, I denounce this as a vile calumny! I denounce this as false. I claim this for my fellow-countrymen of French origin that there is not to be found anywhere under Heaven a more docile, quiet and law-abiding people. I claim this for my fellow-countrymen of French origin and I appeal to the testimony of any of those who know them and have lived amongst them that whatever their faults may be, it is not one of their faults to shield, conceal and abet crime. It is true that upon the present occasion the French Canadians have shown an unbounded sympathy for the unfortunate man who lost his life upon the scaffold on the 16th November last. But if they came to that conclusion, it was not because they were influenced by race preferences or race prejudices, if you choose to call them such. They were no more influenced in their opinion by race prejudice, than were the foreign papers which deprecated the execution of Riel. It is a fact that the foreign press, the American press, the English press, the French press, almost without any exception, have taken the ground that the execution of Riel was unjustified, unwarranted and against the spirit of the age. Certainly, it cannot be charged against that press that they were influenced by race feelings or prejudices, if you choose to call them such. And in the same manner, I say, the French Canadians, in the attitude which they took, were not impelled by race prejudices, but by reasons fairly deducible and deduced from the facts of the case.

But if it had been stated that race prejudices, that blood relations had added keeness, and feeling to a conviction formed by the mind, that would have been perfectly true. I will not admit that blood relations can so far cloud my judgement as to make me mistake wrong for right, but I cheerfully add I will plead guilty to that weakness, if weakness it be, that if an injustice be committed against a fellow-being the blow will fell deeper into my heart if it should fall upon one of my kith and kin. I will not admit anything more than that. That race prejudices can so far cloud my judgement as to make me mistake wrong from right, I do not believe to be true.

Before I go further, I desire to say this: It has been stated, time and again, by *The Mail* newspaper and by other Tory organs, that it was the present intention of the French Canadian leaders to organize a purely French Canadian party, to lay aside all party ties and to have no other bonds of party in this House but that tie of race. I protest against any such assertion. Such an assertion is unfounded, it is calculated to do harm, it not founded on truth. It would be simply suicidal to French Canadians to form a party by themselves. Why, so soon as French Canadians, who are in the minority in this House and in the country, were to organize as a political party, they would compel the majority to organize as a political party, and the result must be disastrous to themselves. We have only one way of organizing parties. This country must be governed and can be governed simply on questions of policy and administration, and French Canadians who have had any part in this movement have never had any other intention but to organize upon those party distinctions and upon no other.

In order to lay this question at rest, I cannot do better than to quote the language of the honourable member for Hochelaga, at a meeting that took place recently at Longueuil. That meeting took place in January, I believe. Mister Benoit, the honourable member for the county, had been invited, but had not put in an appearance, and the fact had been commented on by some speakers who had addressed the meeting.

Mister Desjardins spoke as follows:

Mister Benoit has perhaps done well to hesitate, because I have myself hesitated, seeing at the head of the invitation I received, – 'Parti National'. If it be understood by 'Parti National' that it is a party other than those already existing, I am not of that party; but if it be understood that Liberals and Conservatives shall unite in the same idea and present a united front when their national interests may be imperiled, I am of that party. In our movements we have not desired that a criminal should escape death because he is a French Canadian; but because as regards Jackson and Riel, if the first had his life saved, the second should have had it also. We do not want any more privileges; we are strong enough, but what we want is justice for all.

It has been said by sober-minded people that the execution, even if unjust, of the man who was executed and who is believed to have been insane by those who sympathize with him, does not make this a case for the outburst of feeling which has taken place in Quebec on the occasion of Riel's execution. I differ from that view. In our age, in our civilization, every single human life is valuable, and is entitled to protection in the councils of the nation. Not many years ago England sent an expedition and spent millions of her treasure and some of her best blood simply to rescue prisoners whose lives were in the hands of the King of Abyssinia. In the same manner I say that the life of a single subject of Her Majesty here is valuable, and is not to be treated with levity. If there are members in the House who believe that the execution of Riel was not warranted, that under the circumstances of the case it was not judicious, that it was unjust, I say they have a right to arraign the Government for it before this country, and, if they arraign the Government for it and the Government have to take their trial upon it, it must be admitted as a consequence that certain parties will feel upon the question more warmly than others. It is not to be supposed that the same causes which influenced public opinion in Lower Canada acted in the same manner with all classes of the community; that the causes which actuated the community at large were identical in all classes of the community. Some there were who believed that the Government had not meted out the same measure of justice to all those that were accused and who took part in the rebellion. Others believed that the state of mind of Riel was such that it was a judicial murder to execute him; but the great mass of the people believed that mercy should have been extended to all the prisoners, Riel included, because the rebellion was the result of the policy followed by the Government against the half-breeds. That was the chief reason which actuated them, and it seems to me that it is too late in the day to seriously attempt to deny that the rebellion was directly the result of the conduct of the Government towards the half-breeds. It is too late in the day to dispute that fact. Yet we have heard it disputed in this House. By whom? By the last man who, I should have expected, would have disputed it by the honourable member. He gave us the other day his version of the origin of the trouble. Everybody is responsible for the rebellion except one body. *The Globe* is responsible for it; the Farmers' Union is responsible for it; the white settlers are responsible for it. Everybody you can conceive of is responsible for it, except the Government. The Government is perfectly innocent of it, as innocent as a new-born child! Such was the statement made by the honourable member the other day. But if the honourable member is now in earnest as to that matter, how is it that the half-breeds alone have been prosecuted? If *The Globe* is the cause of that rebellion, *The Globe* should have been the first to be indicted. If the white settlers were the instigators of the rebellion, the white settlers should have been indicted also. There is more than that. The counsel for the Crown received authority and even instructions specially to proceed against the instigators of the rebellion, the white settlers, who certainly would have been more guilty than the half-breeds whom they had instigated to rebellion. Here is part of the instructions given by the late Minister

*Sir Wilfrid Laurier, the seventh Prime Minister of Canada*

of Justice to the counsel for the Crown: 'It must be, and from the information which the Government have, it seems probable…' It seems the Government share the opinion of the honourable member for Provencher, and they profess to act accordingly:

It must be, and from the information which the Government have, it seems probable that the rebellion has been encouraged actively by whites, particularly in Prince Albert. Nothing in the whole duty entrusted to you is, I apprehend, more important than that we should if possible find out some of the men who, with far better knowledge than the half-breeds, stirred them up to rebellion, and your special attention is asked to this point.

The honourable member for Provencher does not seem to have given any help to the counsel for the Crown, notwithstanding the knowledge which enables him to say on the floor of Parliament, with the responsibility attaching to his utterances, that the white settlers are responsible for the rebellion. If they are, how comes it that no white settler has yet been indicted – that every white settler is at large? What are we to infer from this? Are we to infer that the Government has receded from the position which was here taken by Sir Alexander Campbell? Or are we to infer that the statement of the honourable member for Provencher is only one of those wild assertions made as a last expedient in the defence of acts otherwise indefensible? The honourable gentlemen went further. He not only charged the white settlers, the Farmers' Union and *The Globe* newspaper, but he also held responsible the Mackenzie Administration. He said that the administration of that Government, from the time that they took office to the time they left, had been null and that the history of their administration in the North-West had been a perfect blank.

Well, Mister Speaker, it is a charge which cannot be made against the present Administration. Their administration was not at all one blank. Blood! Blood! Blood! Prisons, scaffolds, widows, orphans, destitution, ruin – these are what fill the blank in the administration of this Government of the affairs of the North-West.

Mister Speaker, there might be something to say, as the honourable gentleman will apprehend, upon the administration of the honourable member for East York of the affairs of the North-West Territories, but the present would not be a seasonable time, and the occasion may arise hereafter. Let me, however, tell this to the honourable gentleman: if the administration of Mister Mackenzie was blameable for its treatment of the affairs of the North-West, if they were remiss in their duties, how much more blameable must be the present Administration, which have not yet done that which should have been done by their predecessors?

But I forget; the honourable gentleman has nothing, or, at least, very little, to say against the present Government. It may be possible that they have not been altogether diligent in the duties they had to perform, but still they have shown a great deal of good will at least, so says the honourable gentleman. Here is what he says:

In 1880, Sir John Macdonald took the first opportunity he had, in order to bring in a bill into this House – he himself, the leader of the Conservative party, introduced a bill into

Parliament to extend the same privileges and rights to the half-breeds in the territories as those enjoyed under the Manitoba Act by the half-breeds in the province of Manitoba.

This statement is correct, except with regard to the date which should have been 1879 instead of 1880. Sir John Macdonald, as he says, introduced a bill to extend to the half-breeds of the North-West Territories the same privileges as had been granted to those of Manitoba. That was done in 1879, and the Act which I hold in my hand reads as follows:

> That the following powers are hereby delegated to the Governor in Council to satisfy any claims existing in connection with the extinguishment of the Indian titles preferred by the half-breeds resident in the North-West Territories, outside the limits of Manitoba previous to the 15th day of July, 1870, by granting land to such persons to such extent and on such terms and conditions as may from time to time be deemed expedient.

The provisions of this statute were repeated in the Act of 1883. But before we proceed further, it may be important to at once define what were those privileges and rights which were extended to the half-breeds of Manitoba. By the Act of 1870 it was decreed as follows:

> And whereas it is expedient towards the extinguishment of the Indian title to the lands in the province to appropriate a portion of such ungranted lands to the extent of 1,400,000 acres thereof for the benefit of the families of the half-breeds residents, it is hereby enacted that the Lieutenant-Governor, under regulations to be from time to time made by the Governor-General in Council, shall select such lots or tracts in such parts of the province as he may deem expedient, to the extent aforesaid, and divide the same among the children of heads of families residing in the province at the time of the said transfer to Canada.

And by a further Act, the Act of 1874, the same privileges were extended, not only to heads of families but to minors, the children of half-breeds, as defined in section 32 of that Act. These Acts, as they were administered, assigned, first, to each head of family the plot of land of which he happened to be in possession at the time of the transfer, to the extent of 160 acres; and besides that the half-breeds were also granted, for the extinguishment of the Indian title. One hundred and sixty acres of land or scrip for 160 acres of land; and each minor, 240 acres or scrip for that quantity. In 1879, the First Minister took power to extend the same privileges to the half-breeds of the North-West. It will be seen that the half-breeds of Manitoba were treated as a special class. They were not treated as Indians; they were not treated as whites but as participating in the rights of both the whites, and the Indians. If they had been treated as Indians, they would have been sent to their reserves; if they had been treated as whites, they would have been granted homesteads. But as I have said, they were treated as a special class, participating in both rights of whites and Indians; as whites they were given a homestead of 160 acres on the plot of land of which they happened to be in possession; as Indians, they were given scrip for lands to the extent of 160 acres for each head of family, and 240 acres for minors.

In 1879, as I have said, the Government passed a statute similar to the statute of Manitoba. Did they act upon it? When did they act upon it? When was the first thing done by the Government of Canada to put in force the Act of 1879? The first thing ever done by the Government of Canada to put in force the Act they themselves had passed, was on the 25th January, 1885.

Six long years elapsed before they attempted to do that justice to the half-breeds, which they had taken power from Parliament to do, at the time. During all that time the Government was perfectly immovable. The honourable member for Provencher told us the Government have done their duty by the half-breeds.

Sir, if the Government had done their duty by the half-breeds, how is it that the half-breeds so often petitioned the Government to grant them their rights? How is it that they so often deluged the Department with petitions and deputations? How is it that they so often appealed to the honourable member for Provencher himself? How is it, for instance, that on the 19th of November, 1882, Maxime Lepine, now a prisoner in the Manitoba penitentiary, Baptiste Boucher, wounded in battle, Charles Lavallee, wounded in battle, Isidore Dumas, killed in battle, and several others addressed Mister Duck, the agent at Prince Albert, asking him to try and induce the Government to grant them their rights, representing at the same time that they had petitioned, and that their petitions had been supported by prominent men, amongst others the honourable Mister Royal, the member for Provencher, and all without avail? How is it that these men, in order to obtain the rights which were denied them, have gone through such an ordeal as they have, if the Government did justice by them? An agitation was going on all the time in the North-West, and the Government were perfectly immovable.

# WAR AND PEACE

> **Ours we thought were prosaic days, when the great causes of earlier times had lost their inspiration, leaving for attainment those things which demanded only the petty passing inconveniences of the hour. And yet the nobility of manhood had but to hear again the summons of duty and honour to make response which shook the world.**
>
> *- Arthur Meighen, 1921*

# Sir Robert Borden

## On the Great War

*The Winnipeg Canadian Club, Winnipeg, 29 December 1914*

**'In this struggle against the Prussian oligarchy and against its ideals, Canada, in common with all the Empire, is prepared to fight, and intends to fight, to the death.'**

Borden's address to the Canadian Club was made just as the Great War was entering its fifth month. Those who had been convinced that the conflict would be over by Christmas had been proved wrong. The war would require an even greater contribution in terms of resources and men. Here the Prime Minister imagines the war continuing for another year and speculates that a quarter million soldiers would be required of 'the four free nations of the overseas dominions'. In fact, Borden would commit his country of little more than four million males, of all ages, to a contribution of half a million soldiers. From his determination to meet the ill-considered pledge grew the 1917 Conscription Crisis.

This early effort to bolster support for Canada's participation in the Great War was made before an audience of eight hundred, many of which were obliged to stand due to lack of space. The lines of verse are taken from Tennyson's 'In Memoriam'.

From Halifax to Winnipeg I have journeyed across this vast continent for a distance greater than that which would span the Atlantic; and yet I am only at the threshold of these great western provinces, which have responded so splendidly to the call of duty that came more than four months ago. Through all the vastness of this Dominion, with its scattered centres of population and its diversity of race, tradition and creed, there is but one voice as to the justice of the cause for which we have drawn the sword and but one reply as to the obligation which rests upon us. Nowhere in this Dominion has that response and that voice been more unanimous and more emphatic than in this great gateway city of the west.

In this Dominion, confronted as we are with peaceful tasks that tax to the fullest extent our energies in the development of our vast territory, and in the upbuilding of a great free nation on the northern half of this continent, it is almost impossible to realize a conception which regards the waging of war as a justifiable, desirable and even necessary means of national progress and development. The three great wars in which Germany has engaged during the past fifty years have brought to the nation prestige, territory, huge war indemnities and an astonishing increase of national power and influence. During all that period German soil has never been oppressed by the foot of an invader and its people have been spared many of the miseries which war has brought to the nations over whom they triumphed. The religion of valour; the doctrine that might constitutes the highest and only right; that the state is bound to exercise through war its increasing power for its own advancement and for the diffusion of its ideals and culture; the belief that German ideals, methods and culture embody the highest and best results of civilization and that Germany military dominance represents what is best not only for Germany but for the whole world; the economic and commercial advantages and the colonial expansion which German military prowess would secure for the nation through war; these and the like considerations explain in part the concentration of Germany's thought upon the ideal of force, of war and of conquest.

Their Government possesses a control of public opinion which we find it difficult to realize. All the influences which mould the thought of the people have continuously proclaimed that war, especially war with our Empire, was a stern and inevitable duty. Their ruling classes constitute a military autocracy, and the military caste with its all-commanding authority was bent on war. Beyond question, there were influences in Germany which made for peace and favoured peaceful development; but those forces apparently lacked organization and leadership. Moreover, there has been evident in Germany during the past quarter of a century a rising spirit of democracy which has brought inquietude to the ruling oligarchy and to those who are devoted to the principles of absolutism. There was great confidence that a successful war would be a powerful factor in checking or quelling that spirit.

Between the Prussian autocracy and its ideal of worldwide dominance, British supremacy upon the sea has stood as a barrier which must disappear if the ideal was to be attained; and so it was proclaimed that Germany's future was on the sea. We are only beginning to realize the enormous military strength of the German Empire. We are only commencing to understand how immensely superior she stood in military organization, preparation and resources to all the other nations at the outbreak of war. Wielding that tremendous power, which made any apprehension of attack by our Empire a mere idle dream, Germany has for at least twenty years, with constantly increasing emphasis, pressed her challenge of the seas upon the British Empire. Germany well knew, as Britain knew, what that challenge meant and what would ensue from the failure to accept it. We had either to admit our inability to guard adequately the pathways of the Empire and thus retire ingloriously from the contest forced mercilessly upon us, or we had to make good the Empire's right to exist; and that meant the supremacy of our naval forces against any attack that might reasonably be apprehended. Thus the contest in naval armaments, which British statesmen have vainly endeavoured to prevent, has proceeded from year to year. No shot was fired, no ships were sunk, no battle was fought; but it was, in truth, war between the two nations. International issues are often determined otherwise than by actual hostilities; and Great Britain realized that when her power upon the seas could be successfully challenged by Germany the day of her departure was at hand and indeed had already arrived.

On three recognized occasions during the past ten years Germany has brought Europe to the verge of actual war. On two of these occasions she imposed her will upon Europe, but on the third Great Britain stood firmly resolute and Germany receded. The events of 1911 have never been forgotten; and there is reason to believe that, but for the commanding influence and untiring efforts of Sir Edward Grey, the war which broke out in 1914 would have been forced upon Europe during the previous year.

I have spoken of three occasions; but as was once said to me by a statesman of great experience in the foreign office: 'The international kettle is always on the verge of boiling, although the people know nothing of it until the steam begins to escape.'

When the secrets of diplomatic records come to be fully disclosed I do not doubt that in each of the past ten years German aggressiveness will be found to have made war imminent or at least probable.

Not only here, but in the British Islands, military preparation has been imperfect because development has proceeded along the paths of peace. The instinct of the British people is against militarism and great standing armies are not viewed with favour. But in the British Islands and in the self-governing Dominions alone there are at least sixty millions of people, a population nearly equal to that of Germany. If our preparation for the struggle was insignificant compared with that of Germany, let us not forget that her resources are insignificant compared with those of this Empire. There are many things which count besides armed forces in the field. In the organization of modern war all the resources of the nation must be reckoned with. Consider those of Canada, which even during the coming year can supply food products to an almost unlimited extent. Our great transportation systems are an invaluable asset even for military purposes.

How was it possible to assemble at Valcartier Camp within two weeks after the outbreak of war a force of 35,000 men gathered from a territory nearly as large as Europe?

How was it possible to arm, equip and organize them so that the force was ready to sail within six weeks from the day on which the order was given?

This was possible because of the organizing ability, the great transportation systems and the industrial activities of Canada.

Already our factories are turning out not only clothing and equipment of all kinds, but munitions of war on a great scale and of a character that we did not dream of producing four months ago. Our inexhaustible resources in the forests, the fisheries, the coal and minerals of Canada are tremendous assets in this war. All this must tell in the long run, as Germany will yet know. In a word, we have the resources, while Germany has the preparation.

The ability of the Allied armies to hold in check the powerful forces of Germany pending the preparation which we lack has been amply demonstrated; and the armies of the Empire, as well as its enormous resources, are already being organized on such a scale as leaves no room for doubt as to the issue of this struggle. The preparation must be thoroughly and adequately made. It would be not only useless, but criminal, to send our citizen soldiers into the field of battle without the organization, training and discipline which are essential under conditions of modern warfare.

So here in the west, as well as in the east of this Dominion and throughout the Empire, armies are being organized, equipment and armaments are being prepared and we are making ready for the day when the hosts of Germany shall be driven back within their own frontiers and the march begins which shall not end until the Prussian oligarchy and its dominance over the German people shall have come to a deserved and inevitable end.

During the past three months I have seen at least 60,000 Canadians under arms, and of these 30,000 will shortly be at the battle front. Abroad and at home we have more than 100,000 Canadians preparing for the sternest of all a soldier's duties. Those who are shortly to be at the front will fight side by side with the best troops in the world, and we have a reasonable confidence, inspired by the memories of the past, that they will bear themselves worthily and with honour to themselves and their country. Those who are acquiring the training and discipline of the soldier will do well to remember that they are as truly serving their country as if they were at the front, for without this their service would be ineffective and useless.

It is hardly necessary to emphasize the unity of purpose which actuates the entire Empire in this struggle. For the ruling classes of Germany it is difficult, if not impossible, to comprehend, even imperfectly, the strength of an Empire bound together by ties which to them seem so imperfect and so attenuated. The ideals of government upon which the German Empire is based are so profoundly different from those which constitute the strength and hold firm the unity of the British Dominions, that this result is not surprising. Our self-governing Dominions are united by the ties of a common allegiance to the Crown; but the Crown has become the symbol of the people's sovereignty. According to our conception and practice of government, the King reigns to execute the will of the people who rule. The strength of the Empire rests upon the eternal foundation of liberty expressed in the ideal and consummation of autonomous self-government which is vested in the people of the self-governing Dominions as of right and not of grace. The spirit of Prussian absolutism dominating the people of the German Empire regards any such form of government as weak and ineffective. They conceive that it represents only a passing phase and that the German theory of absolutism cannot fail to impress itself upon the whole world in due

*Sir Robert Borden, Prime Minister of Canada during the First World War*

course. So that this struggle involves issues which transcend even the interests and the future of our own Empire and which embrace the whole theory and practice of government for all the future generations of the world. If the militarist and autocratic ideals of the Prussian oligarchy can assert themselves in worldwide dominance, the progress and development of democracy will either have been stayed forever or the work of centuries will have been undone and mankind must struggle anew for ideals of freedom and rights of self-government which have been established as the birthright of the British people. Thus the powers of democracy are themselves on trial today and the issue of this conflict concerns not only the existence of the British Empire, but all the worldwide aspirations that have found expression in the freedom which its people enjoy.

Insofar as this Empire may be said to possess a constitution, it is of modern growth and is still in the stage of development. One can hardly conceive that it will ever distinctly emerge from that stage or attain a status in which constitutional development is no longer to be anticipated. Indeed, the genius of the British people and all our past history lead us to believe the contrary. The steps in advance have been usually gradual and always practical; and they have been taken rather by instinct than upon any carefully considered theory. But the very liberties of the Empire made possible results which no absolutism could foresee. Thus the unity of purpose inspiring the British Dominions and their participation in this war upon so vast a scale has amused the Prussian warlords. Also it has shattered their confident belief that the military resources of those Dominions were entirely negligible. It is within the bounds of probability that the four free nations of the overseas Dominions will have put into the fighting line 250,000 men if this war should continue for another year. That result, or even the results which have already been obtained, must mark a great epoch in the history of inter-imperial relations. There are those within sound of my voice who will see the overseas Dominions surpass in wealth and population the British Islands; there are children playing in your streets who may see Canada alone attain that eminence. Thus it is impossible to believe that the existing status, so far as it concerns the control of foreign policy and extra-imperial relations, can remain as it is today. All are conscious of the complexity of the problem thus presented; but no one need despair of a satisfactory solution and no one can doubt the profound influence which the tremendous events of the past few months and of those in the immediate future must exercise upon one of the most interesting and far-reaching questions ever presented for the consideration of statesmen.

There are no more loyal and patriotic citizens of Canada than the people of German descent in all parts of our Dominion. Both in the east and in the west they have been earnest and active in endeavour and in aid. And it is particularly to be noted that citizens of German descent in Canada are a peace loving people and averse to all forms of militarism. They thoroughly understand and appreciate the principles of democratic government; they detest absolutism and abhor war. But if the teachings of the most advanced thinkers of Germany are to be regarded and if the course of the German Government is to be considered as expressive of the national spirit, no such ideal animates the German people. Germany is disposed to dismiss with indifference and even contempt all proposals for settling international differences by peaceful methods. Indeed, the German Government seems to consider any such proposals as expressly directed against Germany's interests which, as they conceive, demand that her military power must inevitably be employed for her national development and advancement through the subjugation and humiliation of other nations and the appropriation of such of their possessions as she may find most useful for her purposes. This conception carries with it the ideal that in all the centuries to come brute force shall be the highest right; that the most powerful nation shall be a law to itself; that its treaties and obligations may be put aside when necessity arises, and that the national shall alone be the judge of that necessity. If all the teachings of Christianity and all the ideals of modern civilization point only to this result, mankind has not great reason to regard its ideals and standards as on a higher plane than those of the brute creation. Indeed, one should then say that man was made a little lower than the brutes.

> No more? A monster then, a dream,
> A discord. Dragons of the prime,
> That tare each other in their slime,
> Were mellow music match'd with him.

Such ideals are not helpful to humanity, and the sooner they are dispelled and dismissed the better for the nation which entertains them and the better for the world. If this war was necessary for that purpose, let us not regret that it came when it did.

In common with the whole world, we fully recognize and appreciate the great qualities of the German people and all that they have achieved in the highest spheres of human activity and usefulness. With them we desired no contest, except in generous rivalry for the advancement of all that is best in modern civilization. With them we have no quarrel, save that they have forsaken the cause of liberty and democracy in rendering an unquestioning obedience to the militarist and arrogant autocracy to which they have surrendered the control of their national life. In this struggle against the Prussian oligarchy and against its ideals, Canada, in common with all the Empire, is prepared to fight, and intends to fight, to the death.

Reverses may come, sacrifices will be inevitable, there may be days of doubt and even of gloom; but the fortitude, the determination and the resourcefulness which did not fail the people of this Empire in the storm and peril of more than a century ago and which have maintained the northern half of this continent as part of the Empire, are still our common inheritance and will not fail us now.

There is but one way to deal effectively with the Prussian gospel of force and violence and the Prussian ideal of absolutism. It must be smashed utterly and completely. The sooner that is accomplished the better for the German people and for all the nations. Canada joins wholeheartedly in that great task. What has been done is known to all. What remains to be done shall be limited only by the need.

## Arthur Meighen

The Glorious Dead

*Thelus Military Cemetery, Vimy Ridge, 3 July 1921*

**'Just as the war dwarfed by its magnitude all contests of the past, so the wonder of human resource and the splendour of human heroism have reached a zenith never witnessed before.'**

Arthur Meighen visited Europe during the first of his two brief terms as Prime Minister. This speech, altered somewhat and given the title above, was collected in a slim volume, *Oversea Addresses, June – July 1921.* It was delivered by Meighen upon the ridge at which Canadians had proved victorious four years earlier.

Thelus Military Cemetery, one of several on Vimy Ridge, is the resting place for 244 Canadians, 51 soldiers from the United Kingdom and one German.

The Great War is past; the war that tried through and through every quality and mystery of the human spirit; the war that closed, we hope for ever, the long, ghastly story of the arbitrament of men's differences by force; the last clash and crash of earth's millions is over now. There can be heard only sporadic conflicts, the moan of prostate nations, the cries of the bereaved and desolate, the struggling of exhausted peoples to rise and stand and move onward. We live among the ruins and the echoes of Armageddon. Its shadow is receding slowly backward into history.

At this time the proper occupation of the living is, first, to honour our heroic dead; next, to repair the havoc, human and material, that surrounds us; and, lastly, to learn aright and apply with courage the lessons of the war.

Here in the heart of Europe we meet to unveil a memorial to our country's dead. In the earth which has resounded to the drums and the tramplings of many contests, they rest in the quiet of God's acre with the brave of all the world. At death they sheathed in their hearts the sword of devotion, and now from oft-stricken fields they hold aloft the Cross of Sacrifice, mutely beckoning those who would share their immortality.

No words can add to their fame, nor, so long as gratitude holds place in men's hearts, can our forgetfulness be suffered to detract from their renown. Just as the war dwarfed by its magnitude all contests of the past, so the wonder of human resource and the splendour of human heroism have reached a zenith never witnessed before.

Ours we thought were prosaic days, when the great causes of earlier times had lost their inspiration, leaving for attainment those things which demanded only the petty passing inconveniences of the hour. And yet the nobility of manhood had but to hear again the summons of duty and honour to make response which shook the world. The danger to the treasury of common things – for common things are, when challenged, most sacred of all – the danger to the treasury of common things ever stirred our fathers to action, and it has not lost its appeal to their sons.

France lives and France is free, and Canada is better because she did something worthwhile to help free France to live. In many hundreds of plots throughout these hills and valleys, all the way from Flanders to Picardy, lie fifty-thousand of our dead. Their resting-places have been dedicated to their memory forever by the kindly grateful heart of France, and will be tended and cared for by us in the measure of the love we bear them.

Around and over all are being planted the maple trees of Canada, in the thought that her sons will rest better under trees they knew so well in life. Across the leagues of the Atlantic the heartstrings of our Canadian nation will reach through all time to these graves in France. We shall never let pass away the spirit bequeathed to us by those who fell – 'Their Name Liveth Forevermore.'

*Arthur Meighen, the first Canadian Prime Minister to visit Vimy Ridge*

## William Lyon Mackenzie King

Address on the National Plebiscite on Conscription

*National Broadcast from Ottawa, 7 April 1942*

**'To those who, beyond the events of today, are able to look into the future, it is no longer the unity, it is the very existence of our country as a free nation which they see is in danger...'**

The Canadian federal election of 26 March 1940 was overshadowed by the events of the Second World War. The Conservative Party ran a disastrous campaign in which the leader, Robert Manion, advocated the creation of an all-party national unity government. Under Mackenzie King, the governing Liberals easily won re-election, in part due to their pledge not to introduce conscription. It was a promise they would later regret.

After the fall of France the following June, the government introduced conscription for home service, limiting overseas service to volunteers. King's aim was to avoid a repeat of the Conscription Crisis of 1917, which had so damaged the country and his party. By 1942, the need to send conscripts to Europe was such that King sought release from his election promise. His National Plebiscite on Conscription asked voters to relieve him of the commitment made during the election campaign:

> Are you in favour of releasing the Government from any obligations arising out of any past commitments restricting the methods of raising men for military service?

I wish to speak to you tonight, my fellow Canadians, on a matter which, at this time of war, is of first importance – of first importance to the present position of our country, and to its future security; and, therefore, of real concern to the homes and lives of all.

On Monday, the 27th of this month, you will be asked to give the government a free hand in the discharge of its duty in carrying on the war. This may seem to you a strange request. What may seem stranger still is that this request is being made at a time of war. All of us, I believe, realize that, in wartime, a government has greater need for a free hand than in peacetime. Why then, you ask, does the government at this time of war, come to us for a free hand?

The answer is not, as you might suppose, that the government lacks full legal power for the conduct of the war. The hands of the government are not tied either by the law or the constitution. The government has been given by parliament much wider powers for wartime than it commands in peacetime. It is important that you should understand, that at the present time, as far as legal power goes, the government is perfectly free to take any action which a majority in parliament will support. This will continue to be true of the power of the government at Ottawa to the end of the war.

How then, you ask, are the hands of the government tied? What is it that binds the government? What is the restriction which the government seeks to have removed? Why was the restriction ever imposed? Why should the government and parliament not tackle this question on their own responsibility without resorting to a plebiscite, and why, after two and a half years of war, has it become necessary to have the restriction removed?

These are questions which have been repeatedly raised ever since the government announced its intention to ask you to free its hands. They are very natural questions. They are questions to which you will expect a satisfactory answer.

If the only thing that mattered in the relations between the people and the government was the possession of power, the government would, of course, be free to do as it pleases. That is what obtains under a dictatorship. No account is taken of the will of the people. It is on that principle that the Nazi, Italian and Japanese dictators are acting today. Under democratic government, however, quite as important as the possession of power is its exercise in accordance with the will of the people.

When those who hold representative and responsible positions have given a definite promise to the people, they have created an obligation to act in accordance with that promise, until the people are again consulted. Such an obligation may not be binding according to law, but as an obligation it is no less sacred.

There are those, I know, who make light of what they call 'political promises'. It will, I think, be generally agreed that a political platform or programme is one thing; a definite and concrete promise or pledge is quite another. Because of circumstances, a government may, without breaking faith, fail to carry out, to the letter, its full programme. No change in circumstances could, however, justify a government in ignoring a specific pledge to the people, unless it was clear that the safety of the nation was immediately involved, and there was no possibility of consulting the people.

The pledge from which the present government is asking to be freed is not related to any ordinary day-to-day matter of policy. It is a pledge which was made specifically in relation to the conduct of the present war. It is a pledge which was given, by government and opposition alike, before and since the outbreak of the war, and to which, at the time it was made, no political party took exception. The present House of Commons was returned in the light of that pledge.

The pledge to which I refer is, as you are all aware, that, as a method of raising men for military service overseas, resort would not be had to conscription. In other words, that voluntary enlistment would be the method by which men would be raised for service overseas.

That promise is a restriction upon the government today. It is, as I have said, not a legal restriction. It is a moral obligation and I need not add a moral obligation of the most solemn kind. It is equally the one and only restriction upon the exercise by the government of its full power.

You ask: why was the restriction ever imposed? Why was the promise given? 'Surely,' many will say, 'the government should have known that it would need a free hand in time of war. Why, then, did the government tie its own hands?' The answer to this question is very simple.

The pledge not to impose conscription, as everyone knows, was the result of Canada's experience in the last war. The way in which conscription was then introduced, and the way it was enforced, gave rise to bitter resentment. Moreover, events proved that conscription in the last war had little or no military value.

Before, and at the commencement of the war, the people of Canada, like the peoples of most other countries, continued to think of the present war in terms of the last war. They thought of the situation overseas as they remembered it from 1914 to 1918. They thought of the situation in Canada in terms of the disunity which followed the introduction of conscription. They thought of just another European war. They most certainly did not think of a war in which all the nations of the world would be in danger. Much less did Canadians think of the war as one in which Canada might become the most coveted of all the prizes of war. That, however, is the actual situation today.

The pledge not to impose conscription for service overseas was given in order to maintain the unity of Canada. Without this assurance, I do not believe that parliament would have given, as it did, prompt and wholehearted approval to Canada's entry into the war. It was the trust of the people in the pledged word of the government which then maintained our national unity.

We must never lose sight of the importance of national unity. National unity is, I believe, more essential to the success of the war effort of any country than most other factors combined. 'Every kingdom divided against itself is brought to desolation, and a house divided against a house falleth.'

The restriction upon the power of the government was necessary at the outset to preserve national unity. It has helped until recently to maintain national unity. In the past few months it has, however, become a matter of controversy and a threat to unity. You know full well that a foremost aim of my public life has been the preservation of the unity of Canada. I must say that under the changed conditions of today, and with Canada's record in the war what it has been over the past two and a half years, I see no reason why the removal of the restriction should weaken our unity. Instead, I believe firmly that its removal will help to overcome a source of irritation and disunity within our own country. It will, I believe, also help to remove a source of misunderstanding in the other countries united with Canada in the common effort to preserve freedom in the world.

I come now to the question: why have the government and parliament not tackled this question on their own responsibility without resorting to a plebiscite?

The answer is very simple. Had the government taken the position that, as conditions had changed, it did not intend longer to be bound by any pledge, it would immediately have been said that the government had violated the most sacred undertaking ever given in its name.

It would most certainly have been said that, before so deciding, we should have referred the matter to the people in a general election, or a referendum, or as we are doing, by means of a plebiscite, and asked to be relieved from all past commitments. It would have been asserted that we were no better than the Nazis; that we had ceased to have regard for the will of the people and were now relying upon force to give effect to policies which were the direct opposite of those on which we had been returned to power. Had the present government attempted to do such a thing, does anyone imagine it would have been able to retain the confidence of parliament? For the government to have disregarded its pledged word would, I believe, have helped to destroy faith, not merely in the government, but in democratic institutions. Far from increasing our total war effort, the disunity caused by such a breach of faith would, I believe, have made our effort less effective. By such an arbitrary act, we might well have destroyed the national unity on which our war effort is founded.

There never was a time when the need is what it is today to conserve what still exists of faith in democratic institutions. The present unhappy state of the world is, in large part, the result of broken pledges. Nazi Germany has erected bad faith and the broken pledge into a principle of action. Bad faith, broken pledges, and disregard of the popular will, are the forces against which Canada is fighting today.

But, you may say, no one would expect the government to have taken any such arbitrary action. What the government should have done was to have gone to parliament and asked the members to give it a free hand. It is said that a release would have been granted immediately. But would it? I am certain, in fact, it would not. And that for the simple reason that members of parliament would, for the most part, have taken the position that they were as much bound by past commitments as were the members of the government.

And that brings me to the last of the questions to which you are waiting a reply: 'Why, after two and a half years of war, has it become necessary to have the restriction removed?'

One answer is that this restriction is being represented as the bar to an all-out effort on Canada's part. It makes no difference whether conscription for service overseas would add to Canada's total effort or not, the fact that the government is not free to consider its adoption is made to appear as limiting Canada's war effort.

The truth, of course, is that our army today is just as large as it would have been if conscription for overseas service had been adopted. The absence of conscription for overseas service has not limited our war effort. The lack of power to impose such conscription has, however, placed our war effort in a wholly false light before our own citizens, and, what is worse, before our allies. In other words, conscription has been made the symbol of a total effort, regardless of all Canada is doing to help win the war.

The issue at present is not conscription; it is whether or not the government, subject to its responsibility to parliament, is to be free to decide that question itself in the light of all national considerations. The government is not asking you to say whether or not conscription should be adopted. That responsibility the government is asking you to leave to itself and to parliament, with entire freedom to decide the question on its merits.

The question of conscription, properly viewed, is a military question. The place to discuss it is in parliament. What the government now seeks for itself and for parliament is freedom to

*Prime Minister William Lyon Mackenzie King signing photographs on the day of the National Plebiscite on Conscription*

consider and debate and decide this question, like all other questions connected with the war, unrestricted by any pledge and in the light only of the needs of national security.

A part of our forces should be kept in Canada to protect us against attack; a part of our forces should be sent overseas to help defeat the enemy and thus prevent him from attacking Canada. Both tasks are equally essential to our safety. Anyone who tells you that only one of these tasks is necessary is deceiving you. The government with the information which it alone possesses is in a position to decide where Canada's forces can be used to the greatest advantage in defending Canada, and in helping to defeat Germany and Japan, or how the armed forces required can best be raised. We do not ask the people to make that decision. But we believe the matter is so important that the government and parliament should be completely free to decide the question wholly on its merits.

The people of Canada are not going to hesitate to take any step which they believe to be necessary for the preservation of their freedom. They are certainly not going to hesitate to adopt any measure needed to preserve their national existence, but they will wish to know, and they have a right to know, that before any step is taken, that step is necessary. This is particularly true in the case of a measure which has been the subject of bitter controversy and the source of disunity in the past.

The only place it can satisfactorily be decided whether a particular step is necessary or a particular measure needed, is in parliament. In parliament, the government can state its case and provide the information on which a wise decision can alone be made.

In the greatest of all emergencies, I ask you, are you not prepared to trust the government and your own parliament to see that only those things are done which are wholly in the interest of the country? If there are any who are not, who or what are they prepared to trust? This is the question I should like every citizen of Canada to ask himself, and herself as he or she proceeds to answer 'yes' or 'no' to the question being asked on the 27th of this month.

But there is a greater and more urgent reason why the restriction on the power of the government should be removed. And to this I ask your special attention. I have spoken of unity. To a nation, there is one thing even more important than the preservation of its unity. That is the preservation of its existence. To those who, beyond the events of today, are able to look into the future, it is no longer the unity, it is the very existence of our country as a free nation which they see is in danger today. We are no longer in a world where even the most powerful nation is able, by itself, to save itself from the ambition and greed of the aggressor nations. For the preservation of its very existence, each free country is going to need all the help that other free countries can give. It will require the utmost co-operation on the part of all free countries to save them from becoming victims, one by one, of the gangster nations whose undoubted aim is world conquest. With our immense territory, great resources and small population, no country may come to need the help of the other countries more than our own. Unless we continue to do all we can to help others, we shall have no right to expect them to do all they can to help us. Until the present tide of conquest is turned into overwhelming defeat for the enemy, no country – and assuredly not Canada – can consider itself secure.

The last thing I have been or would wish to be is an alarmist. I would, however, not be true to the trust the people of Canada have reposed in me did I not say that I believe the situation, for all free nations, is far more critical today than it has ever been. Canada's position is by no means an exception. Look at what has happened in the past two and a half years of war; look at what is happening today, and ask yourselves what other view is possible. Practically the whole of continental Europe, except Russia, is under the domination of Germany, and is compelled to serve her war machine. Despite Russia's magnificent campaign and the ground she has regained, much of her European territory is still in Nazi hands. Who can say what the outcome of the struggle between Russia and Germany may be? In the Middle East and in Africa, the situation is also desperately critical. In Asia and in the Pacific, Japan controls a large part of China, and has seized most of the strategic strongholds and territories formerly possessed by the Netherlands, France, Britain and the United States.

Across the Pacific, the tide of Japanese conquest has swept swiftly over thousands of miles of sea. A few weeks ago, it was Hong Kong, Singapore and the East Indies – attacked and taken; a little later, Burma and Australia attacked, with New Zealand also threatened. Today it is Ceylon and India. Who can say how, or when, or where, the sweep of attempted invasion and actual conquest is going to end. Neither sea nor land defences have stopped the advances of the Germans and the Japanese. It becomes increasingly clear that both Germany and Japan are putting forth a supreme effort to achieve world mastery in 1942. At the moment, they are aiming at uniting their forces in a manner which will give them control of the strategic lines of communication in the whole eastern hemisphere.

In the British Commonwealth of Nations, Canada and South Africa are the only countries not immediately subject to attack. Does anyone imagine that if the aggressor nations are successful in the present areas of conflict, they will leave the western hemisphere alone? Is anyone so blind as to believe that already they have not cast their covetous eyes upon the vast territory and resources of our own Dominion? Off our own Atlantic coasts and those of the United States, enemy U-boats have been destroying shipping at an alarming rate. There are strong reasons for believing that Germany hopes, in the course of the next few months, to be able by means of a great naval offensive on the Atlantic, to cut the sea lanes between North America and Britain, and to cripple the merchant fleets of Britain and the United States. Japan has a similar aim on the Pacific. These offensives may come at any time. One thing is perfectly certain. If the enemy is not kept at bay on the oceans, and defeated beyond the waters of the Atlantic and the Pacific, the final battles of the world conflict will be fought in the waters and upon the soil of Canada and the United States.

Here surely is the most powerful of reasons why every effort should be made, as it is being made, alike by the United States and Canada, to help the other united nations to engage the enemy and try to defeat him where he is to be found today. We cannot defend our country and save our homes and families by waiting at home for the enemy to attack us. Every country that has stood behind its own defences in this war has sooner or later been attacked. To remain on the defensive is the surest way to bring the war to Canada. Of course, we should look to our defences; we should protect our coasts; we should strengthen our ports and our cities against attack. But we must also take our full part in the combat, we must go out to meet the enemy before he reaches our shores; we must, if we can, defeat him before he attacks us, before our cities are laid waste and before the women and children of Canada are injured or killed in our streets and our homes.

It is unfortunate that so many have come to think of Canada's war effort as aid for other countries. In reality, it is much more than that. Every sailor, every soldier, every airman in Canada's forces, wherever they serve; every ship, every gun, every plane we manufacture, regardless of the forces that use them; the food we supply to our allies; all these may be aid to other countries against a common enemy, but are equally a contribution to the defence of Canada. Let no one tell you that Canada is in this war to uphold any selfish cause of empire. It is not true. We are fighting to preserve our freedom and our national existence, to defend our homes and families, from an enemy drawing ever nearer. We would do well to remember that, against the piratical ambitions of Germany and Japan alike, the one sure shield of defence is actual combat in the front line of battle, whether on land, at sea or in the air.

Here is the strongest of reasons why no excuse should remain for anyone to say that because of a restriction upon the exercise by the government of its full powers, Canada's war effort is not all it might be. Should the day come – and it may come soon – when Canada is faced with attack, and we need help from the United States or Britain or any of the united nations, how would we feel if we thought their governments were restricted in their power to aid Canada? We would do well, I think, not to permit any misunderstanding to arise in other countries as to our readiness to do our full part in the struggle we are all fighting together.

Aggression has followed aggression with such speed in so many parts of the world that no one can now predict what new areas the war may reach next year, next month or next week. Danger threatens us from the east and from the west. It is in the face of this peril that for the defence of our freedom and of our country, the government asks you to give it a free hand.

## Lester B. Pearson

Address on Accepting the Nobel Peace Prize

*The University of Oslo, 10 December 1957*

***'...I have received an honour that cannot fail to arouse deep emotion in the heart of the recipient.'***

**The awarding of the 1957 Nobel Peace Prize to Pearson – the only Canadian to be so honoured – came through his role as Minister of External Affairs and his proposal that a United Nations Emergency Force be established in order to keep the peace and defuse the Suez Crisis. Made during the dying days of the Saint-Laurent Government, by the time of this address, made before an audience which included Norwegian King Olaf V and Princess Märtha of Sweden, Crown Princess of Norway, Pearson was sitting in the Opposition benches of the House of Commons. He was introduced that afternoon by Gunnar Jahn, Chairman of the award committee.**

**One month after delivering his acceptance speech Pearson was elected leader of the Liberal Party. He won on the first ballot.**

May I thank you, Mister Chairman, for your very kind and generous words. I am sorry that I am not sufficiently educated to have understood them in Norwegian but I was able to detect two words, 'Lester Pearson'. They seemed to me to recur all too frequently, but I suppose that in the circumstance it was hard to avoid that.

I am very conscious of the fact this morning that I have received an honour that cannot fail to arouse deep emotion in the heart of the recipient. My feeling of pride and honour is increased by the presence here today of His Majesty and Her Royal Highness and by the fact, sir, that you are presiding over the ceremonies.

I realise also that I share this honour with many friends and colleagues who have worked with me for the promotion of peace and good understanding between peoples. I am grateful for the opportunities I have been given to participate in that work as a representative of my country, Canada, whose people have, I think, shown their devotion to peace.

*Maryon and Lester B. Pearson on the occasion of the awarding of the 1957 Nobel Peace Prize*

I am deeply aware of the fact that in receiving this honour I am entering a company of men and women who have served humanity with unselfish and constructive devotion. They include, I know, two great Norwegians, Christian Lange and Fridtjof Nansen. I feel very proud and humble at having my name now linked with such men, because of the choice that you, sir, and the members of your honourable committee have made.

I am particularly happy to be able to receive this prize in Norway, a country which has so well discharged its duty to the international community and to peace. Alfred Nobel, not himself a Norwegian, recognised this when he conferred on Norway through your committee the honour and responsibility of making the Peace Award.

On this occasion I wish to pay my sincere tribute to this great Swedish man of vision and action, who worked hard, lived nobly and ensured that his influence for good would extend far beyond his own life time. Alfred Nobel decreed that this award should be conferred on someone who, in the opinion of the committee, should have done the most or the best work to promote fraternity between nations for the abolition and reduction of standing armies and for the holding and promotion of peace congresses.

As to the first, I do not know that I have done very much myself to promote fraternity between nations but I do know that there can be no more important purpose for any man's activity or interests.

So far as abolishing arms are concerned, those of Nobel's day are now out of date, but I know, as you do, that if the arms which man's genius has created today to replace them are ever used they will destroy us all. So they must be themselves destroyed.

As for the promotion of peace congresses we have had our meetings and assemblies, but the promotion through them of the determined and effective will to peace displaying itself in action and policy remains to be achieved.

Alfred Nobel – with a whimsical touch – once said: 'I would not leave anything to a man of action as he would be tempted to give up work; on the other hand, I would like to help dreamers as they find it difficult to get on in life.'

Perhaps this sentiment should have a special appeal for Norwegians who, though adept in overcoming difficulties by practical action, have been described as a 'people who luxuriated in the wealth of their dreams'.

Of all our dreams today there is none more important – or so hard to realise – than that of peace in the world. May we never lose our faith in it or our resolve to do everything that can be done to convert it one day into reality.

The great Ibsen has one of his characters in the play *The Emperor and The Galilean* say: 'There are three Empires. First there is the Empire which was founded on the tree of knowledge. Then there is the Empire founded on the tree of the Cross. The third is still a secret Empire which will be founded on the tree of knowledge and the tree of the Cross – brought together.'

The award which I have received today at this ceremony, which my wife and I will always remember with emotion, is a renewed incentive to work with all other men of good will in the world for the triumph of Ibsen's third Empire, that of the Empire of Peace.

# POLITICS AND CAMPAIGNS

“I would also like to thank and congratulate, in all corners of the country, all those who for the last decade – thousands of them – and even more in the last month, who worked so hard, in a superhuman way, to bring about this result that had come about. A decade is very quick in the history of a people. We are not a small people; we are perhaps something like a great people.”

*- René Lévesque, 1976*

# Tommy Douglas

Mouseland

*CBC Radio broadcast, 1 January 1961*

## *'My friends watch out for the little fellow with an idea.'*

**A Baptist minister, Douglas had a talent for communicating with his electorate, as evidenced by the five consecutive majority governments he led as Premier of Saskatchewan. Dating back to at least 1944, this parable became a favourite on the campaign trail. Douglas repeated the story of Mouseland often, with little variation. The version featured here was broadcast on New Year's Day, 1961, six months after he had led the Saskatchewan Co-operative Commonwealth Federation to yet another electoral victory.**

**In November 1961, Douglas resigned the premiership after having been elected first leader of the federal New Democratic Party. Although he had served in the House of Commons during the Great Depression, his return to federal politics wasn't smooth. In the general election of 18 June 1962, Douglas lost in his bid to serve the constituency of Regina City. His first electoral loss four months later was offset by his by-election victory in the British Columbia riding of Burnaby-Coquitlam. In 1968, he lost his seat to the tide of Trudeaumania, only to return in another by-election. Douglas resigned his leadership of the NDP in 1971, but remained in the House until his retirement from active politics eight years later.**

This is the story of a place called Mouseland. Mouseland was a place where all the little mice lived and played. Were born and died. And they lived much as you and I do. They even had a parliament. And every four years they had an election. They used to walk to the polls and cast their ballot. Some of them even got a ride to the polls. They got a ride for the next four years afterward, too. Just like you and me. And every time on election day, all the little mice used to go to the ballot box and they used to elect a government. A government made up of big fat black cats.

Now if you think it's strange that mice should elect a government made up of cats. You just look at the history of Canada for the last ninety years and maybe you'll see they weren't any stupider than we are.

*Tommy Douglas and his wife Irma. Douglas, who served in both the Legislative Assembly of Saskatchewan and the House of Commons, was elected in thirteen of his fifteen bids for public office*

Now I am not saying anything against the cats. They were nice fellows; they conducted the government with dignity. They passed good laws. That is, laws that were good for cats.

But the laws that were good for cats weren't very good for mice. One of the laws said that mouse holes had to be big enough so a cat could get his paw in. Another law said that mice could only travel at certain speeds so that a cat could get his breakfast without too much physical effort.

All the laws were good laws for cats. But oh, they were hard on the mice. And life was getting harder and harder. And when the mice couldn't put up with it anymore they decided something had to be done about it. So they went en masse to the polls. They voted the black cats out.

They put in the white cats.

The white cats had put up a terrific campaign. They said all that Mouseland needs is more vision. They said the trouble with Mouseland is those round mouse holes we've got. If you put us in we'll establish square mouse holes. And they did. And the square mouse holes were twice as big as the round mouse holes. And now the cat could get both his paws in. And life was tougher than ever.

And when they couldn't take that anymore they voted the white cats out and put the black ones in again. And then they went back to the white cats, and then to the black, they even tried half black cats and half white cats. And they called that coalition. They even got one government made up of cats with spots on them. They were cats that tried to make a noise like a mouse but they ate like a cat.

You see my friends the trouble wasn't with the colour of the cats. The trouble was that they were cats. And because they were cats they naturally look after cats instead of mice.

Presently there came along one little mouse who had an idea. My friends watch out for the little fellow with an idea.

He said to the other mice. 'Look fellows why do we keep electing a government made up of cats, why don't we elect a government made up of mice?'

'Oh,' they said, 'he's a Bolshevik.' So they put him in jail.

But I want to remind you that you can lock up a mouse or a man but you can't lock up an idea.

# René Lévesque

## 1976 Electoral Victory Speech

*The Paul Sauvé Arena, Rosemont, 15 November 1976*

**'...we want and we will work with all our strength to make of Quebec a country that will more than ever be the country of all Québécois who live here and love it.'**

The Parti Québécois victory in the 1976 Quebec provincial election was a surprise to many, not least Premier Robert Bourassa who had called the electorate to the polls only three years into his second term. Although his government had suffered three years of scandal, the Liberal leader had expected to receive a great deal of support from his rescue of the Olympics, which had been held four months earlier in Montreal. The win was decisive, with the PQ taking over 41 per cent of the popular vote to the Liberals' thirty-four. Vote splitting with a revived Union Nationale combined to reduce Bourassa's party from 102 to twenty-six seats. When René Lévesque was sworn in as the 23rd Premier of Quebec, ten days after making this speech, he had a caucus numbering seventy-one members.

I don't think I have to tell you just how unable I am, at this moment, to make any comment on the extraordinary sign of confidence that was hoped for. I have to tell you frankly that we hoped for this with all our hearts, but didn't expect it to come like this this year. I never thought I could be so proud to be Québécois as I am this evening.

I want to thank, from the bottom of my heart, all the voters in every corner of Quebec, who weren't afraid of the necessary changes. I would also like to thank and congratulate, in all corners of the country, all those who for the last decade – thousands of them – and even more in the last month, who worked so hard, in a superhuman way, to bring about this result that had come about. A decade is very quick in the history of a people. We are not a small people; we are perhaps something like a great people.

*René Lévesque at the Paul Sauvé Arena on the evening of the Parti Québécois election victory*

I'd also like to say that my colleagues here, like me, are conscious of the enormous weight that the confidence of the Québécois has placed on our shoulders. There is no man, there is no group that can carry it without making mistakes. All we can promise you, from the bottom of our hearts, that we're going to carry that weight with all the energy, all the honesty and all the enthusiasm that we can. And we're going to do it. And I repeat in the name of everyone this evening, that we are going to keep as best we can each and every one of the commitments that we have made. I won't repeat them this evening, but we won't forget a single one. In particular, I repeat that central commitment, which doesn't at all change the fact that from the bottom of my heart, from the bottom of our collective heart, we hope, in consultation with our fellow citizens of Canada, we can arrive in giving ourselves the country that is Quebec. But this country of Quebec will only arrive when an adult society, conscious of itself, will have approved it with a clear and democratic majority, in a referendum, as we promised.

A little while ago I heard Monsieur Bourasssa who generously congratulated us and who issued a statement extremely appropriate and courageous on an evening like this one. I know what this is like – I lived it also – losing. I know what this is like and I'd like to congratulate him for the way he took it as he demonstrated a little while ago.

I'd like to thank all the elected members of the party who we won't see tonight, but we'll see them in the next few days. I'd also like to warmly thank all those who – often just barely – didn't win their ridings. We'll meet again with them, too. From a personal point of view I'd like to say to them, and it's perhaps a consolation, that this happens one, twice, but not necessarily three times.

If you will allow me, I'd like to very calmly, very sincerely say to our adversaries in Quebec, to our adversaries and to those here, there, who might have feared the results of a victory by the Parti Québécois, that we want and we will work with all our strength to make of Quebec a country that will more than ever be the country of all Québécois who live here and love it.

And once again, I don't know how to thank the voters for the confidence and the responsibility that they granted this evening. In my humble opinion, I don't know how to evaluate it, but I'm sure that politically, this is nearly the most beautiful and perhaps the greatest evening in the history of Quebec.

# Kim Campbell

Leadership Victory Speech

*Ottawa Civic Centre, 13 June 1993*

**'Trust is not just given, it is earned. As your leader and as Prime Minister, I intend to do everything within my power to earn the support of Canadians.'**

The Progressive Conservatives were in the fifth year of their mandate when, in February 1993, Prime Minister Brian Mulroney announced his retirement from politics. The news was anything but a surprise; the Tories were low in the polls and public opinion rated their leader as one of the most unpopular of all time.

In the rush to replace Mulroney, Kim Campbell was the only woman in a field otherwise consisting of men: Jean Charest, Patrick Boyer, Jim Edwards and Garth Turner. Considered far and away the frontrunner at the start, Campbell faced a growing challenge from Charest, which led to analogies with Aesop's fable of the tortoise and the hare. Charest's strong showing forced a second ballot, which Campbell won by a slim margin of 187 votes. The headline in the next day's *Globe* and *Mail* reported 'The Tortoise Runs Out of Time and Luck'.

On 25 June, Campbell was sworn in as the first female Prime Minister of Canada.

I want to begin first of all by saying thank you – thank you to all of you who have worked so hard and so effectively on my behalf. Thank you to those of you who have put your trust in me. You have honoured me by your trust and I return it with my complete commitment to you to lead this party to victory.

Allow me to begin by thanking all the thousands of volunteers who have shown their tremendous confidence in me by working so hard in my campaign. Our victory is their victory. This is your victory, won by your energy and dedication, and I share it with each and every one of you. I want to pay particular thanks to the people in the riding association of Vancouver Centre who believed in me for so long. They have, obviously, a very special place in my heart, and I want to thank them for having faith in me for so long, and for helping me to believe that one can fight tough campaigns – after 1988, anything seemed possible.

I want to also express a debt of gratitude to Prime Minister Brian Mulroney. Prime Minister, your confidence in me gave me a chance to meet some of the greatest challenges in my life, and to grow and to learn and to become even more in love with the political process of this wonderful country. And I want to say to everyone here that Brian Mulroney taught us some very important lessons as a party. He taught us how to think long-term, he taught us how to be united, and he taught us how to win.

To my fellow candidates, Jean, Patrick, Jim and Garth, I offer my genuine congratulations on an absolutely tremendous campaign. Together we have shown Canadians just how much talent and ability is in this party. And if I might be permitted a special word to my friend and colleague Jean Charest. Jean, I don't know whether or not I am a hare, but as Lafontaine would have said, you're quite a tortoise. Jean, you're one hell of a tortoise.

And to all of those who supported other candidates, I want you to know that I certainly respect your decision, that I commend your enthusiasm and your application, and that our party has had and will always need people like you.

To those of you who supported other candidates, let me say how much I respect your decision and I applaud your dedication and enthusiasm. And I want to say that our party has need of you, and that after today we will go ahead, members of our caucus and members of our party, together building the future of this country. This is what counts in this leadership.

I particularly want to thank my friends from Quebec, who have been by my side from the very beginning. Your support was absolutely essential to me, to show the roots of the party in Quebec and the absolute openness of Quebecers, and to show Canada that we bear the future.

This great contest within a family is now over. I invite each and every one of you to join with us for the greater battle that lies ahead, against our real opponents and for the real prize: our third consecutive majority government.

This is not the time for a long speech, so let me simply say this: I said last evening that the biggest challenge before us is to win the trust and confidence of Canadians, to renew in them a new sense of hope about our country. Trust is not just given, it is earned. As your leader and as Prime Minister, I intend to do everything within my power to earn the support of Canadians. We will earn their support by offering to them a party that is open to all Canadians, in which every

*Kim Campbell, the only female Prime Minister of Canada, with other Prime Ministers Pierre Elliott Trudeau, John Turner, Jean Chrétien and Joe Clark*

Canadian, regardless of region or language or gender or origin, can see themselves, and which gives them a chance to participate in sharing our future together by providing them with good government, with thoughtful policies, honestly presented, openly arrived at, and implemented with competence and care for every cent of your tax dollars. Above all, by restoring to Canadians a sense of hope and confidence in themselves that we've always had as a country.

I spoke yesterday of the challenges facing us, offering Canadians, and particularly the young and jobless, a government that will give them back hope, providing Canadians with a government that is not only transparent in appearances, but also transparent in actual fact; offering Canadians a government that will develop its policies in consultation and will implement them with respect and efficiency; but most of all, offering Canadians a government that will restore confidence in themselves and in Canada.

Don't let anyone tell you that Canada's best years are behind us. This is a party with a past and a present, but above all, this is a party and a country with a future. Our task and our challenge as we leave here after this wonderful convention is to seize that future together – and I promise you that I will not rest until we have done just that.

# Kim Campbell

1993 Election Concession Speech

*Campbell Campaign Headquarters, Vancouver, 25 October 1993*

## 'Success was not ours tonight, but success can be ours tomorrow.'

**The Progressive Conservative campaign of 1993 was a disaster of a magnitude that is unlikely to be repeated on the federal level. Where five years earlier, the party had been re-elected with 169 seats – a majority of 43 – it was now reduced to just two. Prime Minister Kim Campbell, defeated easily by the Liberal candidate in the riding of Vancouver Centre, was among those to lose a seat. Her speech is not only one of concession, but a recognition of the extreme injury sustained by her party.**

**Campbell isn't quite correct in her claim that 'as many Canadians voted for the Progressive Conservative Party as voted for the Bloc Québécois or voted for the Reform Party'. In fact, her party fell short of the Reform vote by some 370,000 votes, but outpolled the Bloc by roughly the same number. Curiously, she misidentifies election day as the twenty-sixth of October.**

**Campbell remained Prime Minister for ten more days, when Jean Chrétien was sworn into office. She announced her resignation as leader of the party on 13 December – six months to the day after her triumph at the Ottawa Civic Centre.**

**Before beginning her concession speech, Campbell quipped, 'Gee, I'm glad I didn't sell my car.'**

*Kim Campbell in a photograph taken on New Year's Day, 1993. Within ten months she would win and lose the office of Prime Minister*

My dear friends, Canadian democracy has spoken loudly and clearly today, and I accept the judgement of the Canadian people with disappointment, but without reservation.

My first words are to thank all my friends and supporters at Vancouver Centre who've worked so hard on my behalf both in this election and during the past five years. It has been a privilege to serve you in Ottawa and to represent your views in the House of Commons. I share the disappointment, however, of all my colleagues who were unsuccessful tonight, and I offer to them my thanks and my congratulations for their contribution to Canadian democracy.

The clear winners of today's election are Mister Chrétien and his party, and I congratulate them. I also offer Mister Chrétien and his wife Aline my best wishes for their future; I know, as few do, the dramatic changes that will take place in their lives and how much they will need the support and goodwill of all Canadians. I have conveyed to Mister Chrétien that I will do everything to ensure that the transition for our government to the one that he will be forming is orderly, efficient and rapid.

I also offer congratulations to all the candidates from all parties who were elected or re-elected tonight. In particular, I wish to offer congratulations to the leaders of the Reform Party, the New Democratic Party, and the Bloc Québécois for their personal success.

I want to address a special message to all members and supporters of the Progressive Conservative Party. Our party has a proud heritage in Canada. For 126 years, from the days of Sir John A. Macdonald and Georges-Étienne Cartier, we have brought a broad national vision, a national vision of tolerance, compassion and respect for the diversity of our country. This national vision remains as relevant and needed in Canada today as at any other time in our history. I believe profoundly in the purpose, principles and future of our party. Now is the time for all of us to come together and begin the process of renewal and rebuilding.

I will be meeting in the days and weeks ahead with the cabinet, caucus, candidates and members of the national executive to determine this process.

Success was not ours tonight, but success can be ours tomorrow. When we look at the popular vote tonight we see that as many Canadians voted for the Progressive Conservative

Party as voted for the Bloc Québécois or voted for the Reform Party – that was not reflected in seats, and we accept the reality of the electoral process in Canada, but it should remind us that there are many Canadians who look to us to represent them, to articulate their vision of this country. We must tonight, as Progressive Conservatives, dedicate ourselves anew to the national goals for which our party has always stood.

I would particularly like to thank the men and women of Quebec who supported us. In the last ten years, our party has deepened its roots in Quebec – its roots are still alive. I would like to greet the candidates who share the ideal of a united Canada, which respects diversity; I'd like to thank them for their loyalty and their dedication. I remain convinced that the men and women of Quebec will not achieve their aspirations unless they stay within the country that they helped to build and that they enrich with their distinct personality. Canada is not only an idea or a political system, it's not simply the result of history or geography, Canada is the expression of our values and our hopes and our pride; and my greatest honour would have been to have expressed those values, those hopes and that pride as Prime Minister of Canada.

This election has allowed new members and new parties to bring a strong message to Ottawa. As Canadian citizens let us resolve that no Member of Parliament, no political party will ever be permitted to forget the most fundamental message of all, a message that comes to us from the early days of our history, and that we have the responsibility of carrying on to future generations – that simple, but strong message is that we are above all proud Canadian citizens.

I want to say to you very deeply from the bottom of my heart how grateful I am to you for your support and affection over the years. And I know there is deep disappointment in this room tonight, but I want to remind you of the importance of taking the broad perspective, the historical perspective. Many fine leaders, many fine parties, many fine movements in history have had their setbacks, have had their periods in the wilderness. The most important thing is that we know we had a message and a vision that we believe in deeply, and many Canadians went to the polls today to share that belief. And we have a responsibility to bind our wounds, to perhaps have a good snurf into a Kleenex, and to come back, to continue to work together as we always have, with love and dedication, a good sense of humour, a sense of joy and a sense of purpose. That's what I think of when I think of my life as a Member of Parliament and when I think of the honour that I have had to be the leader of your party.

The past seven weeks I've travelled across this country meeting our candidates and our supporters, and I want to tell you that this party is strong. It is a strong organization peopled with people of vision and enthusiasm and deep love of country. Tonight has been a setback, but October the 26th changes nothing in terms of the strength of our organization or the dedication of our people. The Conservative Party is an important force in Canadian society and our day in the sun will come again – that, I promise.

Thank you again, for your hard work, your devotion and for your affection. You know that I return them. Thank you very much – and consider yourselves hugged.

## Stephen Harper

Speech to the Council for National Policy

*Montreal, June 1997*

### 'Canada is a Northern European welfare state in the worst sense of the term, and very proud of it.'

**In early December 2005, in the midst of a bitter federal election campaign, the Canadian Press was alerted to an eight-year-old speech by Conservative leader Stephen Harper, posted on the website of the Council for National Policy, a secretive group of American conservatives. Then Vice-President of the National Citizens Coalition, Harper made the address during one of the Council's thrice yearly confidential conferences. While the exact date and location of the speech remain undisclosed, it is known to have been delivered in June 1997 in Montreal.**

**The other parties attempted to make the speech an election issue, citing it as further proof of a hidden agenda, but it was soon overshadowed by the news that the Royal Canadian Mounted Police had launched criminal probes into possible government leaks regarding income trust.**

**Harper's speech was subsequently removed from the Council for National Policy website.**

Ladies and gentlemen, let me begin by giving you a big welcome to Canada. Let's start up with a compliment. You're here from the second greatest nation on earth. But seriously, your country, and particularly your conservative movement, is a light and an inspiration to people in this country and across the world.

Now, having given you a compliment, let me also give you an insult. I was asked to speak about Canadian politics. It may not be true, but it's legendary that if you're like all Americans, you know almost nothing except for your own country. Which makes you probably knowledgeable about one more country than most Canadians.

But in any case, my speech will make that assumption. I'll talk fairly basic stuff. If it seems pedestrian to some of you who do know a lot about Canada, I apologize.

I'm going to look at three things. First of all, just some basic facts about Canada that are relevant to my talk, facts about the country and its political system, its civics. Second, I want to take a look at the party system that's developed in Canada from a conventional left/right, or liberal/conservative perspective. The third thing I'm going to do is look at the political system again, because it can't be looked at in this country simply from the conventional perspective.

First, facts about Canada. Canada is a Northern European welfare state in the worst sense of the term, and very proud of it. Canadians make no connection between the fact that they are a Northern European welfare state and the fact that we have very low economic growth, a standard of living substantially lower than yours, a massive brain drain of young professionals to your country, and double the unemployment rate of the United States.

In terms of the unemployed, of which we have over a million-and-a-half, don't feel particularly bad for many of these people. They don't feel bad about it themselves, as long as they're receiving generous social assistance and unemployment insurance.

That is beginning to change. There have been some significant changes in our fiscal policies and our social welfare policies in the last three or four years. But nevertheless, they're still very generous compared to your country.

Let me just make a comment on language, which is so important in this country. I want to disabuse you of misimpressions you may have. If you've read any of the official propagandas, you've come over the border and entered a bilingual country. In this particular city, Montreal, you may well get that impression. But this city is extremely atypical of this country.

While it is a French-speaking city – largely – it has an enormous English-speaking minority and a large number of what are called ethnics: they who are largely immigrant communities, but who politically and culturally tend to identify with the English community.

This is unusual, because the rest of the province of Quebec is, by and large, almost entirely French-speaking. The English minority present here in Montreal is quite exceptional.

Furthermore, the fact that this province is largely French-speaking, except for Montreal, is quite exceptional with regard to the rest of the country. Outside of Quebec, the total population of francophones, depending on how you measure it, is only three to five per cent of the population. The rest of Canada is English speaking.

Even more important, the French-speaking people outside of Quebec live almost exclusively in the adjacent areas, in northern New Brunswick and in Eastern Ontario.

The rest of Canada is almost entirely English-speaking. Where I come from, Western Canada, the population of francophones ranges around one to two per cent in some cases. So it's basically an English-speaking country, just as English-speaking as, I would guess, the northern part of the United States.

But the important point is that Canada is not a bilingual country. It is a country with two languages. And there is a big difference.

As you may know, historically and especially presently, there's been a lot of political tension between these two major language groups, and between Quebec and the rest of Canada.

Let me take a moment for a humorous story. Now, I tell this with some trepidation, knowing that this is a largely Christian organization.

The National Citizens Coalition, by the way, is not. We're on the sort of libertarian side of the conservative spectrum. So I tell this joke with a little bit of trepidation. But nevertheless, this joke works with Canadian audiences of any kind, anywhere in Canada, both official languages, any kind of audience.

It's about a constitutional lawyer who dies and goes to heaven. There, he meets God and gets his questions answered about life. One of his questions is, 'God, will this problem between Quebec and the rest of Canada ever be resolved?' And God thinks very deeply about this, as God is wont to do. God replies, 'Yes, but not in my lifetime.'

I'm glad to see you weren't offended by that. I've had the odd religious person who's been offended. I always tell them, 'Don't be offended. The joke can't be taken seriously theologically. It is, after all, about a lawyer who goes to heaven.'

In any case. My apologies to Eugene Meyer of the Federalist Society.

Second, the civics, Canada's civics.

On the surface, you can make a comparison between our political system and yours. We have an executive, we have two legislative houses, and we have a Supreme Court.

However, our executive is the Queen, who doesn't live here. Her representative is the Governor General, who is an appointed buddy of the Prime Minister.

Of our two legislative houses, the Senate, our upper house, is appointed, also by the Prime Minister, where he puts buddies, fundraisers and the like. So the Senate also is not very important in our political system.

And we have a Supreme Court, like yours, which, since we put a charter of rights in our constitution in 1982, is becoming increasingly arbitrary and important. It is also appointed by the Prime Minister. Unlike your Supreme Court, we have no ratification process.

So if you sort of remove three of the four elements, what you see is a system of checks and balances which quickly becomes a system that's described as unpaid checks and political imbalances.

What we have is the House of Commons. The House of Commons, the bastion of the Prime Minister's power, the body that selects the Prime Minister, is an elected body. I really emphasize this to you as an American group: It's not like your House of Representatives. Don't make that comparison.

What the House of Commons is really like is the United States electoral college. Imagine if the electoral college which selects your president once every four years were to continue sitting in Washington for the next four years. And imagine its having the same vote on every issue. That is how our political system operates.

In our election last Monday, the Liberal Party won a majority of seats. The four opposition parties divided up the rest, with some very, very rough parity.

But the important thing to know is that this is how it will be until the Prime Minister calls the next election. The same majority vote on every issue. So if you ask me, 'What's the vote going to be on gun control?' or on the budget, we know already.

If any member of these political parties votes differently from his party on a particular issue, well, that will be national headline news. It's really hard to believe. If any one member votes differently, it will be national headline news. I voted differently at least once from my party, and it was national headline news. It's a very different system.

Our party system consists today of five parties. There was a remark made yesterday at your youth conference about the fact that parties come and go in Canada every year. This is rather deceptive. I've written considerably on this subject.

We had a two-party system from the founding of our country, in 1867. That two-party system began to break up in the period from 1911 to 1935. Ever since then, five political elements have come and gone. We've always had at least three parties. But even when parties come back, they're not really new. They're just an older party re-appearing under a different name and different circumstances.

Let me take a conventional look at these five parties. I'll describe them in terms that fit your own party system, the left/right kind of terms.

Let's take the New Democratic Party, the NDP, which won 21 seats. The NDP could be described as basically a party of liberal Democrats, but it's actually worse than that, I have to say. And forgive me jesting again, but the NDP is kind of proof that the Devil lives and interferes in the affairs of men.

This party believes not just in large government and in massive redistributive programs, it's explicitly socialist. On social value issues, it believes the opposite on just about everything that anybody in this room believes. I think that's a pretty safe bet on all social-value kinds of questions.

Some people point out that there is a small element of clergy in the NDP. Yes, this is true. But these are clergy who, while very committed to the church, believe that it made a historic error in adopting Christian theology.

The NDP is also explicitly a branch of the Canadian Labour Congress, which is by far our largest labour group, and explicitly radical.

There are some moderate and conservative labour organizations. They don't belong to that particular organization.

The second party, the Liberal Party, is by far the largest party. It won the election. It's also the only party that's competitive in all parts of the country. The Liberal Party is our dominant party today, and has been for 100 years. It's governed almost all of the last hundred years, probably about 75 per cent of the time.

It's not what you would call conservative Democrat; I think that's a disappearing kind of breed. But it's certainly moderate Democrat, a type of Clinton-pragmatic Democrat. It's moved in the last few years very much to the right on fiscal and economic concerns, but still believes in government intrusion in the economy where possible, and does, in its majority, believe in fairly liberal social values.

In the last Parliament, it enacted comprehensive gun control, well beyond, I think, anything you have. Now we'll have a national firearms registration system, including all shotguns and rifles. Many other kinds of weapons have been banned. It believes in gay rights, although it's fairly cautious. It's put sexual orientation in the Human Rights Act and will let the courts do the rest.

There is an important caveat to its liberal social values. For historic reasons that I won't get into, the Liberal Party gets the votes of most Catholics in the country, including many practising Catholics. It does have a significant Catholic, social-conservative element which occasionally disagrees with these kinds of policy directions. Although I caution you that even this Catholic social -conservative element in the Liberal Party is often quite liberal on economic issues.

Then there is the Progressive Conservative Party, the PC Party, which won only 20 seats. Now, the term Progressive Conservative will immediately raise suspicions in all of your minds. It should. It's obviously kind of an oxymoron. But actually, its origin is not progressive in the modern sense. The origin of the term 'progressive' in the name stems from the Progressive Movement in the 1920s, which was similar to that in your own country.

But the Progressive Conservative is very definitely liberal Republican. These are people who are moderately conservative on economic matters, and in the past have been moderately liberal, even sometimes quite liberal on social policy matters.

In fact, before the Reform Party really became a force in the late '80s, early '90s, the leadership of the Conservative Party was running the largest deficits in Canadian history. They were in favour of gay rights officially, officially for abortion on demand. Officially – what else can I say about them? Officially for the entrenchment of our universal, collectivized, health-care system and multicultural policies in the constitution of the country.

At the leadership level anyway, this was a pretty liberal group. This explains one of the reasons why the Reform Party has become such a power.

The Reform Party is much closer to what you would call conservative Republican, which I'll get to in a minute.

The Bloc Québécois, which I won't spend much time on, is a strictly Quebec party, strictly among the French-speaking people of Quebec. It is an ethnic separatist party that seeks to make Quebec an independent, sovereign nation.

By and large, the Bloc Québécois is centre-left in its approach. However, it is primarily an ethnic coalition. It's always had diverse elements. It does have an element that is more on the right of the political spectrum, but that's definitely a minority element.

Let me say a little bit about the Reform Party because I want you to be very clear on what the Reform Party is and is not.

The Reform Party, although described by many of its members, and most of the media, as conservative, and conservative in the American sense, actually describes itself as populist. And that's the term its leader, Preston Manning, uses.

This term is not without significance. The Reform Party does stand for direct democracy, which of course many American conservatives do, but also it sees itself as coming from a long tradition of populist parties of Western Canada, not all of which have been conservative.

It also is populist in the very real sense, if I can make American analogies to it – populist in the sense that the term is sometimes used with Ross Perot.

The Reform Party is very much a leader-driven party. It's much more a real party than Mister Perot's party – by the way, it existed before Mister Perot's party. But it's very much leader-driven, very much organized as a personal political vehicle. Although it has much more of a real organization than Mister Perot does.

But the Reform Party only exists federally. It doesn't exist at the provincial level here in Canada. It really exists only because Mister Manning is pursuing the position of Prime Minister. It doesn't have a broader political mandate than that yet. Most of its members feel it should, and, in their minds, actually it does.

It also has some Buchananist tendencies. I know there are probably many admirers of Mister Buchanan here, but I mean that in the sense that there are some anti-market elements in the Reform Party. So far, they haven't been that important, because Mister Manning is, himself, a fairly orthodox economic conservative.

The predecessor of the Reform Party, the Social Credit Party, was very much like this. Believing in funny money and control of banking, and a whole bunch of fairly non-conservative economic things.

So there are some non-conservative tendencies in the Reform Party, but, that said, the party is clearly the most economically conservative party in the country. It's the closest thing we have to a neo-conservative party in that sense.

It's also the most conservative socially, but it's not a theocon party, to use the term. The Reform Party does favour the use of referendums and free votes in Parliament on moral issues and social issues.

The party is led by Preston Manning, who is a committed, evangelical Christian. And the party in recent years has made some reference to family values and to family priorities. It has some policies that are definitely social-conservative, but it's not explicitly so.

Many members are not, the party officially is not, and, frankly, the party has had a great deal of trouble when it's tried to tackle those issues.

Last year, when we had the Liberal government putting the protection of sexual orientation in our Human Rights Act, the Reform Party was opposed to that, but made a terrible mess of the debate. In fact, discredited itself on that issue, not just with the conventional liberal media, but even with many social conservatives by the manner in which it mishandled that.

So the social conservative element exists. Mister Manning is a Christian, as are most of the party's senior people. But it's not officially part of the party. The party hasn't quite come to terms with how that fits into it.

That's the conventional analysis of the party system.

Let me turn to the non-conventional analysis, because frankly, it's impossible, with just left/right terminology to explain why we would have five parties, or why we would have four parties on the conventional spectrum. Why not just two?

The reason is regional division, which you'll see if you carefully look at a map. Let me draw the United States comparison, a comparison with your history.

The party system that is developing here in Canada is a party system that replicates the antebellum period, the pre-Civil War period of the United States.

That's not to say – and I would never be quoted as saying – we're headed to a civil war. But we do have a major secession crisis, obviously of a very different nature than the secession crisis you had in the 1860s. But the dynamics, the political and partisan dynamics of this, are remarkably similar.

The Bloc Québécois is equivalent to your Southern secessionists, Southern Democrats, states rights activists. The Bloc Québécois, its 44 seats, come entirely from the province of Quebec. But even more strikingly, they come from ridings, or election districts, almost entirely populated by the descendants of the original European French settlers.

The Liberal Party has 26 seats in Quebec. Most of these come from areas where there are heavy concentrations of English, aboriginal or ethnic votes. So the Bloc Québécois is very much an ethnic party, but it's also a secession party.

In the referendum two years ago, the secessionists won 49 per cent of the vote, 49.5 per cent. So this is a very real crisis. We're looking at another referendum before the turn of the century.

The Progressive Conservative Party is very much comparable to the Whigs of the 1850s and 1860s. What is happening to them is very similar to the Whigs. A moderate conservative party, increasingly under stress because of the secession movement, on the one hand, and the reaction to that movement from harder line English Canadians on the other hand.

You may recall that the Whigs, in their dying days, went through a series of metamorphoses. They ended up as what was called the Unionist movement that won some of the border states in your 1860 election.

If you look at the surviving PC support, it's very much concentrated in Atlantic Canada, in the provinces to the east of Quebec. These are very much equivalent to the United States

*Stephen Harper, Canada's 22nd Prime Minister*

border states. They're weak economically. They have very grim prospects if Quebec separates. These people want a solution at almost any cost. And some of the solutions they propose would be exactly that.

They also have a small percentage of seats in Quebec. These are French-speaking areas that are also more moderate and very concerned about what would happen in a secession crisis.

The Liberal Party is very much your northern Democrat, or mainstream Democratic Party, a party that is less concessionary to the secessionists than the PCs, but still somewhat concessionary. And they still occupy the mainstream of public opinion in Ontario, which is the big and powerful province, politically and economically, alongside Quebec.

The Reform Party is very much a modern manifestation of the Republican movement in Western Canada; the U.S. Republicans started in the western United States. The Reform Party is very resistant to the agenda and the demands of the secessionists, and on a very deep philosophical level.

The goal of the secessionists is to transform our country into two nations, either into two explicitly sovereign countries, or in the case of weaker separatists, into some kind of federation of two equal partners.

The Reform Party opposes this on all kinds of grounds, but most important, Reformers are highly resistant philosophically to the idea that we will have an open, modern, multi-ethnic society on one side of the line, and the other society will run on some set of ethnic-special-status principles. This is completely unacceptable, particularly to philosophical conservatives in the Reform Party.

The Reform Party's strength comes almost entirely from the West. It's become the dominant political force in Western Canada. And it is getting a substantial vote in Ontario. Twenty per cent of the vote in the last two elections. But it has not yet broken through in terms of the number of seats won in Ontario.

This is a very real political spectrum, lining up from the Bloc to Reform. You may notice I didn't mention the New Democratic Party. The NDP obviously can't be compared to anything pre-Civil War. But the NDP is not an important player on this issue. Its views are somewhere between the liberals and conservatives. Its main concern, of course, is simply the left-wing agenda to basically disintegrate our society in all kinds of spectrums. So it really doesn't fit in.

But I don't use this comparison of the pre-Civil War lightly. Preston Manning, the leader of the Reform Party has spent a lot of time reading about pre-Civil War politics. He compares the Reform Party himself to the Republican Party of that period. He is very well-read on Abraham Lincoln and a keen follower and admirer of Lincoln.

I know Mister Manning very well. I would say that next to his own father, who is a prominent Western Canadian politician, Abraham Lincoln has probably had more effect on Mister Manning's political philosophy than any individual politician.

Obviously, the issue here is not slavery, but the appeasement of ethnic nationalism. For years, we've had this Quebec separatist movement. For years, we elected Quebec prime ministers to deal with that, Quebec prime ministers who were committed federalists who would lead us out of the wilderness. For years, we have given concessions of various kinds of the province of Quebec, political and economic, to make them happier.

This has not worked. The sovereignty movement has continued to rise in prominence. And its demands have continued to increase. It began to hit the wall when what are called the soft separatists and the conventional political establishment got together to put in the constitution something called 'a distinct society clause'. Nobody really knows what it would mean, but it would give the Supreme Court, where Quebec would have a tremendous role in appointment, the power to interpret Quebec's special needs and powers, undefined elsewhere.

This has led to a firewall of resistance across the country. It fuelled the growth of the Reform Party. I should even say that the early concessionary people, like Pierre Trudeau, have come out against this. So there's even now an element of the Quebec federalists themselves who will no longer accept this.

So you see the syndrome we're in. The separatists continue to make demands. They're a powerful force. They continue to have the bulk of the Canadian political establishment on their side. The two traditional parties, the Liberals and PCs, are both led by Quebecers who favour concessionary strategies. The Reform Party is a bastion of resistance to this tendency.

To give you an idea of how divided the country is, not just in Quebec but how divided the country is outside Quebec on this, we had a phenomenon five years ago. This is a real phenomenon; I don't know how much you heard about it.

The establishment came down with a constitutional package which they put to a national referendum. The package included distinct society status for Quebec and some other changes, including some that would just horrify you, putting universal Medicare in our constitution, and feminist rights, and a whole bunch of other things.

What was significant about this was that this constitutional proposal was supported by the entire Canadian political establishment. By all of the major media. By the three largest traditional parties, the PC, Liberal Party and NDP. At the time, the Bloc and Reform were very small.

It was supported by big business, very vocally by all of the major CEOs of the country. The leading labour unions all supported it. Complete consensus. And most academics.

And it was defeated. It literally lost the national referendum against a rag-tag opposition consisting of a few dissident conservatives and a few dissident socialists.

This gives you some idea of the split that's taking place in the country.

Canada is, however, a troubled country politically, not socially. This is a country that we like to say works in practice but not in theory.

You can walk around this country without running across very many of these political controversies.

I'll end there and take any of your questions. But let me conclude by saying, good luck in your own battles. Let me just remind you of something that's been talked about here. As long as there are exams, there will always be prayer in schools.

# PARLIAMENT

> **I want to make it very clear that, if a majority of honourable members vote against abolition, some people are going to be hanged. Their death would be a direct consequence of the negative decision made by this House on this bill.**
>
> *- Pierre Elliott Trudeau, 1976*

# Sir John A. Macdonald

On the Pacific Scandal

*The House of Commons, Ottawa, 3 November 1873*

***'...the government of the day are unworthy of their position unless they are ready to meet any charges brought against them.'***

**Macdonald's speech, perhaps the most famous made in the House of Commons, was a response to scandal. In February 1873, Sir Hugh Allan's Canada Pacific Railway Company was awarded the charter to build the transcontinental railway. Less than two months later, Liberal Lucius Seth Huntington, 'the honourable member for Shefford', charged in the House that Allan had been awarded the charter in return for contributions toward the Tories' 1872 election campaign. Damning correspondence, including a request from Macdonald for 'another $10,000', was produced. Though the Government managed for several months to weather the scandal, by November it had been severely weakened. As if in reflection, Macdonald himself appeared sickly, sitting through the Opposition's attack, as Tory members slowly departed, reducing the Government to a majority of two seats. After a few days of silence, he finally rose at nine in the evening and, tumbler of gin by his side, began a counter-offensive.**

**This passage, representing roughly one twenty-fifth of the total, captures Macdonald's skills as both an orator and debater. Here he fights not only for his career, but for the future of his Government and that of what has come to be known as the 'National Dream'.**

**Macdonald's speech lasted nearly five hours, concluding at nearly two o'clock the following morning. However, it was not enough to save his governing Liberal-Conservatives. On 5 November, two more members defected, and the Government offered its resignation.**

Let us look back to the circumstances of the case. I invite the careful attention of the house, and especially the attention of those honourable members who were not members of the parliament of Canada at that time, to the circumstances of the case.

In February, I think it was, there was a royal charter given for the purpose of building a Pacific railway, to the Pacific Railway Company. They went home, their president, Sir Hugh Allan, and certain other members of the Board for the purpose of attempting to carry out this charter which had been given to them. The charter had been given to them according to the vote of the Parliament of Canada, with the sanction of the Parliament of Canada, and every clause of it was in accordance with the provisions of the law passed by the Parliament of Canada.

These gentlemen had gone home to England to lay a great scheme, so great a scheme, Mister Speaker, that some of the honourable gentlemen opposite said that it was going to overtax our resources and destroy our credit, and that they could not succeed at all with so small a population in such a young country. They had gone home to England to lay the project before the English world and European capitalists. They were going home to operate, and it depended much on the support they received from this country, from the Parliament and press of Canada, whether they could succeed or not. They had gone home in February. Parliament met early in March, I think. The honourable member for Shefford rose in his place and made his charge against the government on the 2nd of April. The honourable gentleman may have been, I do not say he was not, actuated by principles of fine patriotism in making that charge; but whether he was so actuated or not, whether his motives were parliamentary or unparliamentary, patriotic or unpatriotic, one thing is certain, that the direct aim, the direct object, the point at which that motion and that statement were directed, was to kill the charter in England.

The weapon was aimed with that object, not so much with the desire of destroying the administration, not so much with the purpose of casting a reflection upon the ministry, as with the view of destroying that first on the expectation that the ministry would fall afterwards. That was the aim; there was no doubt about it, and when the honourable gentleman's motion was defeated, and when I took up the resolution the aim was well intended – the desire of killing was well intended – but it failed in the execution.

When I took it up I considered the whole position of events. Sir Hugh Allan and those connected with him went to England in March. Parliament was sitting at the time the honourable gentleman made his motion. I could not know how long Parliament would last, and the chances were that they would return some time before the end of the session. If they did not return then, of course I considered that there could be no examination until they did, but I thought they might return. I declare that I never for a moment supposed that the honourable member, when he made his statement, could be guilty of such great, such palpable, such obvious injustice, as to press his committee in the absence of Sir Hugh Allan, Mister Abbott, and Sir George Cartier, when they had no opportunity of defending either themselves or the charter which they had obtained.

The house must remember also that the motion made by the honourable gentleman went much farther than my motion. The motion of the honourable member, which he moved on the

2nd of April, was not only to inquire into the facts that he mentioned, the statements upon which he based his motion, but to go into the whole of the subject connected with the charter and the granting of the charter to the Pacific railway company. The aim of his motion, I repeat, was to destroy that charter. I will read the motion of the honourable member. After detailing the facts, he moved, 'that a committee of seven members be appointed to inquire into all the circumstances connected with the negotiations for the construction of the Pacific railway, with the legislation of last session on the subject, and with the granting of the charter to Sir Hugh Allan and others.' So that the aim of the honourable gentleman in making that motion was not simply to attack the government, not simply that from improper motives or inducements of any kind they had given the charter, but was for the purpose of destroying that charter and of attacking all the legislation of the previous session on which the charter was based. I never for one moment supposed that any honourable member would be guilty of the gross injustice of attempting to attack the whole of the legislation of the previous session and the charter solemnly granted under an act of parliament, and of attempting to affect vested interest, on which a million of money had been staked, in the absence of the persons primarily interested. That motion was made, and was intended to be a vote of want of confidence. Was that so or was it not so? Will the honourable gentleman say it was not so?

*Mister Huntington*: The motion when made was intended to express precisely what it did express.

*Sir John A. Macdonald*: It is said, sir, that if there had been one honest man in the cities of Sodom and Gomorrah they might have been saved, and so the Opposition may be saved in the same way, for they have one honest man in their ranks – the member for South Wentworth – who stated that that motion was intended to be a vote of want of confidence.

Everybody knew that that was its design, and yet at this day, at this late hour, the honourable gentleman had not the manliness to get up and say so. He dare not say it was not a motion of want of confidence. It was meant in that way, and I can prove that it was by my honourable friend the member for South Wentworth. I call him, and I believe him. He said it was so. Will the honourable gentleman not believe him? Although differing from him in politics, I know he would not say what was not true. If I remember rightly, the honourable member for Shefford said he would make the motion when we went into committee of supply. He gave the necessary notice that is always given in such cases, and I certainly supposed that he intended to make a general motion on our policy connected with the Canadian Pacific Railway. He said he was going to make a motion on that subject, and it was by mere accident that when my friend, the Minister of Finance, rose to make his budget speech, with you in the chair, instead of a committee of supply, the honourable member said he would take another opportunity of making the statement in connection with the Pacific railway. Had we gone into committee of supply the honourable gentleman would have made, in the ordinary parliamentary way, his motion of want of confidence. But he should have given notice of his attack, for a more unmanly attack is unknown. What notice had been given that he was going to make that motion?

True, the government of the day are unworthy of their position unless they are ready to meet any charges brought against them. But had we the most remote information respecting that personal matter? And even when on the second day he announced that he was going to postpone to a future occasion further action, he did not venture to give the slightest intimation to the men he was going to attack; the men whose characters he was going to blacken; of what he was going to say; but he took us by surprise and sought by bringing in documents carefully prepared to get a committee on those statements for the purpose. Certainly it would have been

*Sir John A. Macdonald, Agnes Macdonald and party during their first journey west on the Canadian Pacific Railway*

so if the committee had been granted as he proposed – of killing, as it was designed to kill, as it was bound to kill, the efforts of the Canadian people to get a body of English capitalists, to build the Pacific railway.

He could not possibly have supposed that he would have got the inquiry through that session, but he supposed if the house had granted the committee on his statement, and it had gone home, telegraphed by cable by the associated press, with which some honourable gentlemen opposite seemed to have mysterious connections – it would certainly have been mysterious but it would certainly have affected the construction of the Canadian Pacific Railway, throwing back for years the building of the railway, casting discredit on Canada, and telling British Columbia what they had told them two years before, that they were not going to get the railway.

Mister Speaker, the honourable gentleman did not speak, in his remarks on the motion, of facts within his own knowledge, and as the member for Marquette had done in his statements of facts, he only stated that he was credibly informed that the fact existed, and he would be able to prove it, and I venture to say that in the whole range of parliamentary experience in England, and wherever else fair play is known, no man could be expected to have got any other answer than the one he got from the house.

If the honourable member had risen in his place and said of his own knowledge that he was personally cognizant of certain facts, then the House might have considered those facts as proved, at all events sufficient for a *prima facie* case for inquiry. But the honourable member for Shefford did not pretend to say so, but rose in the House and said he was credibly informed of certain facts, and thereupon asked for a committee to try the Government, and not only so, but to try whether the legislation of the previous session was corrupt or non-corrupt; whether the Members of Parliament who had voted for the Government were right or wrong, and whether that charter, to which great credit was attached, was fraudulent or valid. And on the nonce, when the honourable gentleman made the proposition, we resolved to leave it to the house to say whether they believed that the facts had occurred.

When the honourable gentleman stated that he was credibly informed that such was true, the house voted down the motion. On the next day I gave notice that I would introduce the resolution which I did introduce. I gave notice of the resolution, and there is a little history with the resolution to which I will call the attention of the house. It is reported that at a meeting at New Glasgow the honourable member for Lambton stated that that resolution which I moved was forced upon me by my own followers and that members on this side of the house had come to me to urge me to introduce that resolution. The honourable gentleman has heard my denial. He heard my speech; he was in his place when I made that speech, and interrupted me several times, and I then turned around and asked my friends if any of them had come to me to force any influence, or language, or anything of the kind, to come down to the House with that motion....

# Pierre Elliott Trudeau

## The Debate on Capital Punishment

*The House of Commons, Ottawa, 15 June 1976*

**'...what we will actually be deciding, when we vote on this bill, is not merely how the law of the land will be written, but also whether some human beings will live or die.'**

The last executions in Canada took place on 10 December 1962, when two men were hanged at Toronto's Don Jail, yet it wasn't until the summer of 1976 that capital punishment was removed from the Criminal Code. Introduced by the Liberal government, Bill C-84 replaced the death penalty for first-degree murder with mandatory imprisonment with no chance of parole for 25 years. It was the last in a long line of proposed legislation, stretching back to a 1914 private member's bill, put forward by abolitionists. Following Trudeau's speech in the House of Commons, Bill C-84 was passed on a free vote by a margin of six. Eleven years later, a motion to reinstate capital punishment was defeated by a margin of 21 votes.

From the time of Confederation until the abolition of the death penalty a total of 697 men and thirteen women were executed in Canada.

I am sure that very few of us consciously contemplated, when we decided to run for public office, that we would find ourselves playing a decisive role in the resolution of a question as awesome as that of life and death. Yet, here we are, with all our individual limitations, required by the office we hold to make a decision on as profoundly important an issue as has ever divided Canadians.

It is not open to anyone among us to take refuge in the comforting illusion that we are debating nothing more than an abstract theory of criminal justice, and that it will be the Cabinet's sole responsibility to decide the actual fate of individual murderers, if this bill is defeated.

I want to make it very clear that, if a majority of honourable members vote against abolition, some people are going to be hanged. Their death would be a direct consequence of the negative decision made by this House on this bill.

I say that, Mister Speaker, not from any desire to be morbid or melodramatic, nor from any desire to try to absolve the Cabinet, in advance, of its share of responsibility for the taking of human life in the future, if this bill is defeated. I say it in order to impress upon the House as strongly as I can that what we will actually be deciding, when we vote on this bill, is not merely how the law of the land will be written, but also whether some human beings will live or die.

At this moment, eleven men are being held in Canadian prisons under sentence of death for the murder of policemen or prison officials. Some have exhausted their rights appeal – others have not. Therefore, while it is impossible to pre-judge how Cabinet will treat any individual case when the time comes to decide whether to invoke the royal prerogative of mercy and commute a death sentence to life imprisonment, it is inevitable that the defeat of this bill would eventually place the hangman's noose around some person's neck.

To make that quite clear: if this bill is defeated, some people will certainly hang.

While members are free to vote as they wish, those who vote against the bill, for whatever reason, cannot escape their personal share of responsibility for the hangings which will take place if the bill is defeated.

It is in that context, Mister Speaker, that I wish to place my remarks on the issue before us.

Any discussion of capital punishment must begin with the identification of its intended purpose, which is clearly the security of society, the protection of innocent people against the ultimate criminal violence. It is not that goal which divides us. It is the goal we all share. What divides us is the question of appropriateness of state execution of murderers as a means of achieving that goal.

It is clear that the protection of innocent people against assaults on their lives and liberty is one of the highest duties of the state. It is equally clear that this duty requires aggressive and effective prevention, prosecution and punishment of criminal violence.

It is essential that people have confidence in the law, essential that they have confidence in the ability of the legal process to protect them against the lawless. Reinforcing that vital sense of confidence and security is the primary aim of Bill C-83, the companion piece to the bill we are now debating.

Longer mandatory sentences, and tightening of parole regulations in relation to convicted murderers will give society the assurance it needs that those who have unlawfully taken the life of another will be removed from our midst for a very long time. Other provisions are designed to restrict the availability of guns, the most common murder weapons, and to strengthen the ability of our police forces to prevent and solve crimes. There is every reason to believe that such measures will effectively inhibit criminal activity whereas capital punishment offers no such assurance. That is why the time has come for Parliament to decide whether we should remove capital punishment from the Criminal Code.

The crux of the question before us is whether execution is an effective and therefore justifiable weapon for the state to use in order to deter potential murderers.

There are those who sincerely believe that no man or group of men ever have the right to end a human life. They believe that life is a divine gift which only God has the right to take away. I am not one of those who share that belief.

Our law, from its earliest beginnings, has always recognized the right of an individual to kill another when there exists reasonable grounds for believing that killing an aggressor is necessary to the protection of one's own life or that of another.

Moral philosophers and theologians have recognized for many centuries the right of a country to defend itself in a just war, even when defence involves the killing of enemies.

So the question before us is not whether execution by the state is justified per se. The question is whether state execution is an effective deterrent to murder, and therefore a justifiable act of collective self-defence.

The deterrent effect of capital punishment is at the very core of the issue, and since one's moral view of the justification of capital punishment is entirely determined by one's judgement of its deterrent effect, the proper focus of this debate is factual data and logical induction, not moral philosophy. In that sense, the issue before us must be resolved – by a practical rather than a moral judgement.

I know there are those who say that execution is justified because it prevents a murderer from ever again committing the same crime. It certainly does. But if you rely on that reasoning, you are killing a man not because his death may deter others from following in his footsteps, but because of what he might possibly do at some future time. To justify such preventive execution, there would have to be some reasonable grounds for believing that a convicted murderer, if released into society, would murder again. In fact, the probability lies strongly in the other direction.

We know of only four people who have been found guilty of murder by a Canadian court, and convicted of murder a second time. In order to be absolutely sure that no murderer would murder again, we would have to take the lives of all persons convicted of either first- or second-degree murder, even though the probability is that an infinitesimal percentage of them would ever murder again if allowed to live. That's an unacceptably high price to pay in human lives for a sense of security insignificantly greater than we have now.

I might ask those who would execute a person to prevent a future murder how they could logically avoid advocating the execution of mentally ill people who are found to have homicidal tendencies?

Well, you may say, let's execute the murderer for the crime he has committed. Let's take a life for a life. Let's remove a savage animal from the human race.

I do not deny that society has the right to punish a criminal, and the right to make the punishment fit the crime, but to kill a man for punishment alone is an act of revenge. Nothing else. Some would prefer to call it retribution, because that word has a nicer sound. But the meaning is the same.

Are we, as a society, so lacking in respect for ourselves, so lacking in hope for human betterment, so socially bankrupt that we are ready to accept state vengeance as our penal philosophy?

Individuals who strike back at the murderer of a loved one and kill him in a frenzy of passionate grief have sometimes been excused by the courts because they were thought to have temporarily lost control of their reason. I have received letters from the parents and relatives of victims demanding the death penalty for the murderer, and have been deeply sympathetic to the suffering of those who have suffered such a tragic and cruel loss of a loved one. But the state cannot claim the excuse of blind grief or unreasoning passion when long after the provocative act, and after calm and deliberate consideration, it kills a man.

My primary concern here is not compassion for the murderer. My concern is for the society which adopts vengeance as an acceptable motive for its collective behaviour. If we make that choice, we will snuff out some of that boundless hope and confidence in ourselves and other people, which has marked our maturing as a free people. We will have chosen violence as a weapon against the violence we profess to abhor. Who is so confident that he knows for sure that such an official endorsement of violence will not harden the society we were elected to improve, will not pervade gradually many different relationships in our society? Who is so confident that he knows for sure that acceptance of state violence will not lead to the greater social acceptance of lesser forms of violence among our people?

Vengeance and violence damage and destroy those who adopt them, and lessen respect for the dignity and rights of others among those who condone them.

There is only one other possible justification for capital punishment – the one we started with – the belief that execution of murderers will protect society by acting as a deterrent to the commission of murder by other people.

There are some who adopt an experimental approach to the question of deterrence, like a scientist experimenting with different combinations of chemicals in the search for a new healing drug.

Let's try it, they say, and see if it works. If it does, we'll keep it. If it doesn't, we can always stop using it. Let's not slam the door, they say, on a possibly effective weapon against murder, on some specious philosophical grounds. There are innocent lives at stake. If capital punishment prevents just one murder, they say, it will be adequately justified.

That's compelling rhetoric, but it contains a fatal flaw, namely that we would be experimenting with human lives. Respect for human life is absolutely vital for the rights and freedom we all enjoy. Even the life of the most hardened criminal must be accorded some degree of respect in a free society. If we take that life without proven purpose, without proven necessity, then we weaken dangerously one of the fundamental principles which allow us to live together in peace, harmony and mutual respect. That is why free peoples have always insisted that the onus is on the person who would interfere with another's life or liberty to prove that such interference is necessary for the common good.

Strictly speaking, therefore, it is not up to me, as an abolitionist, to prove that the execution of murderers will not prevent other murders. It is up to the advocates of capital punishment to prove that it will. If they cannot, their case must fail. Otherwise, this debate turns into a guessing game, and the lives of human beings become so many chips on the poker table. That's not good enough. I don't want to hear your guesses about the deterrent value of capital punishment. I don't want to hear about gut feelings. I want proof. Not absolute proof. Not even proof beyond a reasonable doubt. A preponderance of evidence will do. A preponderance of available evidence showing that executions are likely to deter other murderers would serve as an adequate justification for the act, an adequate guarantee that a human life was not being taken capriciously.

Show me the evidence that capital punishment anywhere, at any time, has deterred other people from committing murder. My own reading of the speeches made here on this issue since the first week of May, together with the Solicitor-General's daily monitoring of the debate, have indicated that no such evidence has been placed before the House.

The evidence does not exist, neither in the Canadian experience nor in the experience of any other jurisdiction. At best, the statistics are inconclusive. They prove nothing. There is no evidence proving that the use or non-use of capital punishment has had any effect whatsoever on murder rates anywhere in the world.

I must confess I cannot understand why anyone would agree to kill a man without the least shred of assurance that his death would accomplish any worthwhile social purpose. If penalties applied by the state against law-breakers cannot be justified for their rehabilitative, punitive or deterrent value, they cannot be justified at all – not in a civilized society. Capital punishment fails on all three counts. To retain it in the Criminal Code of Canada would be to abandon reason in favour of vengeance – to abandon hope and confidence in favour of despairing acceptance of our inability to cope with violent crime except with violence.

It is because I have an enduring confidence in mankind, and confidence in society's ability to protect itself without taking human life, that I am eager to support this bill and vote for the abolition of capital punishment.

*The execution of Stanislaus Lacroix on 21 March 1902 in Hull, Quebec*

# Brian Mulroney

## Report on the First Ministers' Meeting at Meech Lake

*The House of Commons, Ottawa, 1 May 1987*

***'We agreed to recognize the distinctiveness Quebec brings to Canada, which includes within it two principal language communities within the federation.'***

**The Meech Lake Accord, referred to here as 'the Meech Lake Agreement', was the first of two attempts made by Mulroney to obtain Quebec's endorsement of the Canada Act 1982. Although public opinion polls indicated initially that a majority in the country supported the agreement, this gradually dissipated due, in part, to the call for Quebec to be recognized as a 'distinct society'. The accord was further endangered when new governments were elected in New Brunswick and Newfoundland. In 1990, when a commission led by Jean Charest recommended changes, Lucien Bouchard left the governing Progressive Conservatives and formed the separatist Bloc Québécois. A revised agreement failed to pass when Elijah Harper, a Member of the Legislative Assembly of Manitoba, blocked the unanimous support that was required.**

*Brian Mulroney, the 18th Prime Minister of Canada*

Mister Speaker, I rise to report to the House on the meeting of First Ministers yesterday at Meech Lake.

I am honoured to inform the House that at about 10 pm last night the Premiers and I reached unanimous agreement in principle on a constitutional package which will allow Quebec to rejoin the Canadian constitutional family.

This agreement enhances the Confederation bargain and strengthens, I believe, the federal nature of Canada. Although it remains to be formalized, it represents in the judgement of First Ministers, of all political stripes, from all areas of the country, an historic accomplishment.

The Meech Lake Agreement springs from the Canadian tradition of honourable compromise, and is a tribute to the statesmanship and leadership of all First Ministers demonstrated yesterday at Meech Lake.

Our task, simply put, was to settle a constitutional impasse which was incompletely resolved in 1981. Our task was to attempt to reconcile Quebec's distinct needs with the interests of all other provinces and the good of the country as a whole.

Mister Speaker, at this time I am pleased to table the statement of principles that constitute the Meech Lake Agreement. The essence of the Agreement is as follows:

We agreed to recognize the distinctiveness Quebec brings to Canada, which includes within it two principal language communities within the federation.

We agreed to give constitutional protection to an expanded immigration agreement with Quebec and to enter into accords with other provinces, appropriate to their circumstances.

We agreed to entrench the Supreme Court of Canada and the requirement that at least three of the nine Justices appointed be from Quebec, and to provide for provincial involvement in Supreme Court appointments.

We agreed that reasonable compensation be granted to provinces that do not participate in future national shared-cost programs in areas of exclusive provincial jurisdiction, if they undertake their own initiatives or programs compatible with national objectives.

We agreed that all provinces must approve changes to national institutions under section 42 of the 1982 Constitution Act, and that the Government of Canada will provide reasonable compensation in all cases where a province opts out of an amendment transferring provincial jurisdiction to Parliament.

We agreed that there will be annual First Ministers' Conferences on the constitution and that the first will be held before the end of 1988 to discuss senate reform, the fisheries and other items to be agreed upon.

Until Senate reform is achieved, appointments to the Senate will be made by the federal government from lists of candidates furnished by the provinces.

We are also entrenching in the constitution the annual First Ministers' Conference on the economy.

Mister Speaker, the Meech Lake Agreement is good for Canada, and good for Canadians. It will unblock the constitutional reform process and enable Canadians to turn their attention to other issues such as Senate reform and fisheries.

Mister Speaker, this agreement represents the best features of a vital federal system, one which I believe responds to the aspirations of Canadians in every corner of the country. It reflects a spirit of partnership – and not one of endless federal-provincial power struggles.

The work of nation-building goes on. Officials will shortly begin drafting a constitutional text which reflects the Meech Lake Agreement. I shall be convening a conference of First Ministers within weeks, the purpose of which will be to seek formal agreement. On the assumption a formal agreement is reached at this conference, the constitutional amending process will proceed. An amending resolution will be tabled in Parliament and in the Legislative Assembly of each province. Proclamation would follow once all the resolutions have been approved.

Mister Speaker, Sir Wilfrid Laurier once said: 'The governing motive of my life has been to harmonize the diverse elements which compose our country.' Surely that is the wish of every member, on all sides of this House. That is our policy. That is our purpose – building a stronger Canada for all Canadians.

# Lucien Bouchard

On the Bloc Québécois as the Official Opposition

*The House of Commons, Ottawa, 19 January 1994*

***'For the first time in contemporary history, this House which is now beginning its work reflects the very essence of Canada...'***

**The federal election in November of 1993 saw an unprecedented change in Canada's political landscape. The Progressive Conservative Party all but vanished, replaced by the regional parties it spawned: the Bloc Québécois and the Reform Party. Although Reform won more votes, they fell two seats below the Bloc. Thus, when Parliament reconvened on 17 January 1994, Canadians were faced with a separatist party as the Official Opposition.**

**This speech by Bloc leader Lucien Bouchard, the first of any length as Leader of the Opposition, outlines the position of the Bloc, drawing more on economics than culture in his argument for Quebec sovereignty. Nevertheless, Bouchard mentions the writings of English-speaking Canadians, Hugh MacLennan and Kenneth McRoberts. The quotation from the latter is taken from 'English Canada and Quebec: Avoiding the Issue', which McRoberts delivered in March 1991 as the sixth annual Robarts Lecture.**

**What follows is the first half of Bouchard's historic speech.**

Mister Speaker, here we are at the beginning not only of a new year but also of a new Parliament, with a new government, a new official opposition elected by the people of Quebec and a new formation representing mainly Western Canada.

The government party and the third party were given clear mandates by their respective voters. I wish to congratulate both leaders for their success at the polls. To the Prime Minister in particular, I wish health, clear-mindedness and broadness of outlook in carrying out his duties in this crucial time in the history of Canada and Quebec.

The people of Quebec will soon decide their future following a debate that we all hope will be marked by a spirit of democracy. This is also a time when the adverse effects of the combined economic and political crisis are threatening to make a growing number of our fellow citizens lose hope.

I also want to pay my respects generally to all the other members elected to this House. On behalf of my colleagues from the Bloc Québécois, I can assure the Speaker, the Government and all members of this House of our full co-operation in respecting decorum in this House. We will see to it, as far as we are concerned, that exchanges remain courteous though intense, rational though impassioned, orderly though vigorous.

The major change in this House is undoubtedly the massive influx of sovereigntist members from Quebec. No one can trivialize the shift represented by the decision some two million voters have made to send 54 members here to pave the way for Quebec's sovereignty.

The dynamics which led Quebec to this decision were such that enough members were elected to form the Official Opposition. Paradoxical as it may seem, this electoral result flows from an implacable logic.

Indeed, it was inevitable that these old walls, which too often resounded with the voices of Quebecers who were ready to approve measures rejected by the voters, such as the Charlottetown Accord and the unilateral patriation of 1982, would one day hear the speeches of members who base their party allegiance on the commitment never to accept to compromise Quebec's interests in Ottawa; members who are freed from the constraints of the old Canada-wide parties and who therefore will not be torn between their obligations as federalist parliamentarians and their loyalty to Quebec; members whose political career is motivated only by the determination to work, with their blinkers off, for Quebec's sovereignty.

Many in English Canada were surprised by the Bloc Québécois' achievement on October twenty-fifth. To tell the truth, I am not surprised by that: the channels of communication from Quebec to English Canada are significantly distorted as they cross the border, so that the Quebec reality is perceived in a very confused way on the other side. That is the first justification for the presence of Quebec sovereigntists in this House.

Institutions often lag behind reality. The previous House of Commons was no exception to this rule; the stinging rejection of the Charlottetown Accord by voters in Canada and Quebec is striking proof. Today, the main architects of that accord have all disappeared from the political scene. They were the same people who showed cold indifference to the misfortune brought on by the long and difficult recession which began in the spring of 1990.

The voters have set the record straight. For the first time in contemporary history, this House which is now beginning its work reflects the very essence of Canada, its bi-national nature and the very different visions of the future which flow from that. Truth is never a bad advisor. As General de Gaulle said, one may well long for the days of sailing ships, but the only valid policy one can have is based on realities.

What are the realities with which this House will be faced? First of all, a really bad economic situation. To realize the full extent of it, it is not enough to look at the total picture as it is now; we must put it in the relevant chronological context.

The latest recession lasted roughly from April 1990 to April 1992, when net job losses stopped. But big business continues to lay off employees and the so-called recovery is so anaemic that only economists dare to call it a recovery. Now, in early 1994, per capita GDP for all of Canada is still nearly five per cent less than it was in 1989. We know that per capita GDP is a more relevant indicator than total GDP, since it is affected by population growth, which is very large in Canada. Not only has Canada declined in relation to its partners, but it is doing worse than before.

The employment situation does not seem any brighter, any more encouraging. By the end of 1993, the Canadian economy had regained only sixty per cent of all the jobs lost during the recession. The situation in Quebec is even more disastrous, since the recovery rate there is only twenty-five per cent. It must be said that for all practical purposes, Quebec had no government for much of 1993, but in that time, many young people arrived on the labour market. Just to absorb the number of net new job seekers, the Canadian economy would have to create over 200,000 jobs a year, about 45,000 of them in Quebec. The 1993 performance of 147,000 jobs in Canada, most of which are part-time, and none in Quebec, is far off the mark.

These chilling statistics hide thousands of human dramas. No one goes gladly to an employment centre for the unemployment insurance benefits to which they are entitled. Underemployment has considerable economic and social costs. It is a real collective tragedy. In this regard, it is very urgent to put people back to work, giving them real hope of recovering their dignity by regaining the right to earn their living.

Therefore, it is no surprise that the unemployment level remains at such a high level. Fortunately, the American economy is not suffering from the same problems as those of the Canadian economy. Consequently, the economic situation has at least one aspect that works for us, namely exports to the United States. But the result is that the gap between American and Canadian unemployment rates has never been so high, the difference being close to five percentage points. The recovery south of the border is much stronger than here. Indeed, major obstacles to a strong recovery continue to exist in Canada. In the last few years, inflation has been lower here than in the United States, but our interest rates remain high.

We hear a lot about the fact that interest rates are presently at their lowest level in thirty years. The reality is that this is only true of short-term interest rates. In 1963, the bank rate set by the Bank of Canada and the preferred rate charged by banks were about the same as today. However, the rate of a twenty-five-year mortgage was seven per cent, and the rate of long-term Canadian bonds was 5.1 per cent, instead of the present 7.25 and seven per cent rates that now apply to a five-year mortgage. This is where the problem lies, and it is a two-fold problem. Indeed, long-term interest rates remain too high, while the purchasing power of Canadian households has dropped significantly.

Soon we will have no choice but to take a close look at the characteristics, the evolution and the magnitude of our economic problems, and also at the hardships that they create for their primary victims, namely the one and a half million unemployed workers, and the millions of children and adults who live below the poverty level. It appears that the new government prefers not to assess the magnitude of the problem, which is not even touched upon in the Throne Speech. Moreover, the government does not realize that we are caught in a vicious circle. The fact is that there will not be a true recovery as long as the political structure remains the same. Indeed, the present political structure is the primary cause of the falling into decay of the Canadian economy.

One of the most obvious, if not spectacular, signs of this is the chronic inability of federal governments to control the budget deficit and the resulting soaring debt. It seems that this voracious monster can at will, like the Minotaur, take its toll in terms of jobs, of the minimal security of the poor, of the financial health of the federal State, and even of the future of our young people. Not only have those deficits been constant for the past eighteen years, but this year's, which stands at some $43 billion, confirms that the system is totally out of order.

In order to get out of this mess, it will not be enough to blame the previous government. In any case, Canadians have already let us know what they thought of its performance. Yet, the careful observer who has not buried his head in the sand cannot fail to identify a certain element of ineffectiveness, which is inherent to the system.

Nevertheless, the government continues to pursue the ostrich's policy followed by its predecessor. By escaping from reality, it cannot put the finger on the main problem: this country is not governable, because it is stuck with a deficient and sclerotic decision-making structure.

Nothing seems to make successive governments in Ottawa come out of the cocoon in which they shelter themselves from reality, and so it is with this new government. Yet, one only has to look at the relative performance of various other countries subject to the same international environment. This is a sure criterion, since everybody is facing the same economic problems and requirements. Therefore, the global context does not justify Canada's mediocre performance in terms of productivity since 1979, the worst of all OECD countries, nor the persistence of such a high unemployment level, nor the uncontrolled growth of the debt which, as we know, reached $500 billion yesterday. Canada is also in first place in terms of relying on foreign investors, since forty per cent of its debt is owed to foreign interests.

Be that as it may, it is not free trade agreements, global markets, or the requirements imposed by the competitiveness of the world markets which, in the last few decades, have forced the federal government to embark upon all kinds of programs and expenditures, to encroach upon provincial jurisdictions, and to create a tentacular bureaucracy. Rather, this extravagance and this inconsistency were motivated by a triple internal concern: to give to the federal government a legitimacy snatched from the provinces; to affirm its role as a strong central government; and to neutralize the centrifugal forces of the structure. It is our political structures which are called into question when we wonder why we have become the most over-governed country in the Western world, with eleven governments for a population of 28 million people.

We only have ourselves to blame if overlapping federal and provincial activities prevent the creation of cohesive programs and generate an outrageous amount of waste in human and financial resources. That reveals a second reality as inescapable as the economic crisis, that certain inefficiencies are at the very heart of our system. These realities feed upon each other, and are a true reflection of the vicious circle which characterizes Canadian federalism. At the core of the economic crisis is a political crisis.

But for the better part of English Canada, there is no political crisis. Or, if there is one, they choose to ignore it. They have sent to Ottawa a new government with the mandate to better manage the present system without changing anything in it.

On the other hand, Quebecers not only sent a completely new team to Ottawa, but they gave their elected representatives the mandate to prepare a new order. The Bloc Québécois was given a double mission: to manage the economic crisis and to handle the political crisis. Does the distribution of elected members in this House not prove the very existence of this second crisis? The government party only got nineteen seats in Quebec, compared to fifty-four for the Bloc. Who do you think speaks for Quebec today?

More than thirty years ago Quebec awakened to the world and decided to catch up. The Quiet Revolution transformed Quebec. It did not take long before the spirit of reform in Quebec collided with the spirit of Canadian federalism in Ottawa. Thirty years ago the horns were locked. Thirty years later we are still at it, as if frozen in a time warp. We should learn from the past, and this we should have learned: The political problem with Canada is Quebec, and the problem of Quebec is Canada.

However, many Canadians refuse to acknowledge the problem which only serves to compound it. For example, the Bloc Québécois has been on the federal scene for more than three years, but until recently we were ranked alongside the bizarre and the outer fringes. Our aim of course is not to win popularity contests in English Canada, but we have here in a nugget the essence of the political predicament which bedevils Canada. A new political party which had led systematically in the polls in Quebec for three years was regularly dismissed as a quirk

*Lucien Bouchard with Gilles Duceppe, his successor in the leadership of the Bloc Québécois*

on the charts or a manifestation of a temporary leave of the senses. Hugh MacLennan's powerful novel *Two Solitudes* was published in 1945. Half a century later the title still mirrors the political landscape.

Some are willing to deny the obvious in order not to upset the status quo. They speak of one Canadian nation, whereas Quebec and English Canada are two different nations. Even when nobody in Quebec was contemplating sovereignty, the Canada that steered Quebecers was not of the same cloth as the Canada that seized the minds and hearts of Maritimers, Ontarians or Westerners. Quebecers were in the vanguard of the struggle for more Canadian autonomy under the Red Ensign and eventually for the political independence of Canada. This tends to be forgotten in certain quarters where Quebec bashing is a popular pastime.

Canada and Quebec have both changed tremendously in the last one hundred years, but they are travelling on parallel tracks and remain as different today as they were yesterday. By and large they both continue to ignore the history and the culture of the other. This is no accident; language, geography and history largely account for it.

However, Quebecers do not deny that English Canada constitutes a nation in its own right with its own sense of community. Every single poll in the last few years has shown that the vast majority of the people in each of the nine provinces want to remain politically united after Quebec becomes sovereign. This small detail is conveniently neglected by all those who question the existence of an English Canada on the shaky basis of regional differences.

In France the people of the north are certainly as different, if not more so, from the people of the south as Maritimers are from the people of British Columbia. But they both feel a strong attachment to France, or to Canada.

In fact, by clinging to the one nation thesis, English Canada is running the risk of undermining itself. As Kenneth McRoberts, the political scientist from York University, wrote in 1991: 'In its effort to deny Quebec's distinctiveness, English Canada has been led to deny its own.'

If one accepts the obvious, one must surely accept the consequences. Every nation has the right to self-government, that is to decide its own policies and future. We have no quarrel with the concept of federalism when applied to uninational states. It is a different matter when it comes to multinational states, particularly to the Canadian brand of federalism.

Canadian federalism means that the Government of Quebec is subordinate to the central government both in large and lesser matters. Within the federal regime, English Canada in fact has a veto on the future development of Quebec.

When the theme of national sovereignty is brought up in English Canada a nice paradox almost always emerges. As I will certainly refer to it in the coming months, I shall call it the paradox of English Canada. First, the tendency to consider passé the concept of national sovereignty, what with the European Community, GATT, NAFTA and so on. This is a patent misreading of the situation. Take a look at the western world. Ninety-five per cent of its population live in nation states.

The fact is that Quebec is the only nation of more than seven million people in the western world not to have attained political sovereignty. I invite members of this House to reflect upon this. As a political structure Canada is the exception rather than the rule, an exception that is not working well, to understate the case.

The particular situation of Quebec was inadvertently recognized by a member of the Canadian delegation to the final GATT negotiations in mid-December. As will be recalled, Canada was seeking to be exempted from the clause attacking subsidies by sub-national governments because, in his words: 'There is only one Quebec.' He was right of course.

Let us ask ourselves: Who was in the driver's seat during the European revolution of 1989-90 which saw German reunification and the accession to political sovereignty of so many nations in central and eastern Europe? Was it the supranational institutions, the EC, NATO, the Warsaw pact, or was it the different nations, each one of them seizing the chance of a lifetime? In short, Quebecers aspire to what is considered normal in the western world.

The paradox of English Canada pops up with the second part of the discussion about national sovereignty, the part that deals with the issue of Canadian sovereignty. A large part of the free trade election of November 1988 was spent, in English Canada, on the impact of the free trade agreement on the sovereignty of Canada. Everybody agreed that this was something important that should not be tampered with. However if Canada's political sovereignty *vis-à-vis* the USA is valuable and must be preserved, why is it that Quebec's political sovereignty *vis-à-vis* Canada is depicted as irrational in the anglophone media of the land? When the preceding Prime Minister said that she preserved Canadian sovereignty during the last stage of the NAFTA negotiations, why is it that nobody rolled their eyes and derided this quaint idea of sovereignty? What mysterious alchemy transforms the quality of a concept according to the people to whom it applies or according to the year of accession to sovereignty? One must not forget that independent nations are not born. They are made.

All this does not prevent Canadians and Quebecers from having quite a few things in common: a respect for democracy, a large degree of openness to people of other cultures, and a fascination with our neighbours south of the border. And they both love their country. However, the problem is and has been for a very long time, that it is not the same country.

Make no mistake about it. We will not stop reminding the people that, in order to legitimize his power play against Quebec National Assembly in 1982, Pierre Trudeau was able to call upon the support of Quebec's Liberal members of Parliament in order to claim to speak on behalf of Quebec.

We will repeat as often as necessary that the government party no longer speaks for Quebec. You can also be sure that we will not lose sight – and will not allow anyone to lose sight – of the fact that the new Prime Minister is the very man who led the assault against Quebec, in 1981, and ignored the quasi-unanimous repudiation by the Quebec National Assembly.

The Charlottetown episode followed a similar pattern. Did we not see a block of Conservative members from Quebec, who had initially got into politics to repair the damage done by the 1982 patriation, side with the Liberals in an effort to seal the fate, once and for all, of Quebec's historical claims?

The 1992 referendum results dispelled any lingering ambiguity. The rejection of the Accord from coast to coast ended all hopes that some may still have had for a renewed federal system in Canada. You take it or leave it as it is.

The Prime Minister himself came to the same conclusion. Did he not announce shortly after coming into office that he would not even attempt such a reform?

Thus we should be able to make in the clear light of day the decision we are supposed to make by referendum in Quebec. We are left with only two choices: either we settle for the status quo that almost every federalist in Quebec since Jean Lesage has denounced or, the alternative is clear, Quebec attains full sovereignty, with full powers to assume full responsibility. The identity and roles of the players would be clarified at the same time.

There certainly seems to be a sort of poetic justice in all this. The henchman of the dastardly deed in 1982, who has since become Prime Minister, will soon have to ask the people of Quebec to turn down the sovereignty deal in favour of the constitutional one which had earned him their reprobation in the first place. And he will have to do it on his own, without the support that his mentor, Pierre Trudeau, claimed to have in Quebec. You can see why he does not want the talk Constitution, as he said.

By its presence and actions in this House, the Bloc Québécois will be doing every Quebecer and Canadian a service, whether they like it or not, by preventing them from going back to square one. Now that the Meech and Charlottetown accords have stripped the varnish of political correctness from the Canadian federal system, revealing its obstinate fixedness, everyone is immune to promises of renewal. So much so that nobody dares make any, not even to score political points.

This imposes upon us a basic civic duty, which consists in sparing ourselves three more decades of fruitless discussion, endless attempts and lost illusions. This waste of resources, this dilution of collective hope, this misuse of our energy has been going on for too long already. All we have to show today for the ordeal the best wills in Quebec and English Canada have suffered is bitterness, suspicion, lack of understanding and a profound collective alienation. We are about to lose the very will to face reality squarely. More importantly, there is the waste of time. I am not only referring to that of the people who, in the excitement of the sixties, dreamed of solving our conflicts and building in Quebec and Canada societies that would be tolerant, imaginative, open to the world and concerned with social justice. I am thinking of our two nations in particular. Because time is running out for them, too. While we mope around, the world is coming apart and rebuilding around us. The boat is going by and we are missing it.

Whether we like it or not, there will be a debate on our political future, and it will take place right here. The government is free to stonewall as has been the practice in this House with regard to the sovereigntist aspirations of so many Quebecers. Is it out of fear or powerlessness that they are evading subjects that put into question the old political structures of Quebec and Canada as well as their capacity to solve social and economic problems? Whether fainthearted or resigned, this total silence is irresponsible and leads to paralysis. The Bloc Québécois has been sent here precisely to break this conspiracy of silence.

We will not be afraid to point out that Quebecers are and will always be in a clear minority position within the federal system. The population ratio is three to one. We can fool ourselves and believe that we can determine the course of events despite this ever-present handicap which relegates Quebec to second-place status when interests diverge. This would imply constant tension and a superior performance on our part. In other words, utopia.

If the truth be told, the Trudeauesque utopia is not foreign to the annals of French Canadian history. For many decades, French Canadians believed that their destiny was prophetic. In many respects, Pierre Trudeau is the last missionary of French Canada.

Here again, we are confronted with a paradox. Canada needed measures to safeguard against the demographic and economic weight of the United States. Hence the creation of the Foreign Investment Review Agency and the implementation of the new energy policy. Quebec, on the other hand, did not require measures to protect itself from the demographic and economic weight of English Canada. Competence was all that was required and everything else would take care of itself. How very naive! And this was seen as reason triumphing over passion.

In reality, Quebecers want to live a normal life. They are tired of fighting for basic things that have been denied them. They are quite willing to confront the challenges of the day, but they want all of the odds to be on their side. On the one hand, they want greater economic integration and a stronger competitive position internationally, while on the other hand, they want political sovereignty in order to face Quebec's competitive partners on a level playing field.

Quebec sovereigntists advocate a modern concept of political sovereignty, one which is exercised within the framework of major economic structures and which is respectful of minorities. Under no circumstances will the 630,000 francophones outside Quebec be sacrificed. Moreover, Quebec sovereigntists were not the ones who rejected the Free Trade Agreement with the United States and NAFTA. There is a difference between withdrawing into oneself and pulling out in order to perform better in the new global economy.

The close economic integration between Quebec and Canada forces us to take a careful look at what is happening in Europe. What lessons can we draw from the European model?

Some pundits like to believe the European Community will gradually transform itself into something resembling Canadian federalism and use this as an argument against Quebec sovereignty. Thus they reveal their lack of familiarity with European developments. In fact, the other way around appears much more likely. To solve the Canadian political crisis our present institutions should and I dare say will evolve along the lines of the European Community.

A few facts seem in order. The European Commission in Brussels has a budget that amounts to 1.2 per cent of the global GNP of the community. It has no fiscal powers and – such a tragedy – cannot run a deficit. The federal government in Ottawa spends twenty-two per cent of GNP and has the whole gamut of fiscal powers. As for deficits we all know what has happened. The commission in Brussels has no army, no police and a small bureaucracy when compared to national governments. Community decisions are in fact executed by national bureaucracies. If we exclude trade matters, national sovereignty remains the basic ingredient of the community. For instance, the twelve members could modify the structure and the workings of the EC without the commission having any say in the decision. For these countries co-operation is the master word, not subordination.

This is a far cry from the Canadian brand of federalism. Who will pretend, for example, that only the provincial governments determine the future of Canada? Who will pretend that the federal government is but a benevolent arbitrator of inter-regional conflicts? For Quebec the central government is the problem. For English Canada it is part of the solution.

The Maastricht Treaty extended the process of economic integration to the field of monetary policy by setting the objective of a common currency before the end of the century, and the process of political co-operation by specifying the objective of a common thread in the fields of defence and foreign policy. These sensitive fields will remain the prerogative of the heads of state assembled in the European Council.

Hence the following question: If the European union is indeed the wave of the future as is frequently alleged in the Canadian media, why not propose this model as a solution to Canada's national problem? If Maastricht represents the embodiment of the next century, why does English Canada not propose the same kind of arrangement to Quebec? The Maastricht arrangements would be much easier to implement between Quebec and Canada than among twelve very diverse countries.

Let there be no mistake. Bloc members will not forget that their commitment to sovereignty constitutes the real reason for their presence in this House. One could say that as far as we are concerned, the pre-referendum campaign has begun. Meanwhile, we will not let the recession be dissociated from its causes.

For the time being, and until Quebecers have made their decision in a referendum, members of the Bloc will seek to safeguard the future by averting present evils to the best of their ability. These evils include unemployment, poverty, lack of budgetary restraint, undue duplication, threats to our social programs, fiscal inequity and loss of confidence in our political institutions and leaders.

All these issues have a direct impact on Quebec's interests but are equally important for the rest of Canada. Our aspirations drive us apart, but our social, economic and budgetary problems are the same.

As Premier Bob Rae would say: 'We are all in the same boat.'

Who can challenge the legitimacy, even for the whole at Canada, of any action the Bloc may take to limit the damage, create jobs, wrestle with the deficit and fight off attacks against our social programs? The universal character of these concerns confers a clear legitimacy on a common response to these issues. In addition, we received an electoral mandate. Our fifty-four seats were allocated by the principal players: the electorate. Do these seats have any less clout because they come from Quebec?

I can already hear our opponents claiming that it was only thanks to an erratic division of seats of English Canada between the Liberals and Reform members that the Bloc was able to come to the fore with the second largest number of members. However, the impact of spoilers and how this translates to the electoral map is also an expression of the will of the electorate. It was a combination of all votes, whether they were from Quebec or the rest of Canada, which made us the Official Opposition. To criticise the fact that this responsibility has now been taken over by the Bloc Québécois shows a lack of respect for the democratic process as a whole.

We intend to take these responsibilities seriously; and we will do so loyally, correctly and with due resolve. We know that is what Quebecers expect us to do, and they would never forgive us if we deviated from this path.

# IDENTITY

"Without the ideal of equality among men, without the vision of human brotherhood, the Canadian nation could never have come into being. The unity of Canada is vital to the continued existence of Canada. But the unity of Canada belongs not to Canada alone – it belongs to mankind. Only by extending throughout the world the ideals of mutual tolerance, of racial co-operation and of equality among men, which form the basis of Canada's nationhood, can nationality come to serve humanity."

*- William Lyon Mackenzie King, 1947*

# William Lyon Mackenzie King

'I Speak as a Citizen of Canada'

*The Supreme Court of Canada, Ottawa, 3 January 1947*

**'To all of us, the most of Canada is still unknown. The vision and courage of men and women have transformed our country – almost within living memory – from small and virtually unknown regions of forest and farm into one of the great industrial nations of the world.'**

King's remarks here, broadcast live, followed his receipt of the first citizenship certificate under the new Canadian Citizenship Act. This legislation created the status of 'Canadian citizen', while maintaining reference to the status of 'British subject'. King was just one of 26 people – among them a farmer, a shoemaker and a metallurgical engineer – who received from Chief Justice Thibaudeau Rinfret a certificate of citizenship at a special ceremony to celebrate the new act.

Chief Justice, ladies and gentlemen, I speak as a citizen of Canada. On behalf of all Canadians, I congratulate the new citizens, who have just received their certificates, on having become citizens of Canada. I welcome you into the full enjoyment of the rights of Canadian citizenship. Some of us who have received certificates tonight have enjoyed those rights all their lives, others only for a time. In homes throughout our land, thousands of our fellow citizens have been listening with pride to tonight's ceremony. I know that all would wish to join in these words of greeting and congratulation.

Citizenship is the highest honour a nation can confer upon an individual who has not been born into this heritage. Without citizenship much else is meaningless. There is no country in the world of which its citizens have greater reason to be proud than Canada. There are older countries, there are larger countries, but no country holds today a higher place in the esteem of other nations. To be a citizen of Canada is to hold a passport which will be honoured everywhere.

Tonight's ceremony symbolizes in a very real way the character of Canadian nationhood. Those of our number who have received certificates of citizenship come from communities widely scattered throughout Canada. Over the years, these widely scattered communities have been welded into a single country. We here, like the people of Canada, generally, are of many different origins. In the past, divergent racial origins have repeatedly been a source of division. Moreover, newcomers, while severing ties with their original homeland, have often felt no binding claim to the land of their adoption. Today we have established a new conception of Canadian citizenship. The new conception of citizenship is designed to bridge the gaps created by geography and by racial decent. As a people, Canadians will be bound more closely together, by the statutory recognition accorded our Canadian citizenship in this new year. Our unity and our strength will be increased by the deeper significance now given to our common citizenship.

The Canada of today has been described as a supreme act of faith. The Canada we know was hewn out of the wilderness, often in defiance of nature. In extent, our country is immense; its chief areas of settlement are divided, one from another, by long distances and by rugged terrain. Many of you who today have become citizens are well aware of this; some of you are from British Columbia and the Prairies, some are from the central provinces, some from the Maritimes.

To all of us, the most of Canada is still unknown. The vision and courage of men and women have transformed our country – almost within living memory – from small and virtually unknown regions of forest and farm into one of the great industrial nations of the world.

But far more than material growth has arisen from the vision and courage of our people; they have also sought continuously to defend and to extend the frontiers of freedom. More than once in the name of Canada, the sons and daughters of Canada have valiantly served; and thousands have died to save the world's freedom. In world affairs, our country has an outstanding record of responsibility and integrity.

Our nationhood is not based on the superiority of a single race, or of a single language, Canada was founded on the faith that two of the proudest races in the world, despite barriers of tongue and creed, could work together in mutual tolerance and mutual respect, to develop a common nationality.

Into our equal partnership of English-speaking and French-speaking Canadians we have admitted thousands who are born of other racial stocks, and who speak other tongues. They, one and all, have sought a homeland where nationhood means not domination and slavery, but equality and freedom.

Without the ideal of equality among men, without the vision of human brotherhood, the Canadian nation could never have come into being. The unity of Canada is vital to the continued existence of Canada. But the unity of Canada belongs not to Canada alone – it belongs to mankind. Only by extending throughout the world the ideals of mutual tolerance, of racial co-operation and of equality among men, which form the basis of Canada's nationhood, can nationality come to serve humanity. Only as nationality serves humanity can mankind hope to substitute co-operation for conflict in the relations between the nations of the world. Making nationality the servant, and not the master in world affairs, Canada today is giving to mankind its greatest hope for the future.

Let me, before I conclude, say just a word or two about the duties and responsibilities of Canadian citizenship; for citizenship is not any chance observance or mere obligation of the moment, it is part of the very structure of our nation. On the degree to which our citizens intelligently use their opportunities, will depend our country's future – and perhaps, in larger measure than we suppose, the possible future of other lands.

A little over twenty-one years ago, I visited the town in which I was born and in which I had spent most of my boyhood days; I had gone there to attend an Old Boys reunion. The theme of my address on that occasion was the opportunities and responsibilities implied in being a citizen of Canada. Last night I read over what I had said at that time. I then sought to define citizenship in terms of public service; that is what citizenship, as something vital, really means – public service in one form or another, in one sphere of activity or another.

To make graphic the impression I'd wish to leave. I recalled how, when very young, some of us had found pleasure in throwing pebbles into a pond, and how fascinating it was to watch the ripples of water radiating in ever expanding circles to the pond's circumference. In this way I sought to bring home the opportunities of citizenship in terms of service to the public. I pointed out the opportunity for service first of all to the local municipality – the town or the city, and to the county in which one lives – then, thinking of expanding areas, to one's province, and then to Canada as a whole. I sought, as well, to bring home the truth that as the circumference of the circle of opportunity expands for the citizen, so do his duties and responsibilities. It is the interest taken by individuals in the expanding circles of citizenship that holds human society together.

In the address I made at that time, I went a step further. I pointed out that citizenship in Canada was not confined to the bounds of the Dominion, extensive as they are. I said that we enjoyed a larger citizenship still, namely our citizenship within the British Commonwealth of Nations. It was the summer of 1925 when I was speaking. That was seven years after the first great war. I went on to say that an even wider citizenship was then coming into being. This I

*Prime Minister William Lyon Mackenzie King in May 1947, four months after his speech at the Supreme Court of Canada*

described as a kind of world citizenship, which was bringing with it for us duties and responsibilities, not only to our own country and to the countries of the British Commonwealth, but to other countries as well. In other words, as we are now able to visualize it, Canadian citizenship is not a citizenship which relates itself merely to the immediate community in which we live. As Canadians we have a national citizenship, a Commonwealth citizenship and a world citizenship. Each carries with it a certain responsibility, a responsibility which it is our duty to recognize and our privilege to assert.

## Lester B. Pearson

Speech to the Royal Canadian Legion

*The Capitol Theatre, Winnipeg, 17 May 1964*

**'I believe that today a flag designed around the maple leaf will symbolize and be a true reflection of the new Canada.'**

Lester B. Pearson's speech before an audience of two thousand at the twentieth bi-annual Dominion Convention of the Royal Canadian Legion remains one of the boldest delivered by any Canadian Prime Minister. The subject, the creation of what he termed as a 'distinctive national flag', had support across the country; indeed, it had been part of the Liberal platform through which the party had been elected some thirteen months previous. Within the Capitol Theatre, however, things were markedly different. Pearson's speech was interrupted repeatedly by boos, threats and heckling. Twice the convention Chairman, Legion President Clare C. Sparling, interjected with failed attempts to quiet the audience.

Among the heckles that the Prime Minister endured was 'God save Diefenbaker!' The leader of the Progressive Conservative opposition, John Diefenbaker was the foremost advocate for the retention of the Red Ensign. It is likely for this reason that Pearson here quotes the popular Premier of Nova Scotia, Robert Stanfield, the man who would one day replace Diefenbaker as Tory leader.

The other figure mentioned in Pearson's speech is Andrew McNaughton, the General who led the Canadian Army at the outset of the Second World War, and later served as Minister of National Defence in the Cabinet of Mackenzie King.

Mister Chairman, honoured guests, and members of the Royal Canadian Legion, I am honoured to be with you tonight as a veteran, as a member of the Legion, and as Prime Minister. I am proud to have witnessed your opening ceremonies and am deeply moved by them. I congratulate most warmly all who participated in your impressive Colour ceremony and in conceiving this visual act of remembrance. I wish all Canadians could witness it.

When it became known that I was going to have the honour of opening this twentieth Legion convention, I got a good deal of advice as to what I should discuss – or not discuss. There was one compelling subject, of course, which I had to refer to: national unity and certain problems which affect that unity, for instance, federal-provincial relations within our confederation.

On this subject, I will say only this: the provinces have new problems and greater responsibilities and must have, among other things, the financial resources to deal with them. The provincial governments will play, I believe, an increasingly important part in our national progress. But this need not be, and must not be, at the expense of the federal government. In our system, the federal government must remain strong in authority, resources, and leadership. I do not consider that I was chosen to preside over its decline or its dissolution – and I do not intend to do so.

I do intend, however, to do everything I can to maintain the closest co-operation with the provinces inside a confederation which must remain strong and united.

There is one subject which I was advised not to mention at all – the flag. That advice, of course, was well meant. It was also impossible to accept. Members of the Legion are aware of my government's commitments, made by our party some years ago, to ask Parliament – to ask Parliament – to decide on a distinctive Canadian flag within a certain period of time. For my part, I am very much aware of the Legion executive's current attitude towards government policy on this subject.

This mutual awareness of our attitudes, I believe, precludes any possibility that I should appear before you tonight and attempt to dodge the flag issue. After all, you are men who know what it means to go into battle.

So I intend to talk briefly, but frankly, about this issue: to put my own feelings, my beliefs, my judgement squarely and honestly before you. You would expect me to do this and I believe it is my duty. I expect dissent. I also respect it.

The question of a national flag, however, is only part of the larger question of national unity which I have already mentioned. There is unease and division in Canada today which is a threat to unity; and this, ironically, at a time when our country is admired, respected and envied throughout the world. The only anti-Canadians I know of are inside our own borders.

When I went overseas in 1915, I had as comrades on my section men whose names were

Cameron, Kimura, English, Bleidenstein, De Chapin, O'Shaughnessy. We didn't fall in, or fall out, as Irish Canadians, French Canadians, Dutch Canadians, Japanese Canadians. We wore the same uniform, with the same maple leaf badge, and we were proud to be known as Canadians, to serve as Canadians, and to die, if that had to be, as Canadians. I wish our country had more of that spirit today, of unity, togetherness and resolve; the spirit that was shown by Canadians in time of war when the survival of our country was at stake.

Well, the survival of our country as a united and strong federal state is at stake today.

What we need is a patriotism that will put Canada ahead of its parts; that will think more of our future destiny than our past mistakes; that rejects emphatically the idea that, politically, we are, or should become, a federation of two associated states – some kind of pre-war Austria-Hungary. We should have none of such separatism or of petty, narrow nationalism of any kind.

I am a Canadian; very proud to be one. But this does not make me less proud of my British heritage or my Irish origins. It makes me all the more anxious to bring that inheritance to the service of my country. So it would be if I were of another race and spoke another language.

I am a Canadian who speaks English. There are millions of others who speak French and have constitutional rights and privileges as French-speaking Canadians which must be respected and recognized. There are also others – and they are an increasingly important segment of our population – who, while they may speak one of the two official languages, also have an ancestral language which they use, traditions and a culture of which they are proud, and which are neither French nor Anglo-Saxon. But we are all, or should be, Canadians – and un-hyphenated, with pride in our nation and its citizenship, pride in the symbols of that citizenship.

The flag is one such symbol. For Canada, it has changed as our country has grown from colony to self-governing dominion to sovereign independence; to a nation respected among nations. Canada made this change by peaceful evolution, gradually and in a way that did not weaken the bonds with the mother country. That phase of our political evolution is now completed.

Our ties to the mother country do not now include any trace of political subordination. They are ties of affection, of tradition and respect. As a Canadian, I don't want them destroyed or weakened. But they have changed, and the symbols of Canada have also changed with them. This is an inevitable process. In World War I, the flag that flew for Canadian soldiers overseas was the Union Jack. In World War II, in January 1944, the Red Ensign came officially on the scene…

*[Cheers.]*

In World War II, in January 1944, the Red Ensign came officially on the scene – though we sometimes forget…

*[The Chairman uses his gavel to quiet the audience.]*

It's all right, Mister Chairman. This is a veterans' meeting. And as Harry Truman once said, 'If you can't stand the heat, keep out of the kitchen.'

But we do sometimes forget the flag designated for the first Canadian forces overseas and presented as such to General McNaughton on his departure from Canada for Europe was one with three joined red maple leaves predominant on it.

And I believe – as sincerely as some of you might believe in another design – I believe that today a flag designed around the maple leaf will symbolize and be a true reflection of the new Canada. Today there are five million or more Canadians whose tradition is not inherited from the British Isles, but who are descendants of the original French founders of our country. There are another five million, or more, who have come to Canada from other far-away lands, whose heritage is neither British nor French. I believe that a Canadian flag – as distinctive as the maple leaf in the Legion badge – will bring them all closer… bring all these Canadians closer to us of British stock and make us all better and more united Canadians.

Would such a change mean any disrespect for the Union Jack or its rejection from our history? No. I would not agree to that. I have served under the Union Jack in war and I have

*Lester B. Pearson, third from left, serving during the First World War*

lived under it in peace. I have seen it flying above the smoke and fire and crashing bombs in London's blitz. I have seen it flying proudly in some desperate times in an earlier war. I know it stands for freedom under law, justice and the dignity of man; for the glorious history of a brave breed of men. The Union Jack should be flown in Canada – not as our national flag, but as a symbol of our membership in the Commonwealth of Nations and of our loyalty to the crown.

In taking this position, I know there are others – and it's quite clear tonight – there are others who disagree longly, honestly and deeply with me. Such an issue is bound to raise strong emotions. Symbols, symbols have a deep emotional meaning. That is why they help to make a nation great, help to inspire and nourish loyalty, patriotism and devotion among those who make up the nation.

*From the audience:* We don't agree with you!

*Pearson:* Well, we have the right in this free country to disagree, thank God! And we also have the right to express our point of view, and to have it listened to.

And so, an emotional reaction is roused when there is any suggestion that old symbols should be discarded or adopted to new conditions and new needs.

You will recall, I'm sure, the great Legion debate just a few years ago – in 1960, I think it was – when you were choosing a new Legion badge. You will remember the arguments put forward in defence of your executive's decision on that new badge. As described by your then President, Mister Justice Woods, it was correct according to heraldry, was distinctive and embodied the right symbolism to represent those things the Legion stood for. It was strictly your own, and could not be confused with the badge of any other organization. Its central dominant feature was the maple leaf.

Writing about this central symbol, Mister Justice Woods said at that time: 'Consideration was given to some other form of emblem to represent Canada. As a matter of fact, a number of those who have criticized the badge asserted that the maple leaf was not a good Canadian symbol. Your council, however,' – and here he was referring to your executive council – 'were of the opinion that it was a widely accepted Canadian symbol. This certainly is true in Europe. Our troops wore it on their caps and uniforms in the First World War. It appears on the flag of the Canadian Army, It appears on our Coat of Arms. It appears on the shields of our provinces.' Mister Woods then added: 'When it was pointed out to us that it was improper to mutilate the Union Jack by placing the maple leaf over it we did not see how we could properly carry this on in the new badge, so we removed the Union Jack and this left the gold maple leaf. We decided to change its colour to red. We put a white background so it would stand out and this in conjunction with the blue on the Legion scroll…'

*[Booing from the audience.]*

I'm talking about the Legion badge! And in the case of your new badge, so it is…

*[Heckling from the audience.]*

*Chairman:* Ladies and gentlemen, I thought you were all ladies and gentlemen. This is our honoured guest, invited here by you. Surely, the Royal Canadian Legion has more courtesy and dignity than that. You may do all of this next week if you wish to, but leave it tonight.

*Pearson:* You will recall also that the suggestion made at the time, that the question of your new badge should be determined by referendum throughout your membership, was rejected by the executive as impractical.

As in the case of your new badge, so it is with any question of changing symbols. It asks a lot of human nature to expect ready acceptance of something that is going to alter that which is venerated and has been for long honoured by so many. Any suggestion for change is bound to provoke strong criticism as well as support. This is all part of the democratic process,

We who are elected to serve Canada in Parliament owe those who elect us more than the advocacy of non-controversial ideas. We owe Canada our best judgement, and we fail Canada if we fail to exercise that judgement, or if we pass our responsibility for judgement back to the electors who sent us to Parliament.

I believe most sincerely that it is time now for Canadians to unfurl a flag that is truly distinctive and truly national in character; as Canadian as the maple leaf which should dominate the design; a flag easily identifiable as Canada's.

No one would deny that we have a responsibility to the past. But we have also a greater responsibility to the present and to the future. Moreover, our responsibility to the past will be best fulfilled by being true to its real substance and meaning. May I quote the words of Premier Stanfield of Nova Scotia in this connection, on 6 April last:

Surely, however, it is not necessarily patriotic for me to insist that something I value highly must be adopted as a national symbol if it is objectionable as a national symbol to a large number of Canadians. Surely the Canadian thing for us to do is to find symbols which are mutually acceptable. Let us emphasize what we have in common. Surely we can have a national anthem and a flag that unites Canada.

In the same spirit the Canadian Chamber of Commerce not long ago adopted the following resolution: 'That the Parliament of Canada formally adopt and authorize a distinctive national flag,' because, as the resolution said: 'A distinctive national flag would be a strong, unifying influence, consistent with the status of full nationhood.'

But I want to add this, ladies and gentlemen, that while I am concerned about this whole question of national symbols, national anthem, national flag, and what they mean to our country, I am even more concerned with making Canada the kind of country – with freedom, economic security, social justice, and opportunity for all – over which we will be proud to have our flag fly.

People are more important than emblems.

# Lester B. Pearson

Address on the Inauguration of the National Flag of Canada

*Parliament Hill, Ottawa, 15 February 1965*

**'And so the new Flag, joining and rising above the milestones of our history, today takes for the first time its proud place as the emblem of Canada...'**

**In June 1964, Pearson rose in the House of Commons and tabled plans for a national flag. The six months of debate that followed finally ended through closure. The resolution was adopted by a 163 to 78 vote. The National Flag of Canada, commonly known as the 'Maple Leaf flag', was approved by Queen Elizabeth on that Christmas Eve. The Royal Proclamation was signed in January 1965 when Pearson and John Diefenbaker were in London to attend the funeral of Sir Winston Churchill.**

**Nine months after his appearance before the Royal Canadian Legion in Winnipeg, the new Canadian flag for which Pearson had argued was raised on a special staff which had been erected on Parliament Hill. Suffering a bout of ill-health, the Prime Minister left his sickbed to witness the sight.**

**In his speech, Pearson quotes the words: 'The Maple Leaf, our emblem dear', which are taken from 'The Maple Leaf Forever', once considered the unofficial anthem of Canada.**

*Prime Minister Lester B. Pearson at a December 1964 press conference concerning the National Flag of Canada*

On September 5, 1945 an Order-in-Council was passed declaring the Red Ensign to be Canada's National Flag pending a decision of the Parliament of Canada.

Such a decision was made in December 1964 after long and vigorous Parliamentary debate and careful Committee consideration and recommendation. As a result of this decision by the Canadian Parliament and on the advice of the Government of Canada, Her Majesty, our beloved Queen, was pleased to issue a proclamation that the flag we are about to raise today should be the flag of Canada.

So, at noon today, in this eighth month of our ninety-eighth year as a Confederation, our new flag will fly for the first time in the skies above Canada and in places overseas where Canadians serve.

If our nation, by God's grace, endures a thousand years, this day, the 15th day of February, 1965, will always be remembered as a milestone in Canada's national progress.

It is impossible for me not to be deeply moved on such an occasion or to be insensible to the honour and privilege of taking part in it.

There are many in this country who regret the replacement of the Red Ensign by the red maple leaf. Their feelings and their emotions should be honoured and respected. But I am sure, now that the decision has been made by the representatives of the Canadian people in Parliament assembled, that all Canadians, as good patriots, will accept that decision and fly with pride our national flag.

This ceremony today is not a break with history but a new stage in Canada's forward march from a group of separate and scattered and dependent colonies, to a great and sovereign Confederation stretching from sea to sea and from our southern border to the North Pole.

No step by which we have advanced to our present position among nations has been an easy one and none has been taken without some nostalgia for the past.

This is inevitable in the succession of new beginnings that mark a nation's progress – as they do the course of human events – for each brings to an end a stage for which deep attachment often lingers.

The patriotic motives that have led Parliament to adopt a new Canadian flag do not include disrespect for our past or for the emblems of that past.

We salute the future, but we honour the past on which the future rests.

As the symbol of a new chapter in our national story, our maple leaf flag will become a symbol of that unity in our country without which one cannot grow in strength and purpose; the unity that encourages the equal partnership of two peoples on which this Confederation was founded; the unity also that recognizes the contributions and the cultures of many other races.

And so the new flag, joining and rising above the milestones of our history, today takes for the first time its proud place as the emblem of Canada, 'The Maple Leaf, our emblem dear.'

May the land over which this new flag flies remain united in freedom and justice; a land of decent God-fearing people; fair and generous in all its dealings; sensitive, tolerant and compassionate towards all men; industrious, energetic, resolute; wise, and just in the giving of security and opportunity equally to all its cultures; and strong in its adherence to those moral principles which are the only sure guide to greatness.

Under this flag may our youth find new inspiration for loyalty to Canada; for a patriotism based not on any mean or narrow nationalism, but on the deep and equal pride that all Canadians will feel for every part of this good land.

God bless our flag!

And God bless Canada!

# CRISIS AND TERROR

> “There are those rare occasions when time seems to stand still, when a singular event transfixes the world. There are also those terrible occasions when the dark side of human nature escapes civilized restraint and shows its ugly face to a stunned world. Tuesday, September 11, 2001, will forever be etched in memory as a day when time stood still.”
>
> *- Jean Chrétien, 2001*

# R. B. Bennett

'This is a critical hour in the history of our country'

*National radio broadcast from Ottawa, 2 January 1935*

**'Canadians are not those from whom unpleasant facts should be concealed. The people of this country were born optimists, but they were born realists as well.'**

Bennett became Prime Minister due in large measure to the Great Depression. During the 1930 federal election campaign, the governing Liberals had accused his Conservatives of exaggerating the issue of unemployment, and had even gone so far as to suggest that the growing problem did not exist. As a self-made man who had rebuilt a moribund party, Bennett was viewed by many as the man who could pull the country out of the Great Depression. Unfortunately for the new Prime Minister, the economic downturn, eight months old when he took office, only deepened. His strategy in dealing with the crisis, based on faith in the market to correct itself, proved ineffective.

Bennett made this radio broadcast, the first in a series, with the knowledge that his term in office had entered its final calendar year. In the months that followed, the Prime Minister abandoned his *laissez-faire* strategy and began to implement policies inspired by Franklin Roosevelt's New Deal. The conversion led to defections within his party and failed to placate the Canadian electorate. When the federal election he'd so dreaded was held that October, Bennett's Conservatives were defeated soundly, receiving less than thirty per cent of the popular vote.

The time has come when I must speak to you with the utmost frankness about our national affairs, for your understanding of them is essential to your welfare. This is a critical hour in the history of our country. Momentous questions await your decision. Our future course must now be charted. There is one course, I believe with all my heart, which will lead us to security. It is for you to decide whether we will take it. I am confident that your decision will be the right one, when, with care and diligence, you have studied the facts. Then you will support the action which your judgement decrees to be imperative; you will strive for its success, for its success will determine the future of Canada.

In the last five years, great changes have taken place in the world. The old order is gone. It will not return. We are living amidst conditions which are new and strange to us. Your prosperity demands conditions in the old system, so that, in these new conditions, that old system may adequately serve you. The right time to bring about these changes has come. Further progress without them is improbable. To understand what changes and corrections should be made, you must first understand the facts of the present situation. To do that, you should have clearly in mind what has taken place in the past five years; the ways in which we have made progress, the ways in which we have not. To do that – to decide wisely – you must be in a position to judge those acts of government which have palliated your hardships, which have preserved intact our industrial and financial structure, and which have prepared the way for the reforms which must now take place.

Canadians are not those from whom unpleasant facts should be concealed. The people of this country were born optimists, but they were born realists as well. They demand the truth, however disturbing it may be. And the truth is disturbing. The world is in tragic circumstances. The signs of recovery are few and doubtful. The signs of trouble are many, and they do not lessen. The world is searching pathetically for safety and prosperity. It will find them only when each nation, resolute to effect its own regeneration, will come to a meeting place with all the others, in the spirit which declares that even the most powerful among them has no real economic independence of the rest.

That time has not yet come. Meanwhile, dangers abound.

This discussion of our national affairs will take time. It must be thorough. All phases of the situation will be dealt with, for it is vital that you be put in complete possession of the facts. To accomplish this, I have decided upon a series of half-hour broadcast talks. I ask you to give me your earnest and patient attention. I wish with all my heart that I had nothing but good news for you. When one has been head of the government of this country for more than four years and has done his level best, and has worked with all his might to bring you security, it is with inexpressible regret that he speaks as I must now speak to you. But the facts, grave as they are, do not cast me down. Nor will they you. I am deeply anxious, but I can never doubt this country's coming triumph if you will range yourselves on the side of progress and reform. For then we will fight on, you and I, and we will win.

First of all, I shall have a few words to say about conditions as they were in 1930, and as they have been since that time. Then I shall tell you what the policy of the Government has been during that unhappy period. I shall discuss the nature of the measures taken by the Government. You will realize that they were the only ones which the circumstances permitted. You will say, I think, that they were the only ones which were wise. I shall then show you that the time has come for a radical change in the policy of the Government. You will, I know, agree upon its necessity and approve its timeliness. I shall exactly explain what this policy is and develop my plans for its execution. After you are fully acquainted with what has taken place and with the conditions of today, I am confident that this policy will receive your enthusiastic support. Without your support, I am unable to carry it out. Therefore, when you have had an opportunity to thoroughly examine the whole condition of affairs, I will ask you for a decision. You will not be hurried. You will have ample time to test this programme of reform and to decide upon its value. I will then invite your considered opinion as to whether reform is in fact necessary, and as to whether my programme of reform is wise. If you say yes, then I will not rest until I have put it into operation. But if you say no – if you are satisfied with conditions as they now are, if you think that there is not need for reform, if you feel that the Government is not required to do anything more – then I am not willing to continue in this office. For if you believe that things should be left as they are, you and I hold contrary and irreconcilable views. I am for reform.

And, in my mind, reform means government intervention. It means government control and regulation. It means the end of laissez faire. Reform heralds certain recovery. There can be no permanent recovery without reform. Reform or no reform. I raise that issue squarely. I nail the flag of progress to the masthead. I summon the power of the state to its support.

Who will oppose our plan of progress? It will be interesting and instructive to see. It seems to me that the party which supports laissez faire, which demands that government do not interfere with business, which says that the state has no such part to play in these critical times – it seems to me that that party may have a change of heart when it sees how the rest of us feel about the matter, and may decide to come along with you and me. Well, if it will denounce its hereditary chieftain, which is reaction, abandon its creed of inaction, and pledge its allegiance to action, to progress, to reform – it will be welcome if it is really sincere. For I am working, and working grimly, to one end only; to get results. And so, honest support from every quarter from men and women of good will, of every party, race and creed, I hope for and heartily invite.

There must be unity of purpose. There can be no success without it. I earnestly entreat you, be in no doubt upon that point. I am not. If I cannot have your whole-hearted support, it is wrong for me to assume the terrible responsibility of leadership in these times.

I am willing to go on, if you make it possible for me still to serve you. But if there is anyone better able to do so, I shall gladly make way for him. And it is your duty to yourselves to support him, and not me. Your country's future is at stake. This is no time to indulge your personal prejudices or fancies. Carefully and calmly, look well into the situation. Then pick the man and the policy best fitted to deal with it. And resolutely back that man and that policy. The nation should range itself behind them. In war you fought as one. Fight now again as one. For the task ahead demands your war-time resolution and your war-time unity.

When my government came into power in 1930, the economic system of the world was rocking to its foundations. An economic disaster, unparalleled in the history of our civilization, had overtaken us. We were in the grip of something more than a serious illness. Its fatal termination was averted only by means never invoked before. We have been sick almost unto death. But we have survived. Given the right sort of treatment, we will completely recover.

In 1930 there was serious unemployment. Unemployment became greater and greater in the two years following. During the last year, we have been able to put large numbers of men to work. That was a real achievement. It is a fine beginning, but it is only a beginning. I told you in 1930 that I would end unemployment. That was a definite undertaking. By it I stand. Unemployment in Canada today is one of the consequences of this awful and unprecedented world depression. The continued faulty operation of the international economic machine has made re-employment impossible. I do not offer that as an excuse. I state a fact. Therefore, now that the time has come, I am determined to try with all my strength to correct the working of the system in Canada so that present unemployment conditions may be put an end to. When I say I will correct the system, I mean that I will reform it. And when the system is reformed and in full operation again, there will be work for all. We then can do away with relief measures. We then can put behind us the danger of the dole. I am against the dole. It mocks our claim to progress. Canada on the dole is like a young and vigorous man in the poorhouse. The dole is a condemnation, final and complete, of our economic system. If we cannot abolish the dole, we should abolish the system.

In my next speech I shall deal more specifically with the unemployment question.

When my government came into office, our trade had already fallen off. As the depression deepened, our trade further diminished. In 1932, it was undoubtedly in a very bad state. There is little purpose in prolonging the melancholy recital of conditions in those first years of the depression. In 1930, conditions were far from satisfactory. In 1932, they were very much worse. The courage of our people, the robustness of our economic structure, the effectiveness of your government, are all overwhelmingly attested by the fact that, though in 1932 we were in a most critical condition, we did not perish. On the contrary, we fought back strongly. I pay my tribute of profound admiration to the gallantry and patience of the people of Canada in those terrible times.

Other nations have also fought bravely and have done well. But no people with burdens comparable to yours have done better. You have reason to be proud of the past. You have reason to be confident of the future.

Out of the depths of this depression you have struggled. By any economic test you may employ, Canada is more prosperous today than it was two years ago. As I say, employment is increasing. Take our trade returns. They are indeed phenomenally better. Take the conditions of industry. Here you have substantial improvement. Agriculture, a double victim of economic and climatic conditions, is entering upon more promising days. I am within my rights when I claim a definite advance. I am not within my rights if I claim that our troubles are over and that all we have now to do is to fold our hands and be patient and expect the best. For that is not the case. We have come part way. The rest of the journey is a hard one. Our greatest obstacles yet remain.

Look at our burden of debt. It has not diminished. Look at the poverty of many of our people. It is very real. Look at the problem of our railways. Its solution is a condition precedent, I earnestly believe, to prosperity.

Our taxes are high. Our national income is not what it should be. Our trade, domestic and foreign, though vastly improved, must be much greater yet. We have worked hard to secure markets for our natural products. The result of our labours has been remarkable, but we must keep on working, for we need more markets still.

In the beginning of its term of office, the policy of the government was determined by the critical nature of the times. The economic system had broken down. Dismay and uncertainty prevailed. We were storm-tossed in turbulent seas. Swift and decisive measures were needed to avert shipwreck. The emergency demanded emergency action. It was no time for changes or reforms in the economic system. The only sensible thing was to get behind the system and make the best of it, until the fury of the storm had abated.

This your Government did. We gave unswerving support to finance. We stood behind industry. We aided agriculture in all the ways we might. You know what we did. It was singularly effective. Look at conditions in your country during the worst period of the depression, and compare them with conditions in other countries. I think you will agree that our relatively fortunate state is the surest proof that your Government faithfully supported our people in their splendid struggle against the depression.

This Government was not long in office before demands for reform were made upon it. Such demands were natural. But, in your interest, they could not then be heeded. The ship was pounding in mountainous seas. That was not the time to try to recondition it. We had first to save the ship and guide it into less troubled waters. I do not think that even my most irrational opponent will cavil at the sanity of that course.

We were determined to resist the impulse to change until we could be satisfied that change was beneficial: until we could be satisfied that change was safe. We were not prepared to make any alterations in our system until we knew that they would improve it. Conditions in those times were very bad. But assuredly they would have been made worse by any intemperate, ill-considered action which we might have taken.

I will not deny that the temptation was great. We were daily faced by the tragedies of the depression: our unemployed, the suffering poor, the perils which assailed business of all sorts, the plight of agriculture. I can assure you that it was not easy to say no. I had to harden my heart. I did so, but with more sorrow and sadness than I have ever known in my life before. I can assure you with equal truth that, had we said yes to those sometimes frantic pleas, Canada would not have been where it is today. We had to defer reform until the time for reform had come. Our duty and your welfare left us no other course. Consider what would have been the consequences of a blunder in those critical times. Determine the cost of ill-founded experiment. You will see that a false step might have led us to disaster. I ask you to pass judgement upon these points. I ask you to say whether the Government's emergency measures were sound. When you have done so, you will then be required to determine whether the Government's new policy of reform is also right and whether we have chosen the proper time to introduce it.

Now, you will understand that by recovery measures I mean measures which work no change in the economic system. They are emergency measures designed to support the system during the depression, but do not interfere with its operation, and do not, of course, contemplate any modification or correction in it. Recovery measures of the proper kind minimize the dangers and ameliorate the hardships incident to the depression. They also stimulate the movement toward recovery. This kind of assistance is sometimes known as 'priming the pump'.

Reform measures, on the other hand, are measures designed to effect a change in the existing system. They are measures to be taken when it has been decided that the existing system is faulty in some major or minor respect, and that this fault must be cured before the system can satisfactorily function again. These reforms may be, as you can imagine, of very many different types and of varying significance; but, whatever their importance or character, they are all refutations of the old idea that government should leave business alone. This old doctrine is known to some people as the doctrine of laissez faire, and it originated at a time when business as we now understand it, was very young and, presumably, very innocent.

Measures of reform should normally, of course, be initiated and carried out, not in times of depression, but in times of comparative prosperity. That is obvious. Indeed, I suppose that ideal and timely measures of reform might avert a depression by removing the causes of it. But we never have worked ideally, and probably we never will. So if, through lack of reform, depression follows, the next best thing is to introduce reform as soon as the conditions of the depression will permit. I did not have a chance to effect reforms before the days of the depression. I will be perfectly candid and tell you that, in those days, I doubt whether anyone fully realized the need of reform.

*R. B. Bennett, the eleventh Prime Minister of Canada, speaking in Toronto*

How much I wish that in this country or in the world there had been a man with vision to see the abyss upon which we were rushing and with power of action to arrest the movement. I say, I did not have a chance before the depression. This is my first opportunity. I am determined to take it. In fact, I have seized upon it already, as will soon be disclosed to you.

Now, let me say a word about the measures which the Government adopted during the depression to help the people and all those agencies of business which were designed to serve you. And I had better admit that I am somewhat at fault for not having talked before to you about these measures. It may not have been quite fair to all our loyal supporters. It may not have been quite fair to you, to have remained so long silent. My only excuse is that I have been so fully occupied with my daily duties and with my plans for your future, that I have had no time to talk about our actions in the past. In any case, they speak for themselves.

But I would not be just to my government and to those who have supported it, if I did not say definitely, and without fear of honest contradiction, that during these terrible times we have served your interests as well as any government in the world has served the interests to which it was pledged. Our recovery measures have been veritable bulwarks against the fury of the depression. To test their value in a spectacular way, you can ask yourselves what would have been the condition of this country now without guidance and direction and the right sort of support from the state. If you will consider the condition of some other countries, you will easily be able to answer this question. As I say, the Government's emergency programme has not been excelled by any other in the world. To me, the clearest proof of the effectiveness of our recovery measures lies in the fact that they have carried us through the depression and today have brought about a degree of improvement in conditions, which alone makes possible the introduction of our programme of reform.

I shall take an early opportunity to fully and accurately inform you, by speeches and through published documents, of all that this government has done. We will render the strictest account of our stewardship. We shall indeed be proud to do so. Tonight, and in my speeches following, I want more especially to talk of the present and the future.

This economic system of ours is something that most of us have never stopped to think very much about. Before the war there was no great occasion to. After the war, when the system was rushing uncontrollably toward the 1929 abyss, I imagine there was not many who were much concerned. Now, alas, we have reason enough to worry; and still more reason, therefore, to do our best to end the cause of all this worry and trouble and to free our minds for happier things. It is a tragedy of these times that men and women, boys and girls, whose minds should be given to constructive pursuits, find themselves handicapped and harassed by the uncertainties of life, and prevented, by the anxieties of this present situation, from giving their best to the things which are most worth while.

But it is now necessary that we give further, and the most careful, thought to our economic system, so that we may the better appreciate its capacity to serve us in the conditions in which we live today. Our best interest leaves us no alternative. We will examine the system without prejudice of any sort. We neither hate nor love it. It is here to do you service. That is its only purpose. If it has failed, then we must change it. Quite properly, we have a regard for those things with which we have long been beneficially associated, but allegiance to a system does not involve our condonation of its defects. Possibly some of you will maintain that, because the system has served us well in the past, there is a presumption in favour of its continuing to do so in the future. But clearly, that is no proof that it will do so. Indeed, present conditions are surely proof enough that it will not. And, as I say, if it does not serve us, we must reform it. There is no conceivable justification for maintaining in its old form any agency designed to promote the happiness and welfare of the people when change in it will more surely achieve that essential purpose.

I do not intend to trouble you just now with the history of the capitalist system. But, in my opinion, it is important that you should carefully examine the origin of capitalism, its place in the early days, and the theory upon which it operated. It would be helpful to a clearer understanding of some of our present difficulties if you were to trace the development which carried the system from the simple practice of a simple theory to the complex practice of a theory strained and wrenched out of its original form. You would then see that for the old checks and balances which ensured the proper working of the original system, the system today has provided no counterpart within itself. You would agree that free competition and the open market place, as they were known in the old days, have lost their place in the system, and that the only substitute for them, in these modern times, is government regulation and control. You would understand that past depressions were caused by maladjustments in the operation of this system, and were corrected only after intense suffering and hardship, that these depressions were so many crises, dangerous and difficult to surmount, but that, in comparison with them, this depression is a catastrophe, and therefore demands the intervention of the Government.

If you examine this capitalist system, you would appreciate more fully some of the facts which underlie the transcendent fact that times have changed, that old conditions are no more, that something new has come into our social and economic life, and that this new element, this new force, insistently demands recognition. And I am compelled to add, you would realize more clearly the folly of some men who try to ignore this irresistible truth.

I do not have to determine how far these crises were incident to the inexorable march of progress, or how far they were brought about by the failure of capitalism to attune itself to this forward movement. Nor is it necessary for us to pass judgement on the question of whether this current depression would have occurred had the capitalist system, in the last decade or two, been directed by supermen, compounded wholly of wisdom and saintliness. The truth is that in all times, faults in the system have been seized upon by the unscrupulous and greedy as vantage points in their battle for self-advancement. And we will be dealing with the matter in a thorough and practical way if we remove these faults, so as to put a final stop to the unfair practices which they made possible.

# Pierre Elliott Trudeau

Address on the Implementation of the War Measures Act

*National broadcast from Ottawa, 16 October 1970*

**'If a democratic society is to continue to exist, it must be able to root out the cancer of an armed, revolutionary movement that is bent on destroying the very basis of our freedom.'**

Trudeau was two years into his first term as Prime Minister when he was confronted by what remains the greatest terrorist event to take place on Canadian soil. The October Crisis was triggered by the 5 October 1970 kidnapping of James Cross, a British Trade Commissioner, by the Front de libération du Québec. Five days later, the FLQ kidnapped Pierre Laporte, the Minister of Labour and Manpower, Minister of Immigration and Vice-Premier of Quebec.

At the request of Jean Drapeau, the Mayor of Montreal, and the Quebec provincial government of Robert Bourassa, Ottawa invoked the War Measures Act, 'An Act to confer certain powers upon the Governor in Council in the event of War, Invasion, or Insurrection', dating back to the Great War. Under the emergency legislation, the FLQ was banned and *habeas corpus* was suspended.

The night after Trudeau's address to the nation, Laporte's body was found in the trunk of an abandoned car at Saint Hubert Airport. On 3 December, Cross was freed after police discovered where he was being held. The captors were given free passage to Cuba in exchange for his release.

I am speaking to you at a moment of grave crisis, when violent and fanatical men are attempting to destroy the unity and the freedom of Canada. One aspect of that crisis is the threat which has been made on the lives of two innocent men. These are matters of the utmost gravity and I want to tell you what the Government is doing to deal with them.

What has taken place in Montreal in the past two weeks is not unprecedented. It has happened elsewhere in the world on several recent occasions; it could happen elsewhere within Canada. But Canadians have always assumed that it could not happen here and as a result we are doubly shocked that it has.

Our assumption may have been naive, but it was understandable; understandable because democracy flourishes in Canada; understandable because individual liberty is cherished in Canada.

Notwithstanding these conditions – partly because of them – it has now been demonstrated to us by a few misguided persons just how fragile a democratic society can be, if democracy is not prepared to defend itself, and just how vulnerable to blackmail are tolerant, compassionate people.

Because the kidnappings and the blackmail are most familiar to you, I shall deal with them first.

The governments of Canada and Quebec have been told by groups of self-styled revolutionaries that they intend to murder in cold blood two innocent men unless their demands are met. The kidnappers claim they act as they do in order to draw attention to instances of social injustice. But I ask them whose attention are they seeking to attack. The Government of Canada? The Government of Quebec? Every government in this country is well aware of the existence of deep and important social problems. And every government to the limit of its resources and ability is deeply committed to their solution. But not by kidnappings and bombings. By hard work. And if any doubt exists about the good faith or the ability of any government, there are opposition parties ready and willing to be given an opportunity to govern. In short, there is available in Canada everywhere an effective mechanism to change governments by peaceful means. It has been employed by disenchanted voters again and again.

Who are the kidnap victims? To the victims' families they are husbands and fathers. To the kidnappers their identity is immaterial. The kidnappers' purposes would be served equally well by having in their grip you or me, or perhaps some child. Their purpose is to exploit the normal, human feelings of Canadians and to bend those feelings of sympathy into instruments for their own violent and revolutionary ends.

What are the kidnappers demanding in return for the lives of these men? Several things. For one, they want their grievances aired by force in public on the assumption, no doubt, that all right-thinking persons would be persuaded that the problems of the world can be solved by shouting slogans and insults.

They want more, they want the police to offer up as a sacrificial lamb a person whom they assume assisted in the lawful arrest and proper conviction of certain of their criminal friends.

They also want money. Ransom money.

They want still more. They demand the release from prison of seventeen criminals, and the dropping of charges against six other men, all of whom they refer to as 'political' prisoners. Who are these men who are held out as latter-day patriots and martyrs? Let me describe them to you.

Three are convicted murderers; five others were jailed for manslaughter; one is serving a life imprisonment after having pleaded guilty to numerous charges related to bombings; another has been convicted of seventeen armed robberies; two were once paroled but are now back in jail awaiting trial on charges of robberies.

Yet we are being asked to believe that these persons have been unjustly dealt with, that they have been imprisoned as a result of their political opinions, and that they deserve to be freed immediately, without recourse to due process of law.

The responsibility of deciding whether to release one or other of these criminals is that of the federal government. It is a responsibility that the Government will discharge according to law. To bow to the pressures of these kidnappers who demand that the prisoners be released would be not only an abdication of responsibility, it would lead to an increase in terrorist activities in Quebec. It would be, as well, an invitation to terrorism and kidnapping across the country. We might well find ourselves facing an endless series of demands for the release of criminals from jails, from coast to coast, and we would find that the hostages could be innocent members of your family or of your neighbourhood.

At the moment the FLQ is holding hostage two men in the Montreal area, one a British diplomat, the other a Quebec cabinet minister. They are threatened with murder. Should governments give in to this crude blackmail we would be facing the breakdown of the legal system, and its replacement by the law of the jungle. The Government's decision to prevent this from happening is not taken just to defend an important principle, it is taken to protect the lives of Canadians from dangers of the sort I have mentioned. Freedom and personal security are safeguarded by laws; those laws must be respected in order to be effective.

If it is the responsibility of governments to deny the demands of the kidnappers, the safety of the hostages is without question the responsibility of the kidnappers. Only the most twisted form of logic could conclude otherwise. Nothing that either the Government of Canada or the Government of Quebec has done or failed to do, now or in the future, could possibly excuse any injury to either of these two innocent men. The guns pointed at their heads have FLQ fingers on the triggers. Should any injury result, there is no explanation that could condone the acts. Should there be harm done to these men, the Government promises unceasing pursuit of those responsible.

During the past twelve days, the governments of Canada and Quebec have been engaged in constant consultations. The course followed in this matter had the full support of both governments, and of the Montreal municipal authorities. In order to save the lives of Mister Cross and Monsieur Laporte, we have engaged in indirect communications with the kidnappers.

The offer of the federal government to the kidnappers of safe conduct out of Canada to a country of their choice, in return for the delivery of the hostages has not yet been taken up, neither has the offer of the Government of Quebec to recommend parole for the five prisoners eligible for parole.

This offer of safe conduct was made only because Mister Cross and Monsieur Laporte might be able to identify their kidnappers and to assist in their prosecution. By offering the kidnappers safe exit from Canada we removed from them any possible motivation for murdering their hostages.

Let me turn now to the broader implications of the threat represented by the FLQ and similar organizations.

If a democratic society is to continue to exist, it must be able to root out the cancer of an armed, revolutionary movement that is bent on destroying the very basis of our freedom. For that reason the government, following an analysis of the facts, including requests of the Government of Quebec and of the City of Montreal for urgent action, decided to proclaim the War Measures Act. It did so at 4:00 a.m. this morning, in order to permit the full weight of government to be brought quickly to bear on all those persons advocating or practising violence as a means of achieving political ends.

The War Measures Act gives sweeping powers to the Government. It also suspends the operation of the Canadian Bill of Rights. I can assure you that the Government is most reluctant to seek such powers, and did so only when it became crystal clear that the situation could not be controlled unless some extraordinary assistance was made available on an urgent basis.

The authority contained in the act will permit governments to deal effectively with the nebulous yet dangerous challenge to society represented by terrorist organizations. The criminal law, as it stands, is simply not adequate to deal with systematic terrorism.

The police have therefore been given certain extraordinary powers necessary for the effective detection and elimination of conspiratorial organizations which advocate the use of violence. These organizations, and membership in them, have been declared illegal. The powers include the right to search and arrest without warrant, to detain suspected

*Soldiers outside the Quebec Provincial Police Headquarters on rue Parthenais in Montreal, 15 October 1970*

persons without the necessity of laying specific charges immediately, and to detain persons without bail.

These are strong powers and I find them as distasteful as I am sure you do. They are necessary, however, to permit the police to deal with persons who advocate or promote the violent overthrow of our democratic system. In short, I assure you that the Government recognizes its grave responsibilities in interfering in certain cases with civil liberties, and that it remains answerable to the people of Canada for its actions.

The Government will revoke this proclamation as soon as possible.

As I said in the House of Commons this morning, the Government will allow sufficient time to pass to give it the necessary experience to assess the type of statute which may be required in the present circumstances.

It is my firm intention to discuss then with the leaders of the opposition parties the desirability of introducing legislation of a less comprehensive nature. In this respect I earnestly solicited from the leaders and from all honourable members constructive suggestions for the amendment of the regulations. Such suggestions will be given careful consideration for possible inclusion in any new statute.

I recognize, as I hope do others, that this extreme position into which governments have been forced is in some respects a trap. It's a well-known technique of revolutionary groups who attempt to destroy society by unjustified violence to goad the authorities into inflexible attitudes. The revolutionaries then employ this evidence of alleged authoritarianism as justification for the need to use violence in their renewed attacks on the social structure. I appeal to all Canadians not to become so obsessed by what the Government has done today in response to terrorism that they forget the opening play in this vicious game. That play was taken by the revolutionaries; they chose to use bombing, murder and kidnapping.

The threat posed by the FLQ terrorists and their supporters is out of all proportion to their numbers. This follows from the fact that they act stealthily and because they are known to have in their possession a considerable amount of dynamite. To guard against the very real possibility of bombings directed at public buildings or utilities in the immediate future, the Government of Quebec has requested the assistance of the Canadian Armed Forces to support the police in several places in the Province of Quebec. These forces took up their positions yesterday.

Violence, unhappily, is no stranger to this decade. The Speech from the Throne opening the current session of parliament a few days ago said that 'we live in a period of tenseness and unease'. We must not overlook the fact, moreover, that violence is often a symptom of deep social unrest. This Government has pledged that it will introduce legislation which deals not just with symptoms, but with the social causes which often underlie or serve as an excuse for crime and disorder.

It was in that context that I stated in the House of Commons a year ago that there was no need anywhere in Canada for misguided or misinformed zealots to resort to acts of violence in the belief that only in this fashion could they accomplish change. There may be some places in the world where the law is so inflexible and so insensitive as to prompt such beliefs. But Canada is not such a place. I said then, and I repeat now, that those who would defy the law and ignore the opportunities available to them to right their wrongs and satisfy their claims will receive no hearing from this Government.

We shall ensure that the laws passed by parliament are worthy of respect. We shall also ensure that those laws are respected.

We have seen in many parts of Canada all too much evidence of violence in the name of revolution in the past twelve months. We are now able to see some of the consequences of violence. Persons who invoke violence are raising deliberately the level of hate in Canada. They do so at a time when the country must eliminate hate, and must exhibit tolerance and compassion in order to create the kind of society which we all desire. Yet those who disrespect legal processes create a danger that law-abiding elements of the community, out of anger and out of fear, will harden their attitudes and refuse to accommodate any change or remedy any shortcomings. They refuse because fear deprives persons of their normal sense of compassion and their normal sense of justice.

This Government is not acting out of fear. It is acting to prevent fear from spreading. It is acting to maintain the rule of law without which freedom is impossible. It is acting to make clear to kidnappers and revolutionaries and assassins that in this country laws are made and changed by the elected representatives of all Canadians – not by a handful of self-selected dictators. Those who gain power through terror, rule through terror. The Government is acting, therefore, to protect your life and your liberty.

The Government is acting, as well, to ensure the safe return of Mister James Cross and Monsieur Pierre Laporte. I speak for millions of Canadians when I say to their courageous wives and families how much we sympathize with them for the nightmare to which they have been subjected, and how much we all hope and pray that it will soon conclude.

Canada remains one of the most wholesome and humane lands on this earth. If we stand firm, this current situation will soon pass. We will be able to say proudly, as we have for decades, that within Canada there is ample room for opposition and dissent, but none for intimidation and terror.

There are very few times in the history of any country when all persons must take a stand on critical issues. This is one of those times; this is one of those issues. I am confident that those persons who unleashed this tragic sequence of events with the aim of destroying our society and dividing our country will find that the opposite will occur. The result of their acts will be a stronger society in a unified country. Those who would have divided us will have united us.

I sense the unease which grips many Canadians today. Some of you are upset, and this is understandable. I want to reassure you that the authorities have the situation well in hand. Everything that needs to be done is being done; every level of government in this country is well prepared to act in your interests.

# Jean Chrétien

## Remarks on the Attacks on the United States

*The House of Commons, Ottowa, 17 September 2001*

**'Today more than ever we must reaffirm the fundamental values of our charter of rights and freedoms: the equality of every race, every colour, every religion and every ethnic origin.'**

On Tuesday, 11 September 2001, the date of the terrorist attacks in the United States, Canada's 37th Parliament was nearing the end of its summer recess. Six days later, the House of Commons resumed its sitting as scheduled with a motion that all be put aside to address the tragic events. Following adoption, the Prime Minister, Jean Chrétien, moved:

> That this House express its sorrow and horror at the senseless and vicious attack on the United States of America in September 11, 2001;
>
> that it express its heartfelt condolences to the victims and to the American people;
>
> and that it reaffirm its commitment to the humane values of free and democratic society and its determination to bring to justice the perpetrators of this attack on these values and to defend civilization from any future terrorist attack.

There followed a moment of silence, before Chrétien began the debate titled 'Attack on the United States'.

*Prime Minister Jean Chrétien and United States Ambassador Paul Celluci at a Parliament Hill Ceremony marking the day of mourning for victims of the attacks of September 11, 2001*

Mister Speaker, I thank the leaders of all parties in the House of Commons, indeed all members, for their co-operation in organizing this historic debate.

In the sad and trying days since the awful news came from New York and Washington, it has been clear that the civilized nations of the world have a solemn duty to speak as one against the scourge of terrorism.

Under these urgent circumstances, Canadians will be pleased to see that their elected representatives have come together in the spirit of unity and resolve to make this debate our first order of business. I look forward to hearing the views of members on the role that Canada should play in shaping a firm and just global response to an unprecedented global threat.

There are those rare occasions when time seems to stand still, when a singular event transfixes the world. There are also those terrible occasions when the dark side of human nature escapes civilized restraint and shows its ugly face to a stunned world. Tuesday, September 11, 2001, will forever be etched in memory as a day when time stood still.

When I saw the scenes of devastation, my first thoughts and words were for all the victims and the American people, but there are no words in any language whose force or eloquence could equal the quiet testimony last Friday of 100,000 Canadians gathered just a few yards from here for our National Day of Mourning. I was proud to be one of them and I was equally proud of the Canadians who gathered in ceremonies right across the country. It was a sea of sorrow and sympathy for those who have lost friends and loved ones: Americans, Canadians, citizens of many countries. Above all, it was a sea of solidarity with our closest friend and partner in the world, the United States of America.

As always, this time of crisis brought out the very best in our people: from prayer meetings and vigils to the countless numbers who lined up to give blood, from a flood of donations by individuals and businesses to patience in the face of delays and inconvenience. We were all moved by the sight of Canadians opening up their hearts and homes to thousands of confused and anxious air travellers who had no place to go.

When I spoke to President Bush last week, he asked me to thank the Canadian people. I ask all members to carry his message back to their constituencies.

The president also told me that he had been told many times by his officials about the tremendous co-operation and assistance they were receiving from the agencies and departments of the Government of Canada in responding to the immediate emergency of the attack and in the investigation that would bring to justice those who committed this crime against humanity.

Indeed, I am proud of the speed and co-ordination that has characterized our response: assessing and pre-positioning disaster assistance supplies, so that we could respond in a timely and effective manner when called upon; seeing to the safety of stranded air travellers; working to protect the safety of Canadians; sharing information with investigators; and responding to calls for information about loved ones.

The relevant ministers will inform the House in detail on what their departments have done, and are doing, on behalf of Canadians. But I want to express my appreciation to our public servants for their round the clock effort.

The House must also address the threat that terrorism poses to all civilized peoples and the role that Canada must play in defeating it. To understand what is at stake, we need only reflect on the symbolic meaning of the World Trade Center towers. In the words of their architect, the towers were: 'a representation of our belief in humanity, our need for individual dignity, our belief in co-operation and, through co-operation, our ability to find greatness.'

So, let us be clear: this was not just an attack on the United States. These cold-blooded killers struck a blow at the values and beliefs of free and civilized people everywhere. The world has been attacked. The world must respond. Because we are at war against terrorism and Canada, a nation founded on a belief in freedom, justice and tolerance, will be part of that response.

Terrorists are not attached to any one country. Terrorism is a global threat. The perpetrators have demonstrated their ability to move with ease from country to country, from place to place, to make use of the freedom and openness of the victims on whom they prey, the very freedom and openness that we cherish and will protect. They are willing, indeed anxious, to die in the commission of their crimes and to use innocent civilians as shields and as tools.

We must prepare ourselves, and Canadians, for the fact that this will be a long struggle with no easy solutions, one in which patience and wisdom are essential.

Let us not deceive ourselves as to the nature of the threat that faces us and that this can be defeated easily or simply with one swift strike. We must be guided by a commitment to do what works in the long run, not by what makes us feel better in the short run.

Our actions will be ruled by resolve but not by fear. If laws need to be changed they will be. If security has to be increased to protect Canadians it will be. We will remain vigilant but will not give in to the temptation in a rush to increase security to undermine the values that we cherish and which have made Canada a beacon of hope, freedom and tolerance in the world.

We will not be stampeded in the hope, vain and ultimately self-defeating, that we can make Canada a fortress against the world.

Finally, I want to make another very important point. Canada is a nation of immigrants from all corners of the globe, people of all nationalities, colours and religions. This is who we are. Let there be no doubt. We will allow no one to force us to sacrifice our values or traditions under the pressure of urgent circumstances.

We will continue to welcome people from the whole world. We will continue to offer refuge to the persecuted. I say again, no one will stop this.

I have been saddened by the fact that the terror of last Tuesday has provoked demonstrations against Muslim Canadians and other minority groups in Canada. This is completely unacceptable. The terrorists win when they export their hatred.

The evil perpetrators of this horror represent no community or religion. They stand for evil, nothing else. As I said, this is a struggle against terrorism not against any one community or faith. Today more than ever we must reaffirm the fundamental values of our charter of rights and freedoms: the equality of every race, every colour, every religion and every ethnic origin.

We are all Canadians. We are a compassionate and righteous people. When we see the searing images of mothers and fathers, sisters and brothers, many of them Canadian, wandering the streets of New York looking for their missing loved ones, we know where our duty lies.

We have never been a bystander in the struggle for justice in the world. We will stand with the Americans as neighbours, as friends, as family. We will stand with our allies. We will do what we must to defeat terrorism.

However, let our actions be guided by a spirit of wisdom and perseverance, by our values and our way of life. As we go on with the struggle, let us never, ever, forget who we are and what we stand for.

*Vive le Canada.*

# UNITY

“*They want to take it away*
*from their children?*
*They want to break it down?*
*No! That's our answer.*”

*- Pierre Elliott Trudeau, 1980*

# Charles de Gaulle

*Vive le Québec libre!*

*Montreal City Hall, 24 July 1967*

**'I have noticed what immense efforts of progress, of development, and consequently of empowerment that you have accomplished here...'**

Made during the height of centennial celebrations, French President Charles de Gaulle's speech from the balcony of Montreal's City Hall holds place as both the most famous and infamous delivered by a foreign head of state on Canadian soil.

In the months leading up to de Gaulle's visit, the Canadian Government had become troubled over relations with the President. It had been noted that France had sent no representative to the March funeral service for Governor General Georges Vanier, who had befriended de Gaulle early in the Second World War. Prime Minister Lester B. Pearson went so far as to dispatch his Secretary of State for External Affairs, Paul Martin, Sr, to meet with the President in Paris.

De Gaulle's invitation to visit Canada was not made through Ottawa, but by Quebec premier Daniel Johnson, to whom the President refers in his speech. Though head of state, de Gaulle chose to arrive not in Ottawa, but in Quebec City. The next day he travelled the Chemin du Roy by motorcade to Montreal where he was met by Johnson and Mayor Jean Drapeau. Although he was not scheduled to speak, the French President reportedly told Drapeau 'I have to speak to those people who are calling for me.'

*Charles de Gaulle making his infamous speech from the balcony of Montreal City Hall*

It is a great emotion that fills my heart to see before me the French city of Montreal!

In the name of the old country, in the name of France, I salute you! I salute you with all my heart!

I would tell you a secret that you cannot repeat. Here this evening, and all the length of my journey, I found myself in the same sense of atmosphere as the Liberation. And all the length of my trip, in addition, I have noticed what immense efforts of progress, of development, and consequently of empowerment that you have accomplished here, and that it is Montreal that I must give this statement, because, if there is a city in the world exemplary of modern success, it is yours! I say it is yours, and I permit myself to say, it is ours!

If you knew what confidence France, waking up after immense troubles, now carries for you, if you knew what affection she has started to feel again for the Frenchmen of Canada, and if you knew to what point she feels obliged to further your march that is before you, to your progress.

It's why she has finalised

*...ive by careful*

*...n said that the United States government is a failure. I don't go so far.*

*...ntage by experience, and endeavour to see if we cannot ar...*

*...ntrary, I consider it a marvellous exhibition of human wisdom. It was as*

*plan as will avoid the mistakes of our neighbours.*

with the Government of Quebec, with my friend Johnson here, the agreements for which the French on this side and the other of the Atlantic can work together towards the same French undertaking. And, of course, the aid that France brings here, each day a little more, she knows well that you will reciprocate because you are building the best factories, enterprises, laboratories, which will be astonishment for all, and which, one day, I know you will allow to aid France.

This is what I have come this evening to say, and that I will bring back from this unforgettable Montreal reunion, an unforgettable souvenir. The entirety of France knows, sees, hears that which is happening here, and I would tell you, she is better for it.

*Vive Montréal!*
*Vive le Québec!*
*Vive le Québec libre!*
*Vive le Canada français!*
*Et vive la France!*

# Lester B. Pearson

Statement on President de Gaulle's Speech

*Ottowa, 25 July 1967*

## 'Canada will remain united and will reject any effort to destroy her unity.'

**Charles de Gaulle's incendiary speech from the balcony of Montreal's City Hall was considered a serious breach of diplomatic protocol. His visit to Expo the next day, a Tuesday, did nothing to improve the situation. The President referred to Quebec as a country and encouraged its citizens to become their own masters. During a dinner at French Pavillion, de Gaulle acknowledged: 'There may have been difficulty, there may have been something, but if the President of the Republic of France has helped the French of Canada, he will rejoice, and so will France, I assure you.'**

**Pearson's cabinet considered several responses, including the cancellation of the President's visit to Ottawa, scheduled for the Thursday. In the end, it was decided that the Prime Minister would issue a statement, broadcast approximately 24 hours after de Gaulle's speech.**

**For Pearson, *'Vive le Québec libre'* were not the most disturbing words delivered in Montreal; it was the President's likening his journey from Quebec City to Montreal to the atmosphere of the Liberation, as reflected in the response.**

**After Pearson issued his statement, de Gaulle cut short his trip and flew back to France from Montreal's Dorval Airport the next afternoon. He never visited Ottawa, nor did he ever again set foot on Canadian soil.**

I am sure that Canadians in all parts of our country were pleased when the President of France received such a warm welcome in Quebec. However, certain statements by the President tend to encourage the small minority of our population whose aim is to destroy Canada; and, as such, they are unacceptable to the Canadian people and its Government.

The people of Canada are free. Every province of Canada is free. Canadians do not need to be liberated. Indeed many thousands of Canadians gave their lives in two world wars in the liberation of France and other European countries.

Canada will remain united and will reject any effort to destroy her unity.

Canada has always had a special relationship with France, the motherland of so many of her citizens. We attach the greatest importance to our friendship with the French people. It has been and remains the strong purpose of the Government of Canada to foster that friendship. I hope that my discussions later this week with General de Gaulle will demonstrate that this purpose is one which he shares.

*French President Charles de Gaulle at Expo 67 the day after his speech from the balcony of Montreal City Hall*

# Pierre Elliott Trudeau

## Final 1980 Quebec Referendum Speech

*The Paul Sauvé Arena, Montreal, 14 May 1980*

### 'My name is a Quebec name, but my name is a Canadian name also...'

**Delivered three months after his return to power, Pierre Elliott Trudeau's final speech of the 1980 Quebec referendum is perhaps his best remembered. However, Trudeau never counted the address amongst his best.**

**Much of the speech is an attack on Quebec Premier René Lévesque and the 'Yes' forces, based on what Trudeau describes as the 'ambiguous, equivocal question' found on the referendum ballot:**

**The Government of Quebec has made public its proposal to negotiate a new agreement with the rest of Canada, based on the equality of nations; this agreement would enable Quebec to acquire the exclusive power to make its laws, levy its taxes and establish relations abroad – in other words, sovereignty – and at the same time to maintain with Canada an economic association including a common currency; any change in political status resulting from these negotiations will only be implemented with popular approval through another referendum; on these terms, do you give the Government of Quebec the mandate to negotiate the proposed agreement between Quebec and Canada?**

**The final third of the speech features a response to a remark made by Lévesque in which he had noted Elliott as Trudeau's middle name, adding that the Prime Minister had 'decided to follow the Anglo-Saxon part of his heritage'.**

Mister Chairman, fellow Canadians, first of all, I want to thank you for this warm welcome. I think it is obvious by this immense gathering – it is obvious that these are historic moments. There are very few examples in the history of democracy of one part of a country choosing to decide, for itself and by itself, whether, 'Yes' or 'No', it wants to be part of the country to which it has always belonged. There are very few occasions when this has happened in the history of democracy. And I believe that all those here this evening, all those who have worked for the 'No' in this province for over a month, will be proud to reply when… when our children and perhaps, if we are lucky our grandchildren, ask us in twenty or thirty years:

You were there in May 1980. You were there when the people of Quebec were asked to decide freely on their future. You were there when Quebec had the option to stay in Canada or to leave. What did you do in May 1980 – 'No, that was our answer.'

I should like to ask you this evening to reflect on the question that is asked of us, and on the consequences of the answers we may give to these questions.

Allow me – perhaps for the last time before going to the polls – allow me to remind you of the essence of the question. There are two issues involved:

The first is the sovereignty of Quebec, and that is defined in the question itself as: the exclusive power to make its laws, levy its taxes and establish relations abroad… in other words, sovereignty.

And while we in this room answer 'No', in other rooms in other parts of the province, there are people who answer 'Yes'; who truly and honestly want sovereignty.

I share your opinion: this is the false option; an option that means, as Jean Chrétien said, that we will no longer send Quebec MPs to govern us in Canada; an option that means independence; an option that means the separation of Quebec from the rest of the country.

To this our answer is 'No'.

But it is not to those who are for or against sovereignty that I wish to address my remarks this evening. After the referendum, I hope we will continue to respect one another's differences; that we will respect the option which has been freely chosen by those who are for or against independence for Quebec.

In this question, therefore, there is sovereignty and there is everything else.

Everything else is a new agreement. It is equality of nations. It is at the same time economic association. It is a common currency. It is change through another referendum. It is a mandate to negotiate.

And we know very well what they are doing, these hucksters of the 'Yes' vote. They are trying to appeal to everyone who would say 'Yes' to a new agreement. 'Yes' to equality of nations. 'Yes' at the same time to association. 'Yes' at the same time to a common currency. 'Yes' to a second referendum. 'Yes' to a simple mandate to negotiate.

It is those who say 'Yes' through pride because they do not understand the question, or because they want to increase their bargaining power, and to those among the undecided who are on the brink of voting 'Yes', to whom I am addressing myself this evening. Because what we have to ask ourselves is what would happen in the case of a 'Yes' vote, as in the case of a 'No' vote. And it is the undecided, those who are on the 'Yes' side through pride, or because they are tired and fed up, who, in these last few days, must be addressed.

So let us consider this. The Government of Canada and all the provincial governments have made themselves perfectly clear. If the answer to the referendum question is 'No', we have all said that this 'No' will be interpreted as a mandate to change the constitution, to renew federalism.

I am not the only person saying this. Nor is Mister Clark. Nor is Mister Broadbent. It is not only the nine premiers of the other provinces saying this. It is also the seventy-five MPs elected by Quebecers to represent them in Ottawa who are saying that a 'No' means change. And because I spoke to these MPs this morning, I know that I can make a most solemn commitment that following a 'No' vote, we will immediately take action to renew the constitution and we will not stop until we have done that. And I make a solemn declaration to all Canadians in the other provinces, we, the Quebec MPs, are laying ourselves on the line, because we are telling Quebecers to vote 'No' and telling you in the other provinces that we will not agree to your interpreting a 'No' vote as an indication that everything is fine and can remain as it was before.

We want change and we are willing to lay our seats in the House on the line to have change. This would be our attitude in the case of a 'No' vote.

Monsieur Lévesque has asked me what my attitude would be if the majority of Quebecers voted 'Yes'. I have already answered this question. I did so in parliament. I did so in Montreal and in Quebec City. And I say it again this evening: if the answer to the referendum is 'Yes' – I have said it clearly in the House of Commons – Monsieur Lévesque will be welcome to come to Ottawa, where I will receive politely, as he has always received me in Quebec City, and I will tell him that there are two doors. If you knock on the sovereignty-association door, there is no negotiation possible.

Monsieur Lévesque continues to repeat, 'But what about democracy – what would you do if a majority of the Quebec people voted 'Yes'? Would you not be obliged, by the principle of democracy, to negotiate?'

No indeed!

It is like saying to Monsieur Lévesque, 'The people of Newfoundland have just voted 100 percent in favour of renegotiating the electricity contract with Quebec. You are obliged, the name of democracy, to respect the will of Newfoundland, are you not?'

It is obvious that this sort of logic does not work.

The wishes of Quebecers may be expressed through democratic process, but that cannot bind others – those in other provinces who did not vote to act as Quebec decides.

So by that reasoning, Monsieur Lévesque, there will be no association. Now, if you want to speak, if you want to speak of sovereignty, let me say that you have no mandate to negotiate that, because you did not ask Quebecers if they wanted sovereignty pure and simple.

You said: 'Do you want sovereignty on the condition that there is also association?'

So, with no association, you have no mandate to negotiate sovereignty; you do not have the key to open that door, and neither do I.

I do not have that mandate either, because we were elected on February 18, scarcely a couple of months ago – for the specific purpose of making laws for the province of Quebec. So don't ask me not to make any, don't ask me to give full powers to Quebec.

On the other hand, if Monsieur Lévesque, by some miracle, and it truly would be a miracle, knocked on the other door, saying, 'I have a mandate to negotiate, and would like to negotiate renewed federalism' – then the door would be wide open to him. and I would say: 'You did not have to go to the trouble of holding a referendum for that; if it is renewed federalism you want, if that is what you wish to negotiate, then you are welcome.'

But is it really possible that Monsieur Lévesque would say that, because what are the 'Yes' supporters saying? The 'Yes' supporters are saying – and I asked Monsieur Lévesque this a couple of weeks ago: 'What will you do if the majority votes "No"?' What will you say then? Will you respect the will of the people, or will you claim that a 'No' vote does not mean as much as a 'Yes' vote, and that a 'No' does not count for the moment, but that another referendum needs to be held? I asked Monsieur Lévesque that, and this was his answer: 'We will not refuse a few crumbs of autonomy for Quebec, but we will still be going around in circles.'

Monsieur Lévesque, if the people of Quebec vote 'No', as I believe they will, won't you say that since the people have rejected sovereignty-association, it is your duty to be a good government and put an end to the status quo on which you place so much blame, and to join us in changing the constitution.

Monsieur Lévesque told us we will still be going around in circles. Well, that should enlighten all those who intend to vote 'Yes' in order to increase Quebec's bargaining power, all those who intend to vote 'Yes' out of pride, and all those who intend to vote 'Yes' because they are fed up.

If Monsieur Lévesque does not want renewed federalism, even if the people vote 'No', then, clearly, if the people vote 'Yes', he is going to say: 'Renewed federalism is out of the question.'

For my part, I will say: sovereignty-association is out of the question. Which means that we have reached an impasse and those who vote 'Yes' must realize right now that a 'Yes' vote will result in either independence, pure and simple, or the status quo – that is what the 'Yes' option boils down to: the independence of Quebec, the separation of Quebec, or else the status quo, no change, because Monsieur Lévesque refuses to negotiate.

That's what we have to say to the 'Yes' side: if you want independence, if you vote 'Yes', you won't get independence because you made it conditional on there being an association, an association being achieved along with independence.

If you want association, your 'Yes' vote doesn't mean anything because it is not binding on the other provinces, which refuse to join in an association with you. And if you vote 'Yes' for a renewed federalism, your vote will be lost as well, because Monsieur Lévesque will still be going around in circles.

So you see, that is the impasse that this ambiguous, equivocal question has led us into, and that is what the people who are going to vote 'Yes' out of pride, that is what they should think about. Voting 'Yes' out of pride means that we are putting our fate in the hands of the other provinces, which are going to say 'No', no association, and then we will have to swallow our pride and our 'Yes' vote.

And those who are saying 'Yes' in order to get it over with, 'Yes' to break away, 'Yes' to get negotiations started, they read in the question itself that there will be a second referendum, and then maybe a third, and then maybe a fourth. And that, my friends, that is precisely what we are criticizing the Parti Québécois Government for; not for having wanted independence – that is an option we reject and we're fighting it openly.

But what we are criticizing the Parti Québécois for is for not having the courage to ask: Independence, 'Yes' or 'No'?

'Yes' or 'No'?

You, the supporters of the 'No' side, you know the divisions this referendum has caused. You have seen the divisions it has caused with families. You have seen the hatred it has created between neighbours. You know it has widened the generation gap. You know that the deep suspicion and mistrust between supporters of the 'Yes' side and those of the 'No' side will last for a long time to come.

*Prime Minister Pierre Elliott Trudeau with Claude Ryan, leader of the Quebec Liberal Party, before his referendum speech at the Paul Sauvé Arena*

You know what kind of trial the referendum is. Well, you have been told by the Parti Québécois Government that there will be other referendums and you know that the hatred, the differences, the enormous waste of energy in Quebec will go on and on. Well, we are saying 'No' to that. 'No', it will not go on.

Here is a party whose goal was separation, then independence, then sovereignty, then sovereignty-association, and then they even said that sovereignty-association was only for the purposes of negotiation. Here is a party that, in the name of pride, said to Quebecers: Stand up, we are going to move on to the world stage and assert ourselves.

And now, this party, on the point of entering the world stage, gets frightened and stays in the wings. Is that pride? Should we use that as a reason to vote for a party that tells us it will start all over again if the answer is 'Yes', that there will be another referendum?

Well, that is what we are criticizing the Parti Québécois for – not having the courage to ask a clear question, a question a mature people would have been able to answer, really a simple question:

Do you want to leave Canada, 'Yes' or 'No'?

No!

Well, it's because the Parti Québécois knew how the vast majority of Quebecers would answer the question: Do you want to stop being Canadians. The answer would have been 'No' and that is why it has failed to enter the world stage.

Well, we know there is a clear answer, there is an unambiguous answer and that answer is 'No'. That answer is 'No' to those who want, as Camil Samson, I think said, to take our heritage away from us and from our children.

The answer is 'No' to those who advocate separation rather than sharing, to those who advocate isolation rather than fellowship, to those who – basically – advocate pride rather than love, because love involves challenges coming together and meeting others half-way, and working with them to build a better world.

So then, one must say, leaving that whole convoluted question aside, one must say 'No' to ambiguity. One must say 'No' to tricks. One must say 'No' to contempt, because they have come to that.

I was told that no more than two days ago Monsieur Lévesque was saying that part of my name was Elliott and, since Elliott was an English name, it was perfectly understandable that I was for the 'No' side, because, really, you see, I was not as much of a Quebecer as those who are going to vote 'Yes'.

That, my dear friends, is what contempt is. It means saying that there are different kinds of Quebecers. It means that saying that the Quebecers on the 'No' side are not as good Quebecers as the others and perhaps they have a drop or two of foreign blood, while the people on the 'Yes' side have pure blood in their veins. That is what contempt is and that is the kind of division which builds up within a people, and that is what we are saying 'No' to.

Of course my name is Pierre Elliott Trudeau. Yes, Elliott was my mother's name. It was the name borne by the Elliotts who came to Canada more than two hundred years ago. It is the name of the Elliotts who, more than one hundred years ago, settled in Saint-Gabriel-de-Brandon, where you can still see their graves in the cemetery. That is what the Elliotts are.

My name is a Quebec name, but my name is a Canadian name also, and that's the story of my name.

Since Monsieur Lévesque has chosen to analyse my name, but let me show you how ridiculous it is to use that kind of contemptuous argument.

Monsieur Pierre-Marc Johnson is a minister. Now, I ask you, is Johnson an English name or a French name? And Louis O'Neill – a former minister of Monsieur Lévesque's, and Robert Burns, and Daniel Johnson, I ask you, are they Quebecers, yes or no?

And, if we are looking at names, I saw in yesterday's newspaper that the leader of Quebec's Inuit, the Eskimos, they are going to vote 'No'. Do you know what the leader's name is? His name is Charlie Watt. Is Charlie Watt not a Quebecer? These people have lived in Quebec since the Stone Age; they have been here since time immemorial. And Monsieur Watt is not a Quebecer?

And, according to yesterday's newspaper, the chief of the Micmac band, at Restigouche, the chief of fifteen hundred Indians – what is his name? Ron Maloney. Is he not a Quebecer? The Indians have been there for a good two thousand years. And their chief is not a Quebecer?

My dear friends, Laurier said something in 1889, nearly one hundred years ago now, and it is worth taking the time to read these lines: 'My Countrymen,' said Laurier, 'are not only those in whose veins runs the blood of France. My countrymen are all those people – no matter what their race or language – whom the fortunes of war, the twists and turns of fate, or their own choice, have brought among us.'

All Quebecers have the right to vote 'Yes' or 'No', as Madame De Santis said. And all those 'Nos' are as valid as any 'Yes', regardless of the name of the person voting, or the colour of his skin.

My friends, Péquistes often tell us: the world is watching us, hold our heads high; the world is watching us, the whole world is watching what is happening in our democracy. Let's show them we are proud.

Well, I just received what is apparently the last pamphlet that will be put out by the 'Yes' committee. Go pick it up somewhere. I recommend it. It's a historic document.

It's a historic document because we find, all through this pamphlet, expressions such as 'negotiate seriously', 'a Quebec project', 'a better contract with the rest of Canada', 'an association between equals', 'negotiations', 'another referendum'.

We don't once find the word 'separatism'. We don't find the word 'independence', either. We don't find the word 'sovereignty'. We don't find, not even once, the term 'sovereignty-association'.

That's what pride is!

That's what deceiving the public is. And I don't know what historians will say about those who lacked courage at this historic turning point, but I know that they will be hard on those who sought to deceive the public and who say, in this last pamphlet – who say this: 'Some would have you believe that the question deals with separation. That's false.'

That's false. Your question is about sovereignty. Take a stand, you PQ supporters. Show us your true colours. Are you for independence?

No. We are against independence. Of course the world is watching us. The world will be a bit astonished by what it sees. I admit, because in today's world, you see, things are unstable, to say the least. The parameters are changing, to use a big word. And that means that there is fire and blood in the Middle-East, in Afghanistan, in Iran, in Vietnam, that means that there is inflation which is crippling the free economy; that means that there is division in the world; that means there is perhaps a third of the human race which goes to bed hungry every night, because there is not enough food and not enough medicine to keep the children in good health.

And that world is looking at Canada, the second largest country in the world, one of the richest, perhaps the second richest country in the world, a country which is composed of the meeting of the two most outstanding cultures of the Western world: the French and the English, added to by all the other cultures coming from every corner of Europe and every corner of the world. And this is what the world is looking at with astonishment, saying: These people think they might split up today when the whole world is interdependent? When Europe is trying to seek some kind of political union? These people in Quebec and in Canada want to split it up?

They want to take it away from their children?

They want to break it down?

No! That's our answer.

I quoted Laurier, and let me quote a Father of Confederation who was an illustrious Quebecer, Thomas D'Arcy McGee: 'The new nationality,' he was saying, 'is thoughtful and true; nationalist in its preference, but universal in its sympathies; a nationality of the spirit, for there is a new duty which especially belongs to Canada to create a state and to originate a history which the world will not willingly let die.'

Well, we won't let it die. Our answer is: No, to those who would kill it.

We won't let this country die, this Canada, our home and native land, this Canada which really is, as our national anthem says, our home and native land. We are going to say to those who want us to stop being Canadians, we are going to say a resounding, an overwhelming 'No!'

# René Lévesque

1980 Referendum Concession Speech

*The Paul Sauvé Arena, Rosemont, 20 May 1980*

***'My dear friends, my dear friends, if I have understood you correctly, you're saying "A la prochaine fois".'***

**Six days after Pierre Elliott Trudeau made his final scheduled appearance of the 1980 referendum campaign, René Lévesque delivered his concession speech from the very same stage.**

**The loss by the 'Yes' side, which garnered 40.4 per cent of the vote, was seen as a great victory by Trudeau and the federalist forces. Despite the defeat, the sovereignist Parti Québécois government was re-elected eleven months later. In 1985, Lévesque split with the party arguing for a decrease in emphasis on sovereignty in the upcoming election. In October, he resigned as Premier. The Parti Québécois was defeated by the Quebec Liberal Party two months later.**

**Though the overall message of Lévesque's concession speech was *'A la prochaine fois'*, he would not live to see another referendum. In November 1987, at the age of sixty-five, Lévesque died of a heart attack.**

**The venue in which the concession speech was delivered is an interesting one. During the October Crisis, the Paul Sauvé Arena had served as the site of a rally in support of the Front de libération du Québec; in 1976 and 1981 it housed Parti Québécois election victory celebrations. In this respect, Trudeau's speech can be said to have taken place in the heart of the 'Yes' camp. In 1996, the arena was demolished.**

My dear friends, my dear friends, if I have understood you correctly, you're saying: '*A la prochaine fois*.' But in the meantime, with the same serenity that has characterized our behaviour during the campaign, we have to swallow – and it is not easy.

I apologize for having waited to come here to see you. I have to admit that we continued to hope for a while. I have to tell you, it's tough, it hurts more, it hurts more deeply than any electoral defeat, and I know what I'm talking about.

I have to ask that you listen a little bit to what we have to tell ourselves at the end of the campaign. It is clear, let us admit it, that the ball is now in the federalist camp. The Québécois people have just clearly given it another chance. In the weeks and months to come it will be up to the federalists and above all Monsieur Trudeau… it will be up to them to give content to the promises they have multiplied over the last thirty-five days. They all proclaimed that if the 'No' carried the day the status quo would be dead and buried and that the Québécois would have nothing to regret.

We will wait. We will wait to see what will follow. We will wait to see what is going to follow this victory of the 'No', even if I must repeat – because we'll remember from this point of view that it's not very promising on the level either of content or of methods, and in particular the scandalously immoral federal campaign itself, the campaign in which all the rules of the game that were agreed upon among Québécois were walked over without the least hesitation—this victory of the 'No', despite it all, it has to be accepted.

But also, in the name of the immense majority of the rising generation, and of those already of age in Quebec today, and also little by little among the Québécois of other backgrounds of the same generations, tonight's federalist victors must be put on notice, seriously on notice against any temptation to claim to take advantage and to impose upon on us any kind of changes they want that are not in keeping with those demanded by Quebec for almost forty years. In any event, until the next elections I can assure you that the Government is going to attempt to be as vigilant as ever, so that at least all the current rights of Quebec are respected and that any change not make any claim to infringe in any way on that margin of autonomy which Quebec, through great difficulties, has managed to secure.

And now, to all those women and men who made this admirable campaign for the 'Yes' which will remain, for whoever participated in it, the most unforgettable memory of fervour, honesty, justified pride and, despite the slanders, of a fraternal pride open to others, I say to you: keep the memory, but keep the hope as well. Since we must, let us accept the results, but don't ever lose sight of an objective as legitimate, as universally recognized among peoples and nations as political equality: it will come.

Today, from the depths of my conscience and the confidence that I also have in the evolution of Quebec that is going to continue forward, it must be said that this May 20, 1980 will perhaps remain as one of the final glimmerings of the old Quebec that must be respected. We are a family that is very obviously still divided from this point of view. But I'm confident that one day there will be a normal rendezvous with history that Quebec will keep it, and I have confidence that we'll all be there together to participate in it. But I confess that tonight it would be hard for me to say exactly when or how. The only thing I would like to add is this: with the same fundamental confidence in us, and taking into account that tomorrow we have to continue to live together, and that it's extremely obvious that there are great divisions among us, can we finish up this evening by singing for everyone that which remains the most beautiful Québécois song to all, without exception, to all the people here? If someone would like to start it up, *'Gens du pays'*. As for me, I don't have any voice left.

*René Lévesque, the first Parti Québécois Premier*

## Jacques Parizeau

1995 Referendum Concession Speech

*Le Palais des Congrès de Montréal, 30 October 1995*

### 'We were so close to having our own country.'

**In terms of popular vote, the September 1994 Quebec provincial election could hardly have been closer. The Parti Québécois captured fewer than fourteen thousand votes more than the governing Liberals, yet achieved a decisive 29 seat majority. During the campaign, PQ leader Jacques Parizeau promised a referendum should he be given a mandate to govern. He made good on his promise when, a year later, he presented a referendum question which would be put to the people on 30 October.**

**Early public opinion polls indicated that the federalist forces would have an easy victory, but the tide turned quickly and dramatically after Lucien Bouchard, a more popular figure than Parizeau, took on a more prominent role in the campaign.**

**In the end, the question was narrowly defeated when the federalists mustered 50.58 per cent of the vote – 54,288 votes more than the 'Yes' side.**

**Few speeches in Canadian history have ended a career in politics, and not one brought down so highly placed a figure as this concession speech – of sorts – by Parizeau. His placing of blame for the referendum loss on 'money and the ethnic vote', references to francophone Quebecers as 'us', and talk of revenge shocked those in both the 'Yes' and 'No' camps.**

**Condemnation was quick to come. Many within the Parti Québécois, including the Vice-President called for the Premier to resign. Parizeau announced his resignation at a news conference the following afternoon. He did not apologize, nor did he retract his remarks, rather he defended his speech, stating, 'I used words that were strong last night, but they underline a reality that exists.'**

My friends, it didn't work, but not by a great deal. But it was a success, it was a success in a way. If you would, let's stop talking about the francophones of Quebec. Let's talk about us! We'll talk about the sixty per cent of us. We voted in favour!

We fought well, we fought well and we showed clearly what it is we wanted. And we missed by a small margin, by some tens of thousands of votes. Well, in a case like this, what do we do? We spit in our hands and start all over again.

I would have liked this to have gone through. I wanted so badly, like all of you, that it would get through. We were so close to having our own country. Well, it's been delayed a little – not for long, not for long. We won't wait fifteen years this time – no, no, no.

What has happened is wonderful. To see in one meeting after another, these young people who were saying that the future of their country wasn't all that important, but more and more of them were coming along and saying we want that country of our own. And when the youth think that we'll get our own country.

It's true, it's true that we have been defeated, but basically by what? By money and the ethnic vote, essentially. So all it means is that, in the next round, instead of being 60 or 61 per cent to vote 'Yes', we will be 63 or 64 per cent and it will suffice. That's all. But now my friends, in the months that will come, we are going to… Listen: there were people got so afraid that the temptation to take revenge is going to be something! And never will it be more important to have in Quebec a Parti Québécois government to protect us until the next time!

The independence of Quebec remains the stuff that binds us. We want a country and we shall have it.

Right now, my friends, we are entering into a stage in the next days and weeks, during which we will want, each and every one of us, to place our fists on the table – not to mention anything else. Stay calm, my friends. Let us resist any provocation. As the Prime Minister of Canada was saying a few days ago, we're really going to have to work through this. Don't give in. Stay calm, smile. Don't be long in the face – smile. The next round is just around the corner and we are going to have our own country!

About this I have no doubt. That you younger people voted in a great majority, to have our own country. But now I want to address my old comrades in arms, those who are my age, who've sought after a country for years and years. I say this: don't be discouraged. The young people are just beginning, they've just had a slight setback. They'll soon be successful. But you, old comrades in arms, remain in the fray. We need you; sovereignty is near.

*Le Québec aux Québécois.*

In the days to come, we will receive insults. We will be told that we don't know what we want. They will say: well yes, everything's fine, everything is as usual. No, no! Everything's not as usual. Never forget that three-fifths of those who we are voted 'Yes'. That wasn't quite enough, but very soon it will be enough. Our country is within our grasp!

Stay calm, keep smiling, even if that doesn't come easily, and tell yourselves that it's from this solidarity we share, year after year, among the generations, among those of the right from the left, among the unions and the small and medium size businesses, through which we live,

*Jacques Parizeau campaigning in Montreal two days before the vote in the 1995 Quebec Referendum*

It's between ourselves, the artists and the students, the unions and the bosses, the unemployed and those who have jobs. It's all together that right now we in Quebec, will not sacrifice ourselves to the move to the right taking place in the rest of Canada! We'll never sacrifice that!

We will show that we are able, even if we don't yet have a country, to raise a French society that has a heart for hard work and has a heart in the right place – until we will have our own revenge and we will have our own country.

Thank you to all my friends for being here tonight.

*Vive l'espoir, vive le Québec!*

# TRIBUTES

"Sir John Macdonald now belongs to the ages, and it can be said with certainty, that the career which has just been closed is one of the most remarkable careers of this century. It would be premature at this time to attempt to fix or anticipate what will be the final judgement of history upon him; but there were in his career and in his life, features so prominent and so conspicuous that already they shine with a glow which time cannot alter, which even now appear before the eye such as they will appear to the end of history."

*- Sir Wilfrid Laurier, 1891*

# Sir John A. Macdonald

On the Assassination of Thomas D'Arcy McGee

*The House of Commons, Ottawa, 7 April 1868*

**'He has lived a short life, respected and beloved, and died a heroic death; a martyr to the cause of his country.'**

Thomas D'Arcy McGee was murdered in the early hours of 7 April 1868, the very same day on which Sir John A. Macdonald made this speech in the House of Commons. McGee was shot from behind as he arrived at the doorway of his boarding house, having just made the short walk from a late night session of the House. The assassination shocked a country that had yet to celebrate the first anniversary of Confederation. Macdonald, who saw something of a kindred spirit in McGee, was among those most affected. Both had worked tirelessly for a union of the colonies that made up British North America, and both were given to drink. Indeed, many considered McGee, ten years the Prime Minister's junior, to be the successor in leading the Liberal-Conservative Party.

In speaking of the loss, Macdonald quotes 'in wit a man, simplicity a child', a line from Alexander Pope's 'Epitaph on Gay', a verse written for his friend and fellow poet John Gay.

The Prime Minister's speech was made to a densely crowded House of Commons when it resumed sitting the afternoon after the assassination. In the account provided by *The Globe*, Macdonald 'rose amidst the breathless silence of the House and manifesting feelings of the most profound emotion, which for some time almost stopped his utterance, said'...

Mister Speaker, it is with pain amounting to anguish that I rise to address you. He who last night, nay this morning, was with us and of us, whose voice is still ringing in our ears, who charmed us with his marvellous eloquence, elevated us by his large statesmanship, and instructed us by his wisdom and his patriotism, is no more, is foully murdered. If ever a soldier who fell on the field of battle in the front of the fight, deserved well of his country, Thomas D'Arcy McGee deserved well of Canada and its people. The blow which has just fallen is too recent, the shock is too great, for us yet to realize its awful atrocity, or the extent of this most irreparable loss. I feel, sir, that our sorrow, genuine and unaffected sorrow, prevents us from giving adequate expression our feelings just now, but by and by, and at length, this House will have a melancholy pleasure in considering the character and position of my late friend and colleague. To all, the loss is great, to me I may say inexpressibly so; as the loss is not only of a warm political friend, who has acted with me for some years, but of one with whom I enjoyed the intercommunication of his rich and varied mind; the blow has been overwhelming. I feel altogether incapable of addressing myself to the subject just now. Our departed friend was a man of the kindest and most generous impulse, a man whose hand was open to every one, whose heart was made for friendship, and whose enmities were written in water; a man who had no gall, no guile; 'in wit a man, simplicity a child.'

He might have lived a long and respected life had he chosen the easy path of popularity rather than the stern one of duty. He has lived a short life, respected and beloved, and died a heroic death; a martyr to the cause of his country. How easy it would have been for him, had he chosen, to have sailed along the full tide of popularity with thousands and hundreds of thousands following him, without the loss of a single plaudit, but he has been slain, and I fear slain because he preferred the path of duty.

I cannot but quote from his speech of last night. 'Sir,' said Mister McGee, 'I hope that in this House mere temporary or local popularity will never be made the test by which to measure the worth or efficiency of a public servant. He, sir, who builds upon popularity builds upon a shifting sand. He who rests simply on popularity, and who will risk the right in hunting after popularity, will soon find the object he pursues slip away from him. It is, sir, in my humble opinion, the leader of a forlorn hope who is ready to meet and stem the tide of temporary unpopularity, who is prepared, if needs be, to sacrifice himself in defence of the principles which he has adopted as those of truth who shows us that he is ready not only to triumph with his principles, but even to suffer for his principles who has proved himself, above all others, worthy of peculiar honour.'

He has gone from us, and it will be long ere we find such a happy mixture of eloquence and wisdom, wit and earnestness. His was no artificial or meretricious eloquence, every word of his was as he believed, and every belief, every thought of his, was in the direction of what was good and true.

Well may I say now, on behalf of the Government and of the country, that, if he has fallen, he has fallen in our cause, leaving behind him a grateful recollection which will ever live in the hearts and minds of his countrymen. We must remember too that the blow which has fallen so

*The funeral procession of Thomas D'Arcy McGee, 13 April 1868, Montreal*

severely on this House and the country will fall more severely on his widowed partner and his bereaved children. Of their sorrows I will not venture now to speak but I would remind the House that he was too good, too generous to be rich. He hast left us, the Government, the people, and the representatives of the people, a sacred legacy, and we would be wanting in our duty to this country and to the feeling which will agitate the country from one end to the other, if we do not accept that legacy as a sacred trust, and look upon his widow and children as now belonging to the State.

## Sir Wilfrid Laurier

On the Death of Sir John A. Macdonald

*The House of Commons, Ottawa, 8 June 1891*

### '... for the supreme art of governing men, Sir John Macdonald was gifted as few men in any land or in any age were gifted...'

**This eulogy to Sir John A. Macdonald remains perhaps the finest yet delivered in the House of Commons, and provides a true reflection of the affection, respect and admiration the future Prime Minister had for a man with whom he'd had many differences of opinion. Laurier unites his grief in the death of Macdonald with that felt for Sir Antoine-Aimé Dorion, who had died from a stroke the week before. Though Dorion had served a brief term as Co-Premier of the Province of Canada with George Brown, he'd later refused to participate in Brown's Great Coalition with Macdonald and George-Étienne Cartier. Dorion led the Canada East opposition to Confederation, but proved a valuable Liberal Member of Parliament after the union had taken place.**

**In the deaths of these two men, Laurier recognizes the passing of those who had created the country he served, and encourages others to take up their work.**

I fully appreciate the intensity of the grief which fills the souls of all those who were friends and followers of Sir John Macdonald, at the loss of the great leader whose life has been so closely identified with their party; a party upon which he has thrown such brilliancy and lustre. We on this side of the House who were his opponents, who did not believe in his policy, nor in his methods of government; we take our full share of their grief – for the loss which they deplore today is far and away beyond and above the ordinary compass of party range. It is in every respect a great national loss, for he who is no more was, in many respects, Canada's most illustrious son, and in every sense Canada's foremost citizen and statesman. At the period of life to which Sir John Macdonald had arrived, death, whenever it comes, cannot be said to come unexpected.

Some months ago, during the turmoil of the late election, when the country was made aware that on a certain day the physical strength of the veteran Premier had not been equal to his courage, and that his intense labour for the time being had prostrated his singularly wiry frame, everybody, with the exception, perhaps, of his buoyant self, was painfully anxious lest perhaps the angel of death had touched him with his wing. When, a few days ago in the heat of an angry discussion the news spread in the House, that of a sudden his condition had become alarming, the surging waves of angry discussion were once again hushed, and every one, friend and foe, realized that this time for a certainty the angel of death had appeared and had crossed the threshold of his home. Thus we were not taken by surprise, and although we were prepared for the sad event, yet it is almost impossible to convince the unwilling mind, that it is true, that Sir John Macdonald is no more, that the chair which we see vacant shall remain forever vacant; that the face so familiar in this Parliament for the last forty years shall be heard no more, whether in solemn debate or in pleasant mirthful tones. In fact, the place of Sir John Macdonald in this country, the fate of this country, can continue without him. His loss overwhelms us.

For my part, I say with all truth, his loss overwhelms me, and it also overwhelms his parliament, as if indeed one of the institutions of the land had given way. Sir John Macdonald now belongs to the ages, and it can be said with certainty, that the career which has just been closed is one of the most remarkable careers of this century. It would be premature at this time to attempt to fix or anticipate what will be the final judgement of history upon him; but there were in his career and in his life, features so prominent and so conspicuous that already they shine with a glow which time cannot alter, which even now appear before the eye such as they will appear to the end of history. I think it can be asserted that for the supreme art of governing men, Sir John Macdonald was gifted as few men in any land or in any age were gifted; gifted with the most high of all qualities. Qualities which would have made him famous wherever exercised and which would have shone all the more conspicuously the larger the theatre. The fact that he could congregate together elements the most heterogeneous and blend them into one compact party, and to the end of his life keep them steady under his hand, is perhaps altogether unprecedented. The fact that during all those years he retained unimpaired not only the confidence, but the devotion – the ardent devotion and affection of his party, is evidence that besides those higher qualities of statesmanship to which we were the daily witnesses, he was also endowed with those inner, subtle, indefinable graces of soul which win and keep the hearts of men. As to his statesmanship, it is written in the history of Canada. It may be said without any exaggeration whatever, that the life of Sir John Macdonald, from the date he entered Parliament, is the history of Canada, for he was connected and associated with all the events, all the facts which brought Canada from the position Canada then occupied – the position of two small provinces, having nothing in common but a common allegiance, united by a bond of paper, and united by nothing else – to the present state of development which Canada has reached.

Although my political views compel me to say that, in my judgement, his actions were not always the best that could have been taken in the interest of Canada, although my conscience compels me to say that of late he had imputed to his opponents motives as to which I must say in my heart he was misconceived, yet I am only too glad here to sink these differences, and to remember only the great services he has performed for our country – to remember that his actions always displayed great originality of views, unbounded fertility of resources, a high level of intellectual conceptions, and, above all, a far-reaching vision beyond the event of the day, and still higher, permeating the whole, a broad patriotism – a devotion to Canada's welfare, Canada's advancement, and Canada's glory. The life of a statesman is always an arduous one, and very often it is an ungrateful one. More often than otherwise his actions do not mature until he is in his grave. Not so, however, in the case of Sir John Macdonald. His career has been a singularly fortunate one. His reverses were few and of short duration. He was fond of power, and, in my judgement, if I may say so, that may be the turning point of the judgement of history. He was fond of power, and he never made any secret of it. Many times we have heard him avow from the floor of this Parliament, and his ambition in this respect was gratified as, perhaps, no other man's ambition ever was.

In my judgement, even the career of William Pitt can hardly compare with that of Sir John Macdonald in this respect; for although Pitt, moving in a higher sphere, had to deal with problems greater than our problems, yet I doubt it in the intricate management of a party William Pitt had to contend with difficulties equal to those that Sir John Macdonald had to contend with. In his death, too, he seems to have been singularly happy. Twenty years ago I was told by one who at the time was a close personal and political friend of Sir John Macdonald, that in the intimacy of his domestic circle he was fond of repeating that his end would be as the end of Lord Chatham – that he would be carried away from the floor of the Parliament to die. How true that vision into the future was we now know, for we saw him to the last. With enfeebled health and declining strength, struggling on the floor of Parliament until the hand of fate pinned him to his bed to die. And thus to die with his armour on was probably his ambition.

Sir, death is the supreme law, though we see it every day, in every form, although session after session we have seen it in this Parliament striking right and left without any discrimination as to age or station. Yet the ever recurring spectacle does not in any way remove the bitterness of the sting. Death always carries with it an incredible sea of pain, but the one thing sad in death is that which is involved in the word separation, separation from all we have in life. This is what makes death so poignant when it strikes a man of intellect in middle age. But when death is the natural termination of a full life in which he who has disappeared had given full measure of his capacity, has performed everything required from him and more, the sadness of death is not for him that goes, but for those who love him and remain. In this way I am sure the Canadian people will extend unbounded sympathy to the friends of Sir John Macdonald, to his surviving children, and above all to his companion in life.

Mister Speaker, one after another we see those who have been instrumental in bringing Canada to its present state removed from amongst us. Today we suffer the loss of him who we all unite in saying was the foremost Canadian of his time and who held the largest place in Canadian history. Only last week was buried in the city of Montreal another son of Canada, one who had at one time been a tower of strength to the Liberal Party, one who will ever be remembered as one of the noblest, purest and greatest characters that Canada has ever produced. Sir Antoine-Aimé Dorion. Sir Antoine-Aimé Dorion had not been in favour of Confederation, not that he was opposed to the principle, but he believed that the union of these provinces at that day was premature. When, however, Confederation had become a fact, he gave the best of his mind and heart to make it a success. It may indeed happen, sir, when the Canadian people see the ranks thus gradually reduced and thinned of those upon whom they have been in the habit of relying for guidance, that a feeling of apprehension will creep into the heart last perhaps the institutions of Canada may be imperilled. Before the grave of him who above all was the father of Confederation let not grief be barren grief, but let grief be coupled with the resolution, the determination, that the work in which the Liberals and the Conservatives, in which Brown and Macdonald united, shall not perish, but that though united Canada may be deprived of the services of her greatest men, yet still Canada shall and will live.

*The monument to Sir John A. Macdonald, Ottawa*

# Joe Clark

Eulogy Delivered at the Burial of John Diefenbaker

*The University Of Saskatchewan, Saskatoon, 22 August 1979*

**'John Diefenbaker opened the politics of our country to those to whom it had always been closed.'**

**Former Prime Minister John G. Diefenbaker died alone in his study on 16 August 1979, less than three months after having been elected to the House of Commons for the thirteenth time. Though he didn't live to return to his seat, Diefenbaker did see the Progressive Conservatives return to power, breaking sixteen years of Liberal governments. Thus this affecting eulogy, delivered by the current Progressive Conservative Prime Minister for the previous Progressive Conservative Prime Minister, a man who had been more than twice his age.**

**The historic federal campaign of 1957 had played a significant role in drawing the new Prime Minister to a career in politics, yet Clark had also been amongst those who had a decade later called for a review of Diefenbaker's leadership. While the wound caused by the stance never healed, there is no trace in this affecting tribute.**

John Diefenbaker is home – at the end of a life which started in another century, and embraced most of the history of our Canada. He came to this West when it was raw and young, in the year Saskatchewan became a province. As a child, he talked with the buffalo hunters. As a man, he led his country and dominated its Parliament. Along the way, he touched the lives of his fellow Canadians as no one ever will again.

It is easier to change laws than to change lives. John Diefenbaker changed both. His Bill of Rights, his social programs, his resource and regional development policies, changed permanently the laws of Canada. But, more fundamental than that, he changed our vision of our country. He opened the nation to itself, and let us see our possibilities. It is fitting that his last work, from which death took him, was to prepare a speech to open the Dempster, his highway to our Northern Sea.

We are not here to pass judgement on John Diefenbaker. We are here to celebrate the frontier strength and spirit of an indomitable man, born to a minority group, raised in a minority region, leader of a minority party, who went on to change the very nature of his country – and to change it permanently. When any man dies, after nearly eighty-four full years, there is a mixture of memories. With this man, there is the certain knowledge that he leaves his country better, broader, prouder than he found it.

He was the great populist of Canadian politics. John Diefenbaker opened the politics of our country to those to whom it had always been closed. He gave politics a lively reality to those to whom it had seemed remote. He brought daylight to a process too long obscured in shadow and mystery.

He was a man of passion. Whatever the issue, whomever the person, he had a view – strongly held, forcefully offered, vigorously defended. John Diefenbaker did not tiptoe through the public life of Canada; he strode through – and, as he offered passion to his fellow Canadians, he drew passion in return. John Diefenbaker attracted every reaction from the people of this country, except indifference.

He was a patriot. To John Diefenbaker patriotism was never out of fashion; it was the essence of his life. Not every Canadian shared his view of Canada, but all knew and were touched by his devotion to his view. His faith shaped and formed all his other beliefs. His belief in Canada as a land of equality for all its citizens is in his Bill of Rights. His awareness of the full breadth of this land is in the northern development he spurred and in the regional development he fostered. His abiding commitment to social justice and human dignity is in the health care system he initiated, and in the programmes he sponsored to help the disadvantaged.

He was much more than a statesman. Statesmen are strangers, and John Diefenbaker was personal to most of the people of Canada. He mainstreamed through life. And in those last days, the mourners, who lined the train's long route, who came at midnight to say farewell, who sang and applauded as he left, they were not remembering a Bill of Rights, or a debate in Parliament, or a particular cause or party. Their homage was to a singular man, who entered and enlarged our lives and whom we wanted to see home.

In a very real sense, his life was Canada. Over eight decades, he spanned our history, from the ox cart on the Prairies to the satellite in space. He shaped much of that history, all of it shaped him.

Now that life, that sweep of history, has ended. And we are here today to see John Diefenbaker to his final place of rest.

It is appropriate that it be here. For, while John Diefenbaker was of all of Canada, he was, above all else, a man of the Prairies. His populism was inspired in this open land. His deep feelings for the needs of individuals were shaped by what he saw and felt during the Depression years. The South Saskatchewan dam, one of his physical legacies, reflected his determination that farmers in the region never again suffer dust when there should be grass. It was from Prince Albert that he looked north and caught the vision with which he stirred the minds and hearts of all of us.

And so we commit his mortal remains to the Prairie soil, here, on the campus where he studied and was chancellor, above the river which was a route of our first westward pioneers, in the province which formed him. He showed what one man can do in a country like Canada.

As we commit his body to the land he loved, we commit his soul to the Creator he sought to serve. And we – each of us – commit our memories of him to all of our hearts.

Eternal rest grant unto him, Oh Lord, and let Perpetual Light shine upon him.

God bless and keep John Diefenbaker.

*John Diefenbaker, thirteenth Prime Minister of Canada, with his Bill of Rights*

# Justin Trudeau

## Eulogy for His Father, Pierre Elliott Trudeau

*Notre-Dame Basilica, Montreal, 3 October 2000*

***'My father's fundamental belief in the sanctity of the individual never came from a textbook. It stemmed from his deep love for and faith in all Canadians...'***

**The death of Pierre Elliott Trudeau was followed by five days of mourning during which his body had lain in state on Parliament Hill and at the Montreal City Hall. The state funeral was attended by 1,700 invited guests and one thousand members of the general public. Among the honorary pallbearers were Jimmy Carter, Fidel Castro, Leonard Cohen and the Aga Khan.**

**Justin Trudeau's eulogy followed those by the former Prime Minister's long-time friend Jacques Hébert and Roy Heenan, chairman of the law firm at which the former Prime Minister worked after his retirement from politics.**

**The conclusion of Justin Trudeau's eulogy paraphrases on the last stanza of Robert Frost's 'Stopping by Woods on a Snowy Evening':**

> **The woods are lovely, dark and deep.**<br>
> **But I have promises to keep,**<br>
> **And miles to go before I sleep,**<br>
> **And miles to go before I sleep.**

Friends, Romans, countrymen, I was about six years old when I went on my first official trip. I was going with my father and my grandpa Sinclair up to the North Pole. It was a very glamorous destination. But the best thing about it was that I was going to be spending lots of time with my dad because in Ottawa he just worked so hard.

One day, we were in Alert, Canada's northernmost point, a scientific military installation that seemed to consist entirely of low shed-like buildings and warehouses. Let's be honest. I was six. There were no brothers around to play with and I was getting a little bored because dad still somehow had a lot of work to do. I remember a frozen, windswept Arctic afternoon when I was bundled up into a Jeep and hustled out on a special top-secret mission. I figured I was finally going to be let in to the reason for the existence of this high-security Arctic base.

I was exactly right.

We drove slowly through and past the buildings, all of them very grey and windied, and we rounded a corner and came upon a red one. We stopped. I got out of the Jeep and started to crunch across towards the front door. I was told, no, to the window.

*Justin Trudeau delivering the eulogy for his father*

So I clambered over the snowbank, was boosted up to the window, rubbed my sleeve against the frosty glass to see inside and as my eyes adjusted to the gloom, I saw a figure, hunched over one of many worktables that seemed very cluttered. He was wearing a red suit with that furry white trim.

And that's when I understood just how powerful and wonderful my father was.

Pierre Elliott Trudeau. The very words convey so many things to so many people. Statesman, intellectual, professor, adversary, outdoorsman, lawyer, journalist, author, and prime minister – but more than anything, to me, he was Dad.

And what a dad. He loved us with the passion and a

devotion that encompassed his life. He taught us to believe in ourselves, to stand up for ourselves, to know ourselves and to accept responsibility for ourselves.

We knew we were the luckiest kids in the world. And we had done nothing to actually deserve it. It was instead something that we would have to spend the rest of our lives to work very hard to live up to. He gave us a lot of tools. We were taught to take nothing for granted. He doted on us, but didn't indulge. Many people say he didn't suffer fools gladly, but I'll have you know he had infinite patience with us.

He encouraged us to push ourselves, to test limits, to challenge anyone and anything. There were certain basic principles that could never be compromised.

As I guess it is for most kids, in grade three, it was always a real treat to visit my dad at work. As on previous visits this particular occasion included a lunch at the parliamentary restaurant, which always seemed to be terribly important and full of serious people that I didn't recognize. But at eight, I was becoming politically aware. And I recognized one whom I knew to be one of my father's chief rivals. Thinking of pleasing my father, I told a joke about him – a generic, silly little grade school thing.

My father looked at me sternly with that look I would learn to know so well, and said: 'Justin, we never attack the individual. One can be in total disagreement with someone without denigrating him as a consequence.'

Saying that, he stood up, took me by the hand and brought me over to introduce me to this man. He was a nice man who was eating with his daughter, a nice-looking blond girl a little younger than I was. He spoke to me in a friendly manner for a bit and it was then that I understood that having different opinions from those of another in no way precludes holding this person in the highest respect. Because mere tolerance is not enough: we must have genuine and deep respect for each and every human being, regardless of their beliefs, their origins and their values. That is what my father demanded of his sons and that is what he demanded of our country. He demanded it out of love – love of his sons, love of his country. That is why we love him so. The letters, the flowers, the dignity of the crowds who came to bid farewell – all of that is a way of thanking him for having loved us so much.

My father's fundamental belief in the sanctity of the individual never came from a textbook. It stemmed from his deep love for and faith in all Canadians – and over the past few days, with every card, every rose, every tear, every wave and every pirouette, you returned his love.

It means the world to Sacha and me.

Thank you.

We have gathered from coast to coast to coast, from one ocean to another, united in our grief, to say goodbye. But this is not the end. He left politics in '84. But he came back for Meech. He came back for Charlottetown. He came back to remind us of who we are and what we're all capable of. But he won't be coming back anymore. It's all up to us, all of us, now.

The woods are lovely, dark and deep. He has kept his promises and earned his sleep.

*Je t'aime Papa.*

# CELEBRATION

**"Tonight we let the world know that this is Canada's year in history. It is a time to measure, with grateful hearts, the achievements of our past. It is a time to face with confidence the test and opportunity of the future. It is a time to assess our national condition. It is a time to appreciate the honourable place we hold in the world community gained by sacrifice in war and service in peace."**

*- Lester B. Pearson, 1966*

## Lester B. Pearson

On the Lighting of the Centennial Flame

*Parliament Hill, Ottawa, 31 December 1966*

**'It is my hope and my belief that as we continue to work out Canada's destiny, our national spirit and our national purpose will shine – as this Centennial Flame now shines before us here...'**

As Prime Minister of Canada, Pearson ushered in Canada's centennial year on a crisp and clear winter evening. The ceremony included the debut of Healey Willan's 'Anthem for the Centennial of Canadian Confederation'/'Hymne à l'occasion du Centenaire de la Confédération canadienne' with words by Robert Choquette and John Glassco.

Today's reader may not recognize Charles Bruce, whose poetry the Prime Minister quotes. The winner of a 1951 Governor General's Award for his collection *The Mulgrave Road*, Bruce is perhaps best-known today for *The Channel Shore*, his only novel.

One hundred years ago our country was born. For this we honour men of vision and purpose and high endeavour. Lesser men would have failed or, more likely, would not have tried at all. The task at times seemed impossible. So did that which followed: the consolidation and expansion of the new country until, strong and free, it spanned the continent from sea to sea and reached toward the Arctic.

Tonight, one hundred years later on Parliament Hill in Canada's capital, with the lighting of this flame, with pride in our present and faith in our future, we open officially our centennial celebration.

As this symbolic flame burns, so let pride in our country burn in the hearts of all

*The lighting of the Centennial Flame*

Canadians, where the real meaning of Canada must ever be found. If I may put it in the words of Canadian poet Charles Bruce:

> This heaped geography...
> What is the blend of fear, strength, song and dream
> Slowburning in its heart?
> ...There is no answer but the wordless answers
> That live in flesh, in nerves, heart, blood and bone;
> The moving images that crowd our dreams...

Tonight we let the world know that this is Canada's year in history. It is a time to measure, with grateful hearts, the achievements of our past. It is a time to face with confidence the test and opportunity of the future. It is a time to assess our national condition. It is a time to appreciate the honourable place we hold in the world community gained by sacrifice in war and service in peace.

Economically, we have become a rich society and a great industrial power. We have built new dimensions of progress and welfare into the Canadian way of life. The boundaries of freedom and opportunity have been expanded for every Canadian.

Out of our experience in nation-building, we are forging a new principle of democracy, the principle of political and economic unity in racial and cultural diversity. History and geography, man and the map, have made Canada a particular kind of community where we can show this unity in diversity that all mankind must find if we are to survive the perils of a nuclear age.

Much has been done in Canada. Much remains to be done for Canada. We have laid a strong foundation on which to build in our second century. If we have the will and the goodwill there is no limit to our progress. It is my hope and my belief that as we continue to work out Canada's destiny, our national spirit and our national purpose will shine – as this Centennial Flame now shines before us here – humbly but strongly before all the world as an example of what men and women working together can do to build the good society.

Tonight we begin a new chapter in our country's story, Let the record of that chapter be one of co-operation and not conflict; of dedication and not division; of service, not self; of what we can give, not what we can get. Let us work together as Canadians to make our country worthy of its honoured past and certain of its proud future.

God bless Canada.

## Lester B. Pearson

On the Opening of Expo 67

*Île Notre-Dame, Montreal, 27 April 1967*

***'By the time the gates of Expo are closed six months from now, its success will have made all Canadians prouder of our own country than ever before...'***

**Expo 67 was originally granted to Moscow as part of the fiftieth anniversary of the Russian Revolution. In the autumn of 1962, the fair was awarded to Montreal after the Soviets cancelled. While the Diefenbaker government had been reluctant supporters of the event, Pearson's Liberals considered the fair to be a focal point of Canada's centenary.**

**The official opening ceremony at which Pearson made his remarks was broadcast in colour live via satellite to an audience estimated at 700 million.**

**The description of Expo 67 as 'The Big Blast Up North', referred to in the speech, was a headline in the 22 April 1967 edition of *The Saturday Evening Post*.**

This is a proud day for Montreal, for Quebec and above all for Canada. The heading of an article about Expo in a recent issue of an American magazine referred to it as, 'The Big Blast Up North'. Certainly Expo is going to be that – and much more. Behind this big Canadian birthday 'blast' are achievements in planning, organization and construction that are little short of miraculous.

The men behind these achievements should be proud and happy. We should be grateful to them, as we recall the sceptics who once said Expo 67 was too big a project for Montreal, Quebec or Canada to accomplish in less than four years. But it was done – and well done.

We are witnesses today to the fulfilment of one of the most daring acts of faith in Canadian enterprise and ability ever undertaken. That faith was not misplaced. But Expo is much more than a great Canadian achievement of design and planning and construction. It is also a monument to Man. It tells the exciting and inspiring story of a world that belongs not to any one nation but to every nation.

No theme could have been more fitting for our times than 'Man and His World'. Here in Expo we have one of the most impressive collections of Man's works and Man's ideas ever brought together.

Today we pay our tribute to the dedication and the effort of many men and women that have made all this possible. Montreal has proven its capacity to carry through such an undertaking and its mayor has shown the inspired and dynamic leadership which was essential. So have the people of Canada as a whole, through the co-operation of the three levels of government that was required.

We acknowledge also the tireless and effective work of the staff of Expo, all of whom, beginning with the Commissioner-General, I would like to thank very sincerely.

It is also a truly international effort – made possible by many men from many countries.

The scope of international support for the Expo theme, as shown by the record-breaking participation, is a wonderfully encouraging display of Man's faith in himself and his world; in his capacity to improve and progress; in his power to cope with the challenges of his world and himself. In all the wonders of Man which we now have on display at Expo, we can see in inspiring actuality how much every nation has to gain from co-operation and how much to lose in conflict.

I am sure all Canadians will share with me the hope that the lasting impact of Expo will be in the dramatic object lesson we see before our own eyes today: that the genius of Man knows no national boundaries but is universal.

If that hope is fulfilled, then Canada's sponsorship of such a dramatic display of the global fraternity of aspiration and achievement within the great diversity of nations may become an important contribution to this era.

Our own country's existence has always depended upon achieving unity of human purpose within the diversity of our linguistic cultural and social backgrounds.

Expo '67 offers perhaps the most striking proof ever assembled in one place that the future well-being of the whole world community of man also depends on achieving the unity of peace within the vast diversity of national policies.

By the time the gates of Expo are closed six months from now, its success will have made all Canadians prouder of our own country than ever before; and more conscious of the interdependence and the brotherhood of all men and all nations.

*Prime Minister Lester B. Pearson in front of the Canadian Pavilion at Expo 67*

# Adrienne Clarkson

## Installation Speech as Governor General of Canada

*The Senate, Ottawa, 7 October 1999*

**'To be complex does not mean to be fragmented. This is the paradox and the genius of our Canadian civilization.'**

The first seventeen Governors General of the Dominion of Canada were titled men from the British Isles. It wasn't until the 1952 installation of Vincent Massey that a Canadian became the vice-regal representative.

The appointment of Adrienne Clarkson, during Jean Chrétien's sixth year as Prime Minister, marked another milestone in the evolution of the position. The second woman to become Governor General, Clarkson was the first immigrant and the first member of a visible minority to accept the role.

In her installation speech, Clarkson quotes several figures in her speech, Governors Samuel de Champlain and Lord Elgin, the painter Paul-Émile Borduas, Grand Chief John Kelly and Prime Minister Wilfrid Laurier, but it is the writers of Canada, including her husband, novelist and philosopher John Ralson Saul, who are accorded the place of prominence.

Prime Minister, you have expressed to me the affection, loyalty and esteem of the Canadian people, which it will be my honour to convey to our gracious sovereign, Queen Elizabeth II. I am pleased to accept the responsibility of being Her Majesty's representative in Canada, with all that entails, through our history and our custom. Knowing better than anyone my own shortcomings, I undertake this task with humility and ask you all, as Canadians, to help me.

I take on the responsibility of becoming Canada's 26th Governor General since Confederation, fully conscious of the deep roots of this office, stretching back, to the Governors of New France and to the first of them, Samuel de Champlain. In our beloved Georgian Bay, which lies on the great water route he took from the French River to Huronia, there is a cairn, placed on a small island, between a tennis court and Champlain's Gas Bar & Marina, which commemorates his passage and quotes from his journal:

> Samuel de Champlain by canoe 1615
> 'As for me, I labour always to prepare a way for those willing to follow.'

Those willing to follow have embodied the institution of the Governor General in ways which have demonstrated the evolution and constant reaffirmation of this country. Canada's institutions have never been static. They are organic – evolving and growing in ways that surprise and even startle us. In a mere thirty years, between 1952 and 1982, we repatriated the Governor Generalship and our Constitution. We adopted our flag, we formalized our understanding of Rights and we strengthened and expanded the bilingual nature of our country. The Governor General is one skein in the woven fabric of what Eugene Forsey characterised as our 'independent sovereign democracy'.

Champlain's successors have had many activists among them. Lord Elgin, who helped Baldwin and LaFontaine to anchor the Canadian model of democracy in 1848, stands out as somebody who appreciated the originality of a country which would promote such a project. He loved to wander about our few small cities, on foot, glorying in snowstorms, eschewing the formality of his office and speaking of his admiration for 'this glorious country' and 'its perfectly independent inhabitants'. He also said, that in order to have insight into the future of all nations, it was necessary to come here.

Vincent Massey, our first Canadian Governor General, laid the groundwork for practically all of our modern cultural institutions – the Canada Council, the National Arts Centre, the Order of Canada, among others. And my predecessor, Roméo LeBlanc, reinforced the central fact of French Canada across this country, culminating in the success of last month's Summit that put New Brunswick and Acadia at the centre of the map of francophone reality. This was only fifty years after the great painter, Paul-Émile Borduas, had exhorted Quebec, and by implication, all of us, to abandon 'the smooth and slippery walls of fear' by refusing 'to act knowingly (or consciously) ... beneath (our) psychic and physical possibilities'.

Allow me a moment of personal reflection. The Poy family, arriving here as refugees, in 1942, was made up of my parents, my brother and myself. Three of us are in this Chamber today. We did not arrive as part of a regular immigration procedure. There was no such thing for a Chinese family at that time in Canadian history.

My mother's intense and abiding love is here in spirit today. My brother, Doctor Neville Poy, was seven when we arrived. And my father, Bill Poy, is here – extraordinary, in his 92nd year. Lance-Corporal Poy, dispatch rider with the Hong Kong Volunteer Corps, received the Military Medal for his bravery during the Battle of Hong Kong. Like many soldiers, he never speaks of those actions, but it is his bravery, which is the underpinning of his children's lives. To have been brought up by courageous and loving parents, was a gift that made up for all we had lost.

As I have said before, the city of Ottawa, then, was small and white – like most of Canada. Much of its psyche was characterized by what Mavis Gallant has called 'the dark bloom of the Old Country – the mistrust of pity, the contempt for weakness, the fear of the open heart'. But it was also the place where our family was befriended by the Molots, who owned the local drugstore, the Marcottes and the Proulx, among whom we lived in Lower Town, and our guardian angels, the Potters.

Because my father had a job with the Department of Trade and Commerce and because we lived among French Canadians, I became fixated, from the age of five, with the idea of learning French. I remember the day when I was dressed up in my patent leather shoes and pink smocked dress, and was taken up the street by my parents to the convent of Sainte Jeanne d'Arc, where I was interviewed by a kindly woman wearing white all around her face, while a dim crucifix glowed in the background. Walking home, I sensed that there was dejection in the air and disappointment. It had been explained to my parents that it was not possible for a Protestant to receive French language education in Ottawa. In my lifetime, this has changed to such a radical degree that I don't even need to comment on it. But that early sense of something being impossible, which actually was nonsensical, put steel into me.

Farley Mowat has pointed out that a little adversity in childhood is a very good thing for animals – including human ones. Our family, like many others, had lost a great deal but we had also gained an enormous amount: a country with lakes, with small mouth bass and with free public education. We became addicted to the wilderness because, as Pierre Morency says, 'Le nord n'est pas dans la boussole; il est ici'.

*Governor General Adrienne Clarkson inspects the Ceremonial Guard*

As John Ralston Saul has written, the central quality of the Canadian state is its complexity. It is a strength and not a weakness that we are a 'permanently incomplete experiment built on a triangular foundation – aboriginal, francophone and anglophone'. What we continue to create, today, began 450 years ago as a political project, when the French first met with the aboriginal people. It is an old experiment, complex and, in worldly terms, largely successful. Stumbling through darkness and racing through light, we have persisted in the creation of a Canadian civilization.

We are constructing something different here. As Jean-Guy Pilon describes in one of his poems:

> Racines tordues à vaincre le feu
> À cracher au visage des étoiles.
> C'est ici que respirent, grandissent
> les constructeurs.

We have the opportunity to leave behind the useless blood calls of generations, now that we are in the new land that stretches to infinity. Wilfrid Laurier understood this clearly: 'We have made a conquest greater and more glorious than that of any territory,' he said, 'we have conquered our liberties.'

There seem to be two kinds of societies in the world today. Perhaps there have always been only two kinds – punishing societies and forgiving societies. A society like Canada's, with its four centuries of give-and-take, compromise and acceptance, wrong-doing and redress, is basically a forgiving society. We try – we must try – to forgive what is past. The punishing society never forgets the wrongs of the past. The forgiving society works towards the actions of the future. The forgiving society enables people to behave well toward one another, to begin again, to build a society in hope and with love.

We know, that in joining Canadian society, we will be able to accept the invitation, offered, in 1970, by Grand Chief John Kelly: 'As the years go by, the circle of the Ojibway gets bigger and bigger. Canadians of all colours and religions are entering that circle. You might feel that you have roots somewhere else, but in reality, you are right here with us.' That the aboriginal circle enlarges to include all of us – native and immigrant – arriving by boat and plane to a vast and beautiful land, has been characterized by Michael Ondaatje, as a 'vision of nature beyond the human ego'. This is a place, he said, 'fixated by the preoccupying image of figures permanently travelling or portaging their past one-quarter we are all still arriving. From the Filles du Roy to Dionne Brand's new Canadians is a miniscule step'.

We must not forget that this complexity is whole. To be complex does not mean to be fragmented. This is the paradox and the genius of our Canadian civilization.

In the contemplation of our wholeness, lies the symbolic importance of the Governor General: the identification of this post with inclusiveness – the inclusiveness that lies at the core of Canadian society, at its best. This is the essence of our notorious decency, our infamous desire to do good. And it is important to recall that with the great waves of immigration, there has been, since the beginning, an underlying motif: the lost, the rejected, and those who dreamed of another life would come here and would make a contribution to the whole.

In a 1913 photograph, a group of Scandinavian immigrants in Larchmont, Ontario is huddled around a blackboard on which is written:

Duties of the Citizen
1. Understand our government.
2. Take an active part in politics.
3. Assist all good causes.
4. Lessen intemperance.
5. Work for others.

It would be easy to focus obsessively on all the pitfalls and prejudices that undoubtedly landmined this path of good intentions. But in examining the intent, you see the underlying central assumption. It was expected that the immigrant, along with everyone else, would join in the social process, which was democratic, co-operative and other-directed. The fact that it would take another fifty years for this kind of inclusiveness to become colour blind, means, simply, that it took another fifty years. Too long, of course. Far too long. But in other countries, it would take a hundred. In some, it has never come.

The essence of inclusiveness is that we are part of a society in which language, colour, education, sex and money need not, should not divide us, but can make us more aware and sensitive to difference.

I learned to be a Canadian through a series of eternally virginal public school teachers, who treated me only as bright – and not bright yellow. They were mostly small-town Ontario women who, given some of our history might have been narrow-minded; but without exception they had the ability to reach out and understood, instinctively, the need for compassion and the stirring of imaginative curiosity.

I believe that my parents, like so many other immigrants, dreamed their children into being as Canadians. And, as the explorers pushed, every day, beyond the limits of their knowledge, what were Cavelier de la Salle, La Verendrye, Hearne and Mackenzie doing, if not imagining themselves spanning this astonishing space. Luckily, all of us came to a land where the aboriginal peoples have always dreamed life into being.

It is customary to talk about how hard immigrants work and how ambitious they are, but those of us who have lived that process, know that it is mainly the dream that counts.

I'm not talking here of fantasy. I am talking of the true dream that is caught in the web of the past as it meets the wind of the future. All of us have this, even if we do not express it. This is what gives a nation, such as ours, its resonance, its depth and its strength.

The dream pulls us on and transforms us into Canadians. The dream gives us the strength to avoid being stereotyped by the past or limited by the expectations of others. The dream brings openness, adventure and, of course, pain and confusion. But, as Leonard Cohen observes, 'There is a crack in everything. That's how the light gets in.'

Through the light that is in us, we have created a place of dynamic innovation. Innovation in political structures. New approaches toward social relationships, towards citizenship. Military innovation in peace keeping. Economic innovation in cutting edge industries, from the railway of 150 years ago to aeronautics, today.

We must not see ourselves as a small country of thirty million people, floundering in a large land mass. We are among the healthiest, best-educated people in the world, with great natural riches. We have two of the world's great languages.

We must not see ourselves as people who simply react to trends but as people who can initiate them.

We must not see ourselves as people to whom things are done but as people who do things.

Our history demonstrates that we have the self-confidence to act and to act successfully. We can – when we trust ourselves – seize hold of the positive energy, flowing out of the choice we have made to be here and to continue what remains an unprecedented experiment.

The streetcar our family often took on Sunday afternoons to Rockliffe Park, used to pass the closed gates of Rideau Hall. I'm so glad that has changed. I'm delighted that crowds of people now come through the grounds and the Visitor Centre. I look forward to continuing the tradition of welcoming Canadians to what is, in effect, your national house.

But we will not always be in Ottawa. John and I intend to travel and re-travel this whole country by plane, train, car, canoe and kayak. We are initiating the holding of a public levee in each province and territory we visit. You are all invited. In ten days we will be in Alberta for our first official provincial trip. Our first levee will be held on Saturday, October 16th at 4 p.m. at the Museum of the Regiments in Calgary. In November, we will be in British Columbia and our levee will be on Sunday, November 21st in Vancouver.

We want to meet as many of you as we can, not only on special occasions at Rideau Hall and at La Citadelle in Quebec City, but where you live and make your lives.

We bring to this new work, a deep commitment to the relationship between francophone and anglophone, which is the essential and central fact of our political history. We have already long-established, personal interests in French immersion schooling, shelter for the fragile in our society and human rights. And I am committed, as I have always been, to affirming and furthering the full expression of that more than half of society to which I belong – a group which modestly calls itself women. We also have a history of deep involvement in and love for the arts. Beauty and excellence are not the property of a select group. They are the means by which we most profoundly express our society and they belong to every one of us.

As I take up this task, I ask you to embark on a journey with me. Together, I hope that we will be able to do it with the Inuit quality of isuma, which is defined as an intelligence that includes knowledge of one's responsibility towards society. The Inuit believe that it can only grow in its own time; it grows because it is nurtured. I pray that with God's help, we, as Canadians, will trace with our own lives, what Stan Rogers called 'one warm line through this land, so wild and savage'.

And in the footsteps of Samuel de Champlain, I am willing to follow.

# BIOGRAPHIES

**Richard Bedford Bennett** (1870–1947) was the eleventh Prime Minister of Canada. He was born at Hopewell Hill, New Brunswick, and grew up in nearby Hopewell Cape. He worked for several years as a schoolteacher and principal before studying law at Dalhousie University. He entered politics as a town alderman and was later elected to the Legislative Assembly of the Northwest Territories. In 1905, after the creation of Alberta, Bennett became leader of the provincial Conservative Party. He was elected to the House of Commons in 1911, and later served brief terms as Minister of Justice and Minister of Finance under Arthur Meighen. Bennett succeeded Meighen as Tory leader in 1927 and became Prime Minister after Mackenzie King's Liberals were defeated in the 1930 federal election. He had the misfortune of taking power during the very worst years of the Great Depression. Though his Conservatives suffered a devastating loss at the polls in the 1935 federal election, Bennett stayed on as party leader. He retired to Great Britain three years later. In 1941, as Viscount Bennett, he was elevated to the House of Lords, the only Canadian Prime Minister to have been so honoured.

**Sir Robert Borden** (1854–1937) was born in Grand-Pré, Nova Scotia. He had no university education, rather he articled at a Halifax law firm and in 1878 was called to the bar. Borden was first elected to the House of Commons in the 1896 federal election and five years later became the leader of the Conservative opposition. In 1911, Borden became the eighth Prime Minister of Canada. He led the government through the First Word War under the Conservative and Unionist party banners. In July 1920, ill-health forced his retirement from politics. After leaving office he served six years as Chancellor of Queen's University.

**Lucien Bouchard** (1938– ) was born in St-Cœur-de-Marie, in Quebec's Lac-Saint-Jean region. He studied social science and law at Université Laval, after which he was called to the bar. Though active in politics, for two decades he practised law in Chicoutimi. A Quebec nationalist, he wavered between federalism and separatism, and appeared mobile in the political spectrum. He worked for the Quebec Liberal Party in the 1970 provincial election, then supported his friend Brian Mulroney in his unsuccessful 1976 bid to become leader of the Progressive Conservatives. Bouchard fought for the 'Yes' side in the first Quebec referendum, yet five years later accepted an appointment as Canadian Ambassador to France. He joined Mulroney's Progressive Conservative government in 1988 as Secretary of State and later Minister of Environment. After eighteen months Bouchard broke with Mulroney over the Meech Lake Accord and, over the next few months, formed the Bloc Québécois. With Jacques Parizeau and Mario Dumont. he was one of the leaders of the 'Yes' side in the 1995 Quebec referendum. Following Parizeau's resignation, in January 1996 Bouchard was sworn in as Premier of Quebec. He retired from politics five years later.

**Avril Phaedra 'Kim' Campbell** (1947– ) was the first woman to be Prime Minister of Canada and the last Progressive Conservative to hold the office. Born in Port Alberni, British Columbia, she spent much of her youth in Vancouver. After studying at the University of British Columbia and the London School of Economics, Campbell practised law for two years in the mid-1980s. Her early career in politics was marked by a stint as a school trustee, and a weak 1986 run for the leadership of the British Columbia Social Credit Party. Later that same year she succeeded in her second attempt to win a seat in the British Columbia Legislative Assembly. She later resigned her seat and launched a successful campaign as a Progressive Conservative candidate in the 1988 federal election. In the government of Brian Mulroney, she served as Minister of State for Indian Affairs and

Northern Development, Minister of Justice, Attorney-General and Minister of Defence. After Mulroney announced his retirement, Campbell was elected leader of the Progressive Conservative Party. On 25 June 1993, she was sworn in as Prime Minister, a position she held for 133 days.

**Jean Chrétien** (1934– ) was born in Shawinigan, Quebec, the eighteenth of nineteen children. He studied at Université Laval and practised law in his hometown before winning a seat in the 1963 federal election. Five years later, Chrétien was appointed Minister of National Revenue in the Cabinet of Pierre Elliott Trudeau. It was the first of many portfolios, including Minister of Indian Affairs and Northern Development, Minister of Industry, Trade and Commerce, Minister of Finance, Minister of Justice, Attorney General, Minister of State for Social Development and Minister of Energy, Mines and Resources. Chrétien played a key role in the 1980 Quebec referendum and later served as Minister Responsible for Constitutional Negotiations during the patriation of the constitution. Chrétien retired from politics after losing to John Turner in the 1984 Liberal leadership race. Six years later, he returned to lead the party. He became Prime Minister following the collapse of the Progressive Conservatives in the 1993 federal election. His term in office was marked by severe budget cuts, a successful effort in eliminating government deficit and payments made on the national debt. After retiring from office in December 2003, Chrétien joined the same Montreal law firm that had once employed his old friend Pierre Elliott Trudeau.

**Charles Joseph 'Joe' Clark** (1939– ) was the sixteenth Prime Minister of Canada and the first to have been born west of Ontario. Clark studied at the University of Alberta, Dalhousie Law School and at the University of British Columbia Faculty of Law. In 1972, at age thirty-three, he was elected to the House of Commons, and within four years became leader of the Progressive Conservatives. The party's slim victory in the 1979 federal election ended over sixteen years of Liberal government rule. Clark was sworn in as Prime Minister on the day before his fortieth birthday, becoming the youngest person to hold the office. However, his minority government was shortlived. Parliament lasted only sixty-seven days before being dissolved when the Tories failed to pass a Motion of Confidence. In February 1980, Pierre Trudeau's Liberals returned to power with a majority of seats. Clark lost the leadership of his party to Brian Mulroney three years later. After the Tories regained power in 1984, Clark served as a senior cabinet minister and was instrumental in the promotion of the Meech Lake and Charlottetown accords. He retired from politics in 1993, but returned to politics in 1998 to again lead the Progressive Conservative Party. He announced his intention to step down in 2002 and was replaced in a leadership convention the following year. Clark was critical when his party later merged with the Canadian Alliance. He refused to join the new party and remained sitting as a Progressive Conservative until his 2004 retirement.

**Adrienne Clarkson, née Poy** (1939– ) was the forty-ninth Governor General of Canada. She was born in Hong Kong, the daughter of a businessman who worked for the Canadian Trade Commission. In 1942, her family arrived in Canada and settled in Ottawa. Prior to her installation as Governor General, Clarkson was known primarily as an award-winning journalist and broadcaster on such shows as *Take Thirty*, *The Fifth Estate* and *Adrienne Clarkson Presents*. She also served as Agent General for Ontario in France and as chair of the boards of the Canadian Museum of Civilization and the Canadian War Museum. In 1963, she married political science professor and author Stephen Clarkson. Twelve years later the couple divorced. In 1999, she married author and philosopher John Ralston Saul.

**Charles de Gaulle** (1890–1970), the first President of France's Fifth Republic, was born in Lille. A member of the French military since the age of twenty-two, in the first year of the Second World War he served as Undersecretary of State for Defense. After the fall of France he was exiled in England from where he led the Free French movement. He later served as President of the Provisional Government of the French Republic. De Gaulle left politics in 1946, returning twelve years later. In January 1959 he became President of France, a position he held for over a decade. De Gaulle resigned in April 1969 after his proposal to transform the French Senate was defeated in a referendum.

**Thomas Clement 'Tommy' Douglas** (1904–1986) was born in Falkirk, Scotland and was raised in Glasgow and Winnipeg. He studied at Brandon College, McMaster University and the University of Chicago, and later served as a minister at the Calvary Baptist Church in Weyburn, Saskatchewan, In 1935, as the local Co-operative Commonwealth Federation candidate, Douglas was elected to the House of Commons. While a Member of Parliament he was elected leader of the Saskatchewan CCF. He led his party to victory in the 1944 provincial election, forming the first democratic socialist government in North America. Douglas' seventeen year term as Premier saw the creation of Saskatchewan Power and several other Crown corporations. His government also brought in free hospital care and a Bill of Rights. Although credited as the Father of Medicare, in 1961 Douglas resigned his premiership before the programme was launched. That same year he became the first leader of the New Democratic Party and in 1962 returned to the House of Commons. He led the federal party for a decade, and remained in Parliament until his 1979 retirement from politics.

**Stephen Harper** (1959– ) was born and raised in Toronto. He studied at the University of Toronto and the University of Calgary. A Progressive Conservative in his youth, Harper left to join the Reform Party, and was for five years the party's Chief Policy Officer. After an unsuccessful run in 1988, Harper won election to the House of Commons in the 1993 federal election. A little over three years later, he quit his seat to become Vice-President of the National Citizens Coalition. In 2002, Harper was elected leader of the Canadian Alliance and after a by-election win returned to Parliament. The following year he worked to merge the Alliance with the Progressive Conservative Party to form the Conservative Party of Canada. Harper won election as leader of the new party in 2004 and became Prime Minister with the defeat of Paul Martin's Liberals in the 2006 federal election.

**William Lyon Mackenzie King** (1874–1950) was the tenth Prime Minister of Canada. Born in Berlin (now Kitchener), Ontario, King was the grandson of William Lyon Mackenzie, the first mayor of Toronto and leader of the 1837 Upper Canada Rebellion. A highly educated man, he held three degrees from the University of Toronto, and one each from the University of Chicago and Harvard University. Though he did not hold a seat in the House of Commons, in 1900 King became the country's first Deputy Minister of Labour. He was elected to Parliament in 1908, but lost his seat three years later. In 1919, he was elected leader of the Liberal Party, returned to the House, and became Prime Minister for the first time after defeating Arthur Meighen's National Liberal and Conservative Party in the 1921 general election. King served over twenty-one years in office, longer than any other Prime Minister in the history of the Commonwealth. During his time in office, Canada acquired greater autonomy through the Statute of Westminster and adopted a number of social programmes.

**Sir Wilfrid Laurier** (1841–1919) was born in Saint-Lin, Canada East, a small town fifty kilometres north of the Island of Montreal. Educated in both French and English, he earned a Bachelor of Civil Law from McGill

University. In 1874, Laurier was first elected to the House of Commons. He served briefly as Minister of Inland Revenue in the Cabinet of Alexander Mackenzie, and in 1887 was chosen as Liberal leader. Laurier brought his party to victory in the 1896 federal election. As Canada's first francophone Prime Minister he oversaw a period of industrialization, immigration and greater autonomy from Great Britain. After winning four consecutive federal elections, he was defeated by Robert Borden's Conservatives. Laurier stayed on as Grit leader until his death through a cerebral hemorrhage. The fifteen years, two months and 25 days that Laurier spent in office remains the longest uninterrupted term for any Prime Minister. He also holds the record for most years of service in the House of Commons at forty-four years, ten months and seventeen days.

**René Lévesque** (1922–1987) was the first Parti Québécois Premier of Quebec, a position he held from 1976 until 1985. Born in Campbellton, New Brunswick, Lévesque was raised in the small Quebec town of New Carlisle. He studied law at Université Laval, but left for a career in broadcasting before completing his degree. A popular figure, he entered politics in 1960 as a cabinet member in the government of Liberal Premier Jean Lesage. As Minister of Hydroelectric Resources and Public Works and Minister of Natural Resources, he played an instrumental role in the establishment of Hydro-Québec. In 1967, Lévesque left the Quebec Liberal Party and founded the Mouvement Souveraineté-Association, which later merged with the Ralliement National to form the Parti Québécois. As Premier, he oversaw the passage of the Quebec Charter of the French Language, commonly referred to as 'Bill 101'.

**Sir John A. Macdonald** (1815–1891) was born in Glasgow. At age five, he and his family emigrated to Upper Canada, and settled in Kingston. While still a boy, Macdonald began articling for a local lawyer. He was called to the bar shortly after his twenty-first birthday. Macdonald's political career began in 1843 when he won election as a Kingston alderman. The following year he was elected to the legislature of the Province of Canada. A Conservative, he left the party and helped found the Liberal-Conservatives. After the new party took power in 1854, Macdonald was appointed Attorney-General, and later became Joint Premier. He served in a variety of roles over the next few years, both in government and as Leader of the Opposition. One of the greatest proponents of Confederation, in August 1867 he became the Prime Minister when his party won the first federal election. He served more than nineteen years in office, during which he oversaw the purchase of Rupert's Land, the creation of the RCMP, the construction of the transcontinental railway and the additions of British Columbia and Prince Edward Island to the Confederation. Macdonald died in office at age seventy-six, three months after having won his sixth majority government.

**Arthur Meighen** (1874–1960) was the ninth Prime Minister of Canada, and the first to have been born after Confederation. Born in Anderson, Ontario, he studied mathematics at the University of Toronto. Meighen pursued a variety of careers before entering into politics. He was first elected to the House of Commons in 1908 as the Conservative Party candidate in the Manitoba riding of Portage la Prairie. Under Sir Robert Borden, Meighen held a number of portfolios, some concurrently, including Solicitor-General, Minister of Mine, Secretary of State, Minister of the Interior, Superintendent of Indian Affairs and acting Minister of Justice. He became Prime Minister in 1920 after Borden stepped down. The following year, Meighen's government was defeated by Mackenzie King's Liberals, due in part to his roles in implementing Conscription in the First World War and in suppressing the Winnipeg General Strike. Meighen is perhaps best remembered for his part in the 'King-Byng Affair', in which he was invited by the Governor General, Lord Byng, to form the government after King's Liberals were defeated in the House. Meighen's second government lasted less than three months; the Conservatives were swept from power in the subsequent election and he himself lost his seat. Meighen resigned as party leader and later served as Leader of the Government in the Senate and Minister without Portfolio. In 1942, he resigned his Senate seat and made a failed attempt to win a seat in the House of Commons.

**Brian Mulroney** (1939– ) was born in the lumber town of Baie-Comeau, Quebec. He attended Saint Francis Xavier University, where he joined the Progressive Conservative Party. After graduation, Mulroney studied law at Dalhousie University and Université Laval, and later practised as a labour lawyer. In 1976, he made an unsuccessful bid for the leadership of the Progressive Conservatives, losing to Joe Clark. Although offered a position in the shadow cabinet, Mulroney withdrew from the political arena and took the job of Executive Vice-President of the Iron Ore Company. He was elected leader of the Progressive Conservatives in 1983, and following a by-election victory took a seat in the House of Commons. The following year Mulroney became Prime Minister, defeating John Turner's Liberals. His term in office is best remembered for the privatization of Crown corporations, the Free Trade Agreement, the creation of the Goods and Services Tax, and the failed Meech Lake and Charlottetown accords. When he announced his retirement in February 1993, his party stood at twenty-one percent in public opinion polls.

**Jacques Parizeau** (1930– ) was born in Montreal, educated at the London School of Economics and was an advisor to the Lesage government during the Quiet Revolution. He later joined the Parti Québécois and when the party took power in 1976 became provincial Minister of Finance. Eight years later, after falling out with then-Premier René Lévesque, Parizeau retired from politics. He returned in 1988, and was elected party leader. Parizeau became Premier of Quebec in the 1994 provincial election, a position he held for thirteen months. He retired the day after the 1995 Quebec referendum.

**Lester B. Pearson** (1897–1972) was born in Newtonbrook, Ontario, now a part of the City of Toronto, and studied at the University of Toronto. His education was interrupted by the First World War, in which he served as a stretcher bearer and, later, as a pilot in the Royal Air Corps. After the armistice, Pearson returned to the University of Toronto and was awarded a scholarship to Oxford. After a brief career as a university professer, Pearson joined the Department of External Affairs. In 1948, he was appointed Minister of External Affairs and won a seat in the House of Commons. For his work in defusing the Suez Crisis, he was awarded the 1957 Nobel Peace Prize. The next year he was elected leader of the Liberal Party and in 1963 became Prime Minster after defeating the Progressive Conservative government of John Diefenbaker. Though Pearson never led a majority government, he oversaw significant social changes, including Medicare, the Canada Pension Plan and the establishment of the National Flag of Canada. As the centennial year drew to a close he announced his intention to retire from politics. He left the Prime Minister's office the following April.

**Louis Riel** (1844–1885) was born at Red River Settlement in what is now Manitoba. The son of a Métis father and French Canadian mother, he was educated in Montreal. Shortly after his return to the west, in 1868, Riel led the Red River Rebellion, which led to the creation of the Province of Manitoba. There followed nearly fourteen years of exile, the bulk of which was served in the United States. Although voted to the House of Commons in three successive elections, Riel dared not assume his seat. In 1884, at the request of a group of Métis settled on the South Saskatchewan River, Riel returned to Canada.

The following year he led the ill-fated North-West Rebellion. Riel surrendered, was found guilty of high treason, and was executed.

**Louis Saint-Laurent** (1882–1973), the twelfth Prime Minister of Canada, was born in Compton, Quebec, a small village in the Eastern Townships. He was educated at Université Laval. A respected lawyer and professor, Saint-Laurent declined the offer of a seat as a justice in the Supreme Court of Canada. For decades he was courted by both the Liberal and Conservative parties, yet didn't enter into politics until his sixtieth year when he was appointed Minister of Justice and Attorney General in the cabinet of Mackenzie King. He later served as Secretary of State for External Affairs. In 1948, upon King's retirement, Saint-Laurent became Prime Minister. He held the office until the 1957 federal election, when his Liberal government was defeated by the Progressive Conservatives under John Diefenbaker.

**Joseph Roberts 'Joey' Smallwood** (1900–1991), the self-described 'last Father of Confederation', is considered the most important person in bringing Newfoundland into Confederation. Born in the small town of Gambo, Newfoundland, he was raised in Saint John's. He worked as a newspaperman, and was for a time campaign manager for the Prime Minister of Newfoundland, Sir Richard Squires. In 1932, as a Liberal, Smallwood made an unsuccessful bid for a seat in the colony's House of Assembly. Through the Great Depression he continued his newspaper work and hosted a radio programme with the Broadcasting Corporation of Newfoundland. In 1946, Smallwood was elected to the Newfoundland National Convention, which was charged with making recommendations to the British government as to the colony's future. As a delegate, he argued for union with Canada and founded a newspaper to promote his viewpoint. After Newfoundland joined Canada, Smallwood was elected Premier. He was re-elected seven times and remained in office until 1972, a span of nearly twenty-three years.

**Justin Trudeau** (1971– ) is the son of Pierre Elliott Trudeau. Born in Ottawa, during his father's first term as Prime Minister, he was educated at McGill University and the University of British Columbia. He holds the Liberal Party nomination for the Montreal riding of Papineau.

**Pierre Elliott Trudeau** (1919–2000) was born into a wealthy Montreal family. He studied at the Université de Montréal, the Sorbonne and the London School of Economics. A lawyer, journalist and professor of law, he entered politics as a Liberal candidate in the 1965 federal election. As Minister of Justice, he was responsible for the liberalization of divorce laws and the removal of homosexual acts from the Criminal Code. In 1968, he succeeded Lester B. Pearson as the fifteenth Prime Minister of Canada, a position he held for most of the next sixteen years. The more notable legislation passed during his time in office includes the Official Languages Act, Bill C-84 (which abolished capital punishment), and the Constitution Act, 1982. After his 1984 retirement from active politics, Trudeau served as counsel for a Montreal law firm. Trudeau's last significant appearance on the political stage occurred several years later in his opposition to the Meech Lake and Charlottetown accords.